This book is to be returned on or

The Seven Cs
of Consulting

FT Prentice Hall

FINANCIAL TIMES

In an increasingly competitive world, we believe it's quality of thinking that will give you the edge – an idea that opens new doors, a technique that solves a problem, or an insight that simply makes sense of it all. The more you know, the smarter and faster you can go.

That's why we work with the best minds in business and finance to bring cutting-edge thinking and best learning practice to a global market.

Under a range of leading imprints, including Financial Times Prentice Hall, we create world-class print publications and electronic products bringing our readers knowledge, skills and understanding which can be applied whether studying or at work.

To find out more about our business publications, or tell us about the books you'd like to find, you can visit us at **www.business-minds.com**

For other Pearson Education publications, visit **www.pearsoned-ema.com**

PEARSON

Education

The Seven Cs of Consulting

The definitive guide to the consulting process

Mick Cope

FT Prentice Hall
FINANCIAL TIMES

An imprint of Pearson Education

London • New York • San Francisco • Toronto • Sydney • Tokyo • Singapore
Hong Kong • Cape Town • Madrid • Amsterdam • Munich • Paris • Milan

PEARSON EDUCATION LIMITED

Head Office
Edinburgh Gate
Harlow CM20 2JE
Tel: +44 (0)1279 623623
Fax: +44 (0)1279 431059

London Office:
128 Long Acre, London WC2E 9AN
Tel: +44 (0)20 7447 2000
Fax: +44 (0)20 7447 2170
www.business-minds.com

First published in Great Britain in 2003
© Pearson Education Limited 2003

The right of Mick Cope to be identified as Author of this Work has been asserted
by him in accordance with the Copyright, Designs and Patents Act 1988.

ISBN 0 273 66333 X

British Library Cataloguing in Publication Data
A CIP catalogue record for this book can be obtained from the British Library

10 9 8 7 6 5 4 3 2 1

Designed by Sue Lamble
Typeset by Northern Phototypesetting Co Ltd, Bolton
Printed and bound in Great Britain by Biddles Ltd, Guildford & King's Lynn

The Publishers' policy is to use paper manufactured from sustainable forests.

About the author

Mick Cope is founder of WizOz – a network-based organization that seeks to help people and businesses optimize their potential. WizOz offers a range of different products and services, all of which are based around the ideas outlined his books. More information on WizOz can be found on his website at www.wizoz.co.uk

As an author Mick Cope has published seven books: *Leading the Organisation to Learn; Seven Cs of Consulting; Know Your Value? Value What You Know; Lead Yourself; Float-You; Personal Networking;* and *Collaborative Coaching.* He has a number of goals in life. The simple one is to live a life of personal freedom where he is able to think, feel and behave according to his values and not succumb to the demands of others. The more challenging one is to help 1,000 people achieve the same in their life.

He would love any feedback on any concepts offered in this book. Contact him at mick@wizoz.co.uk

Seven Cs training programmes

Since this book was first published many people have been trained in the Seven Cs and have seen business performance improve. Feedback from delegates and users includes many examples of how the training programmes have been used, including how they have:

- driven up the level of project success from the current 20 per cent;
- clarified a major bid, thus saving £500k;
- created a cross business language that will facilitate more effective team working and knowledge management;
- enhanced the sales consultants' ability to manage the client in a more professional manner and helps to differentiate consultants from competitors;
- created a client-centric perspective in managers previously centred on their own departmental interests;
- supported the migration from commodity to added-value sales;
- helped migration up the decision-making tree;
- enabled the consultant to discuss change issues with the client that would previously have been left as assumptions;
- helped clients understand the necessity of tackling the human aspects of change as well as the process, structural and system factors;
- ensured companies only take on work that is valuable for the business as a whole;
- provided a consistent house style for the delivery of a broad range of otherwise quite different consulting services;

As a network organization, WizOz is always keen to meet with people or organizations that would like to deliver the Seven Cs. If you have the desire and capability to develop a working partnership with WizOz, please drop us a line via the website.

For more information on the 7Cs training programme visit www.wizoz.co.uk

Contents

Preface to the Second Edition

This edition of the book seeks to introduce a range of new topics that build upon the ideas introduced in the first edition. The aim has been to expand certain ideas that have proved to be popular on the courses and with clients. I would also like to introduce new tools that develop further the constructs in each of the seven stages in the framework.

Client

■ **Heart, Head and Hand Dimensions** – The effective consultant will understand that a human being is a complex system involving the interaction of behaviours, emotions and thoughts. The three elements of *Behaviour*, having to do with activity and doing, *affective*, having to do with feelings, emotions, values and motivation, and *cognitive*, having to do with thinking and believing.

■ **MPH Mapping** – The art of great client management is often built on the ability to see the world as the client sees it. One way to do this is by understanding their 'frame of reference'. This is a process by which you understand the various types of frames or schemas that people use to make sense of the world. If the consultant can map what particular frame is being used by the client then they will be able to tune into and step into the same viewpoint and from this match their thoughts, feelings and behaviours.

■ **Compound Contracting** – Consulting contracts that are focused on selfish outcomes may deliver short-term gain but will offer little opportunity to create a long-term relationship. Effective contracting is founded on the notion of achieving shared and sustainable outcomes. The key to this choice is the absolute focus on mutual benefit and the generation of shared success through the delivery of sustainable value.

Clarify

- **Shadow Map** – The shadow map is a simple tool that allows the consultant to to understand what shadows (hidden factors) might reside between them and the client (or consumer) and understand how to take remedial action to surface the factors that need to be addressed.

Create

- **Convergent Choice** – There are many factors that help determine what makes the difference between a good or bad solution but often it comes down to the rigor of the selection at the end of the Create stage. The challenge is to ensure that the right solution is picked from the range of potential options.

Change

- **Y-Curve** – A key factor in any change stage comes with the ability and desire of the consumer to let go of the old ways of thinking, feeling and behaving and willingly adopt the new way of operating. This is dependent on a switch point where the past is discharged and the future is welcomed with relish. This willingness to switch and welcome new knowledge is often driven by the need to know 'why' the change must be made and 'why' is it important to then internalize a new set of knowledge constructs.

- **Change Spectrum** – All change sits on a simple spectrum. One end is change that is coercive, where the consultant is fully in command. At the other end of the spectrum the client or consumer is left to manage the training in their own way and under their own steam. The consultant and client must make a decision as to the appropriate level of intervention on this spectrum and understand the associated consequences.

Confirm

- **Climb the Ladder** – The Change Ladder (introduced in the Client stage) is used again as a powerful tool to map and measure the effectiveness of the change. By using this tool it becomes possible to draw a deeper understanding of the systemic factors that can cause change to fail in the long run.

- **Cockpit Confirmation** – The one common reference point in all change programmes will be people. In most cases, the success of the project will be impacted by the people's desire, understanding and capability to use the resulting product. The effective consultant will tune into and actively measure not just how the system is being deployed but also how people are thinking, feeling and behaving.

Continue

- **D-E Dissonance** – It is interesting to consider change programmes that have obviously failed to materialize their intended benefits, but the (overt) acceptance of this failure is zero. People avoid information that is likely to increase dissonance. The closer we look at this behaviour, the clearer a number of subtle avoidance patterns can be seen. Recognition of these patterns bring to life the fact that on one hand 80% of change programmes often fail but on the other it is no one's fault.

- **Learning Levels** – All change interventions should be designed to help the client and consumers achieve a specific level of knowledge that will result in improved and sustainable performance. This residual knowledge is not some add-on that can be included as an afterthought in the tender document or initial proposal. In the same way that schools, colleges and universities seek to assure the students level of knowledge before departure, so consultants should understand what knowledge the clients need before closing the engagement.

Close

- **Look back and learn** – The consultant is responsible for ensuring not just that the job is done, but for also helping the client group understand how it was done, why it worked and how the client can repeat the same exercise by flying solo. The After Action Review is a powerful tool that can assist with this process.

- **Build Framework** – No matter what the scenario, the best time to build on a relationship is the point when the customer voluntarily says how successful the previous product or service has been. At this point they are happy with the offering and will make the decision to purchase again. Logically the point on the 7Cs life cycle where this will happen is in the Close stage.

Consultant's capital

- **Knowledge Bandwidth** – So just how does a consultant create value? How do they pay the mortgage, feed the kids, buy the latest toys and pay for next year's holiday? Like all professionals, they go to market with their talent and tools. The effective consultant will have a clear and conscious appreciation of their explicit and tacit talent and how it can best be deployed in the market.

The development of the 7Cs tools is an ongoing and dynamic process that will continue for as long as clients and delegates express interest in taking them further. New tools and ideas can always be found on the WizOz website (**www.wizoz.co.uk**) under the Toolkit section.

If you have any ideas or comments about the 7Cs tools or suggestions for new ideas that can be included on the website then please submit them and they can be included in the toolkit.

Preface to the First Edition

Conventional wisdom suggests that an author should focus on the needs of the reader. I confess I took the decision to be selfish. I wanted to write a book I would use as a personal guide, memory-jogger and communication tool. However, my belief (and the argument in this book) is that the principles of consulting are sufficiently generic to ensure that what I find of use will also be of interest to colleagues in other companies and industries. The underlying principles are:

- Consulting is fundamentally about change, about helping another person, team or organization make the transformation from one state to another. This might be a physical, cognitive, emotional, structural, technological or organizational change. Unless something changes, then why should any reward be forthcoming from the client?

- Any consulting project will benefit from the application of a change model that makes sense to the client as well as the consultant.

- Change is change. Scale, context and outcomes may differ, but the basic steps are common to all assignments.

- Since content and context drive a consulting project, no two will be the same. So any consulting framework can only act as an indicative rather than a directive model.

- Successful consulting is about making a difference for the client and consumer – the goal is to deliver the contracted change, not a successful consultancy project.

These guiding principles are used to underpin the Seven Cs, from meeting the client to closing the contract and saying goodbye. However, they are not offered as sacrosanct principles that must be employed in all situations. Such a rigid approach ultimately leads to the desire to implement wholesale replicated change programmes, which in turn lead to only limited success. That approach is often behind the cynicism about the consulting industry. The aim of this book is to offer an outline framework within which each consultant can understand the context of a situation and then develop a solution that is appropriate (Lissack and Roos, 1999).

I hope that you accept my ideas in the spirit in which they are offered. Although the intention is always to offer ways and means, not must and should, this is difficult when certain ideals and beliefs are felt with passion. So although parts of the book might appear to be directive in nature, if you ever feel that the style or content is offering the 'right solution', then feel free to consign it to the waste bin.

About the reader

As I sit at the keyboard trying to visualize what you look like, where you are reading this book and what you plan to do with it, many thoughts come to mind. I see a person who has just left a large company and is about to jump into the white-water rapids of consultancy; an internal consultant who is looking for practical ways to improve how they fight their way through the political maze; and an experienced consultant browsing in a bookshop to see if there are any new change tools on the market. I can picture a range of people who might be able to use the ideas in the book. They are not looking for a definitive answer to their problems, just a way to put more structure and consistency into their personal engagement framework.

Evidence suggests that there is value in this book for anyone who helps others to change. However, it might be useful to indicate the potential reader base and the value they might get from the book.

■ **Experienced practitioners:** Although they might already be familiar with some of the ideas in this book, they will find a number of frameworks that they have not encountered before. The underlying idea behind the book is to offer new diagnostic models, not just existing ones.

■ **Competent consultants:** They will be competent in a range of roles and might have managed change both as a consultant and practitioner. The book will offer a range of new tools and techniques and, importantly, a valuable structure that will enhance their ability to manage change across various scenarios.

■ **Absolute beginners:** They have seen the change consulting process in action but have never taken direct responsibility for a client project. The book will provide a valuable insight into the way that assignments can be managed and in particular how to leverage, rather than control, change.

Across this broad range of experience and competencies there are two primary groups of people who might be reading the book:

■ **External consultant:** As an external agent you are selling services in an open market. You are possibly targeted against utilization, revenue and client contact time. Life is tough, with the job market in constant upheaval as companies respond to the constant changes in market demand for your services. In addition there is a constant cycle of new products and services with which you need to stay attuned. The company you work for might have a house consulting style that acts as a guiding methodology for you to follow. Or, it might be a smaller business where people are left to their own devices and are free to manage the process on a flexible basis. The Seven Cs of Consulting has been written to help you take a step back and think about how you currently manage your engagements. In particular I hope it will challenge you to think about some of the later stages in the framework – to consider the extent to which you really measure the success of the change programme. Do you just measure the extrinsic factors or do you try to climb inside the human element and find out about how people feel about the new way of working that you have instigated? This book should help you think about the level of sustainability that you embed into your projects. Finally, it might help you understand why closure is often the most underrated stage in any consulting life cycle. So often it is like the hurried kiss goodbye after an uncomfortable sexual liaison, when in reality it should be the point of celebration and an entry point to build on the relationship to create further work with the client.

■ **Internal consultant:** As an internal agent of change you have one of the most difficult roles there is. You desperately seek to deliver value and help the business you work for be more successful. You are full of great ideas and thoughts that the company has helped you develop through its in-house development programmes. But the trouble is that no one listens. You promote your wares to the senior team but it insists on importing in external agents who seem to charge a fortune and have no discernable value over and above what you can offer. The evidence (from people who have been through the training) is that the Seven Cs framework will help give you 'confidence'. This confidence comes from your ability to place a value on things that you do intuitively. There are two factors that cause a problem for internal consultants. The first is the absence of a house consulting style and hence a lack of common language or operating system. They just do what they do – unable really to codify how they do it. As a result they are compared against the external agents who have mega-consulting-processes that can be spread across an entire wall. Secondly, you are forced into a subordinate role by virtue of the fact that your client is (indirectly) your boss – who has absolute control over both the engagement and your career. When this happens it is easy to get into a subordinate state of mind, where you can never say no to the client and always seem to end up as the 'run-around' lackey. This subordinate role often emerges because the client (your senior managers) will always know more about the business than you, just because of the information to which they have access. However, by using the Seven Cs you will be able to make explicit your personal consulting model and use this to demonstrate your professionalism to the client. Moreover, by using the rapid mapping process you will be able to demonstrate your professionalism in a 15-minute coffee conversation – something that immediately positions you as a professional who knows what they are doing and can help deliver business value through sustainable change.

It is also important to emphasize that the consulting process does not just focus on the business consultant. The Seven Cs can be used in any situation where value is being delivered through a change activity, not just a typical business scenario:

- **Systems consultant:** The information technology (IT) sector has to understand how it can provide high-quality but cost-effective support to a range of demanding customers. This includes the systems analyst who is planning to upgrade an entire system; the help-desk operator who has to manage over 100 diagnostic interviews in a day; and the floor technicians who provide support to people at the front line.

- **Personnel manager:** Over recent years there has been a dramatic change in the human resources (HR) sector. No longer are personnel officers expected to act as back-office support to the line. They are now being rebadged as HR consultants – with a clear responsibility to provide a consultative service to a range of company departments.

- **Independent financial adviser:** The plethora of independent financial advisers offers a vivid example of the consulting process in action. These people take someone else's financial situation, create options and (hopefully) take the client through to a position where he or she has a robust financial plan in place.

- **Customer service assistant:** A client engagement is made every time a waiter deals with a customer, a bartender serves a drink or a railway conductor responds to a customer query. In each case someone has a problem to be resolved (the client), and the recipient of the question (the consultant) has an implied contract to take action.

- **Account director in advertising agency:** This role is the key interface between the client/brand and the creative output and strategic capability of the agency. Every element of the Seven Cs is critical to the success of this particularly challenging role – yet this is rarely reflected in formal training or in role support.

- **Finance director:** Finance functions in many organizations are trying to re-invent themselves. They would like to be, and be seen to be, internal experts to be consulted in the early stages of any decision with a financial element – not people whose scrutiny is to be avoided if at all possible! To make this a reality, they are beginning to learn and practise the behaviours of effective consultants.

- **Life coach:** The key emphasis in any coaching relationship is about helping someone achieve their potential through a process that is more focused and supportive than a typical training process. To be effective, the coach must follow a set of underlying actions that ensure that the client leaves the relationship with real and sustainable value and does not revert back to old habits once the comfort support offered by the coach is taken away.

- **Sports coach:** A tennis coach can take a naïve teenager all the way through to the Wimbledon finals. This is simply one long change process filled with a number of smaller change projects.

- **Doctor:** The doctor asked to diagnose a child's illness is a basic consulting engagement, in which the parents are the client and the child is the end consumer of the change.

If you can see yourself in the lists above then the chances are that this book will add value to the way you deliver value for your clients. Treat the book like an airline timetable – not as something you might read every day, but as a guide when you are planning your next round-the-world trip and certainly as something to keep in your briefcase. Although you will have your own experiences and maps, this book will help when you come across new problems or opportunities.

The Seven Cs of Consulting is written on the assumption that you have the capability and knowledge to effect the perfect change consultancy. However, consultants are neither rocket scientists nor miracle workers: they are human beings who want to learn, sometimes forget techniques, and who need the occasional tool in a tight spot. This book will be an invaluable companion to help you on the odd occasions when *you* are human too.

Acknowledgements

I would like to thank all those people who have helped me in the development of this book. I have found it inspiring that friends and strangers have been prepared to give up their valuable time to help review and comment on the early draft of the book.

In particular, I thank Tony Korycki for his amazingly detailed review of the book; Dave Chitty for helping me through the growing pains; and Andy Mcclarnon and Franchesa Cerletti for helping to transform an idea into a living thing.

I would also like to pass on my immense gratitude to the following people who offered their help in reviewing the manuscript: Dr Omar Abu-elbashar, Clay Albright, Joe Arnold, Brougham Baker, Marcio Barbosa, Richard Barron, Angela Barst, Scott Bolden, John Bruce, G. Matthew Bulley, Phillip Bump, Karen Burke, L. A. Burke, Mike and Betty Capuzza, Jane Y. Chin, Dr Frances Clark, James Cobbett, Mark Conde, Brian Connoly, Marella Cook, Kate Cooper, Gilli Coutts, Peter Cullens, Jay Curry, Patrick Damon, John Dickson, Nicol Dixon, Brook Doty, David Foster, Paul Freeman, Cynthia Froggatt, William Furlow, Ross Gabrick, Art Gelven, Verger Gerad, Peter Gibb, Paul Glen, Henry Goldman, Peter Grazier, William Gregg, Pankaj Gupta, Bill Haddock, Lynn Hauka, Nicholaas Herholdt, Dutch Holland, Matt Holt, Thomas H. Jaekel, Brian Kersh, Bryan Kester, Edward Kohl, Wort-Jan Koridon, Paul Laurence, Pat Leach, Brad Leggett, Raymond Lembong, Bob McHenry, Peter McHugh, Ken Miller, Mike Mister, Jackie Mulrooney, Benyamin R. Naba, Lars-Ola Nordqvist, Pam North, Doug Odgers, Julie O'Mara, Steve Ormsby, Thomas Oswold, Graham Parson, David Pickard, Henry Ratter, Jeff Saponja, John Self, Dave Simon, John Sloan, Sylvester Smith, Edward Stern, Lynda Stevens, Stan Stockhill, Ray Taylor, Michel Thirty, Dr Roy Thurston, Carl Vega, Gerad Verger, Andrew Vermes, Chris Welsh Martin Wilkins, Stephen Wilkinson-Carr, Stacey Williams, Dale Winsor, Michael Wright.

For thoughts on the confirmation of change ladder levels, I thank Martyn Cockram, Keith Goodwin and John Castledine. The development of the learning levels model used in the Close stage was undertaken in partnership with Paul Oliver. The Seven Cs questions were developed with assistance from Chris Fox. Thanks to Stuart Neath and Mike Moir for constant challenge and inquiry into the models and how they are presented.

Not forgetting the Financial Times Prentice Hall team, especially Amelia Lakin for helping me yet again to wade through the publishing world, George Bickerstaff for untangling and editing my original ideas into a cohesive presentation, and Pradeep Jethi, my initial publisher, who encouraged me to turn a vague idea into a tangible form. Finally Rachael Stock, who has supported me more than can be expected on my journey.

Finally, without the support of my wife and family none of this would have been possible. Thank you Lin, Michael, Joe (Mathew) and Lucy.

1

The need for sticky change

The underlying proposition that drives this book is that change is failing to deliver the anticipated benefits. There is both documented and anecdotal evidence that this failure to deliver sustainable change at times reaches 80–90 per cent – something that would not be tolerated in most professions or industries. As a result, consultants are being associated (and blamed) with the failure to deliver sustainable change. This has led to the ever-increasing reduction in the perceived brand value of the consultant. If you don't believe this, then simply go to your favourite search engine and type in the two words 'consultant' and 'joke'. The chances are that your machine will spew forth page after page of sites with jokes about consultants and the associated industry, most of which are pretty derogatory (a search by Google found 70,000 sites). A selection includes:

Did you hear that the Post Office just recalled their latest stamps? They had pictures of consultants on them . . . and people couldn't work out which side to spit on.

A man walked into a consultant's office and inquired about the rates for a study. 'Well, we usually structure the project up front, and charge $50 for three questions', replied the consultant. 'Isn't that awfully steep?' asked the man. 'Yes', the consultant replied, 'and what was your third question?'

What is the difference between a consultant and a cablecar? The cable car stops when it loses track.

It might be that you do a great job, don't chase the money, follow an ethical path and always seek to satisfy the customer. However, call yourself a consultant with caution and trepidation because the brand is suffering. It seems that in so many cases clients believe that they are not receiving value through sustainable change. Instead they are getting (or believe they are getting) short-lived, faddish solutions that collapse the moment the consultant walks out of the door.

The Seven Cs framework is designed to help deliver value through sustainable change for the client. This phrase – 'value through sustainable change' – is the foundation stone that underpins and drives the whole concept and framework presented in this book. This is because these factors must be present and managed in any effective consulting process:

- **Change:** A change must always take place. If the client or consumers do not think, feel or behave any differently at the end of the engagement, then what is the value? It is imperative that the consultant and client are both clear as to the change that is required.

- **Value:** There must be explicit value realization. Only by understanding and taking responsibility for the change and the value derived from the change can the consultant and client develop their capacity to repeat the activity and so enhance performance further at a later date.

- **Sustainability:** There is little point in making a change that has value if it does not stick. This is it the root problem with so many change programmes. The consultant and client have a great time, make amazing leaps in performance, celebrate their success and then move on, only to find that little value remains three to six months later.

This failure to hold on to the gains and drive 'sticky' change often stems from a simple failure to understand and manage many of the deep forces that drive change. No matter what the engagement, the process will be quite simple: the consultant enters, does something and then leaves. Although much of the energy is focused on the middle stage (while the consultant is around), much more effort needs to be expended to understand and manage what will happen once the change is implemented and the consultant departs.

> **❝ the consultant's job is to put opposing forces in place that will compensate and counteract the repressive forces ❞**

The reality is that once the consultant departs one of three things can happen: the change can build on the early gains and get better, it stays the same, or decays and gets worse. The factors that will drive this post-intervention decay will generally be the systematic or contextual forces that cause all change programmes to fail. These include apathy, resource shortage, political action and environmental changes. The list is almost endless and probably impossible to complete. However, the consultant's job is to understand just what detrimental forces will impact the change and take action (whilst still in the engagement phase) to put opposing forces in place that will compensate and counteract the repressive forces. This might be to create internal champions or agents of change, ensure the budget is held back, develop symbolic artefacts to reinforce the need for change, or arrange for post-intervention activities. No one action is the right one. What is important is that the consultant and client consider what repressive forces will kick in post-engagement and ensure that pre-emptive action is taken to compensate.

Repressive forces

The primary determinant that drives any successful outcome will be the balance between the repressive forces that cause the client and company to revert to the old way of operating and the positive forces that help them hold on to the gains (*see* Figure 1.1). Although the repressive forces will often depend on the content of the client's project, there are a number of common repressive forces that will cause the engagement to fail to deliver sustainable value:

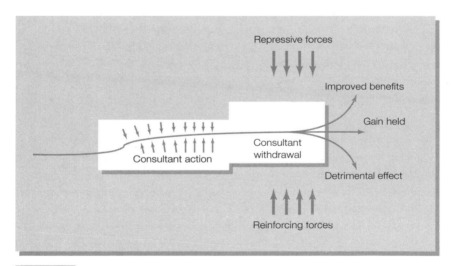

Figure 1.1   Consultancy process

■ The client has not been sufficiently challenged in the opening stage to ensure they really understand their current position and test the seriousness of their intent to take action. The result is they embark on the journey only to find that they do not really want to make the necessary sacrifices when under pressure.

▓ There is a failure to clarify what root issues really caused the present situation. The consequence is that solutions are generated that resolve surface symptoms but do not touch the root cause.

▓ Imported or ill-thought-out solutions are created that will not resolve the problem. This often occurs when clients think they have ready-made solutions that 'worked elsewhere'. The trouble is that all solutions are context-dependent and can rarely be transported without some form of modification.

▓ The end users or consumers of the engagement are not helped to work through the pain of change and to let go of the old way of thinking, feeling and behaving. The client might be prepared to take on board a new way of working while the consultant is around to act as an external prop, but if the change feels uncomfortable then there will be a natural tendency to revert back to the old way of operating once the consultant has left.

▓ There is no accurate measurement and confirmation that the change has delivered the desired outcome. This is often the hard part – actually confirming that the desired change has taken place. It is easy enough to measure the extrinsic factors to demonstrate that the change has been successful, but unless the intrinsic factors are measured then any change may well be a short-term fix. No matter how pretty and big the new computer is, how all encompassing the re-engineered process is, unless people want to use the new ideas then they will fail to deliver long-term value for the business.

▓ Once the client's eye is off the ball and focused on new ideas, often they fail to continue to operate in a new way. There is a natural human tendency to revert back to the comfort zone. It is easy to stay on the diet when in constant contact with the food coach, but what happens when you are out on your own and are confronted by a large chocolate cake? Unless you have really embedded a sense of self-reliance and inner security then the old urges will take over and destroy all the good work.

▓ The change is not properly closed down and the end of the engagement just drifts. When this happens it can leave both the client and consultant with a sense of frustration and uncertainty – neither is really sure if they have added the contracted value to the engagement.

When the client and consultant do not address these issues with passion and professionalism, the result is an engagement that fails to deliver value through sustainable change. Conversely, when the consultant and client jointly address these issues, the chances of delivering sustainable value through change are enhanced.

Reinforcing forces

The Seven Cs framework offers a number of drivers that will act as reinforcing factors to compensate for the repressive forces. These are:

- At the very outset, ensure that the whole picture is understood and that the client is not just offering a restricted view or interpretation of their situation. The consultant must seek to understand all the parameters that will impact on the current situation and the desired outcome that the client wishes to achieve. This is important for two reasons. First, it ensures that the client confirms that they really need the support of the consultant or if the situation is something they can resolve on their own. Second, it allows the consultant to test the client's seriousness of intent. The consultant will not want to spend time and energy working with a client who decides halfway through the engagement that they do not really want to complete the project after all because of budget cuts/market changes/political issues (delete as appropriate). As a partnership it is right that both parties should fully challenge each other to test for seriousness of intent and that both have the right to forgo the opportunity to work together.

- It is a vary rare problem that does not have roots in a lower-level problem – maybe one instigated weeks, months or even years ago. Although it is very easy for the client and consultant to dig only so far to clarify and understand the root cause, the consultant has a responsibility to ensure that the full depth of the problem is explored and resolved and so prevented from resurfacing at a later date. The consultant must always seek to ask why, why and why again and not be prepared to be shrugged of by deflective strategies offered up by the client when they feel that the questioning is becoming difficult.

- There will always be time pressure in any engagement. Both the coach and client are busy people and are probably being pressured by their boss or organization to get things moving so they can 'get back and do some real work'. It is this repressive force that causes both parties to seek out instant solutions – quick fixes that can get the problem sorted so they can get on with things. The positive force applied here must be the emotional courage and strength of both players to resist any short-term pressure and really try to seek out a solution that is most appropriate for this particular situation – and not just borrow a quick-fit solution from an earlier engagement.

- Once the diagnosis is compete and the solution is established then the client will be put under real pressure. Until this point everything is conceptual and the client can talk about what they are 'going' to do. At some stage they will have to 'do'. It is at this point they have to move out of the comfort zone and really start to address what change they will need to make to achieve the desired outcome The positive force at the stage may well have to come from the consultant. This might be empathic or soft support to help encourage the client through the change, or, at the other end of a spectrum, it might involve adopting a more commanding presence to drive the change.

- There is a natural human tension that means we are scared to stand on the scales at the end of a week's dieting, so we need a positive force to counter this negativity. Often the positive force comes from developing a more robust understanding of the measurement process. So often measurement is a black art that only the brave dare to understand, but measurement is a really powerful process when used in a positive way. Sometimes you have to be brave and look under the bed in order to find out that there are no monsters lying in wait.

- There is no feeling like putting on that comfortable pair of old shoes. You have worn them for years and they have always served you well. One day you decide to change and invest in a new pair. After a day or two your feet ache as the new leather fails to bend to the way you walk and you decide to go back to the old shoes just to save your aching feet. It is this natural resistance to new ways of thinking, feeling and behaving that often kills the engagement. The consultant and client must counteract this repressive force with a positive one. This positive force is often one of preparation, preparation and preparation. In any change process you know that a change is coming, so the time to start getting ready for the shift is from the outset of the engagement. Be acutely tuned into what will help make the new way of working comfortable and what factors will cause discomfort. Manage both to amplify the positive forces and attenuate the areas that hinder the change.

> **“ be acutely tuned into what will help make the new way of working comfortable and what factors will cause discomfort ”**

- Finally, you have just spent the last six months running a gruelling project at work and it has really taken its toll on your work and home life. You are sure that everything is wrapped up and complete. You are so confident that when one of the team suggests that you run a closure workshop to dot the i's and cross the t's you politely tell them to take a hike. The job is done, so now everyone can go on holiday. This is a natural process of coming down from a big high. But sometimes you have to resist this pressure to ignore the last element because it is at this last stage that the learning takes place, the value is realized and any hidden problems are identified. The positive force required at this stage is one of perseverance – to hold on to the end and hopefully celebrate the success of the change project.

By looking at the change engagement as a battle of reinforcing and repressive forces it becomes easier to map and measure what factors will enable the change to live beyond a short-term fix and deliver value through sustainable change.

2

The Seven Cs framework

The Seven Cs framework is constructed around a number of dynamic stages, each of which emphasizes a different aspect within the consultancy life cycle. Each stage represents a particular phase that a consultancy process will follow. Within each stage is a set of sub-elements and diagnostic tools that are used to ease the engagement process. These all come together to form a total framework that will act as a guide to any engagement. Each of the stages can be undertaken independently, jointly or in parallel with each other. The seven stages are (*see* Figure 2.1):

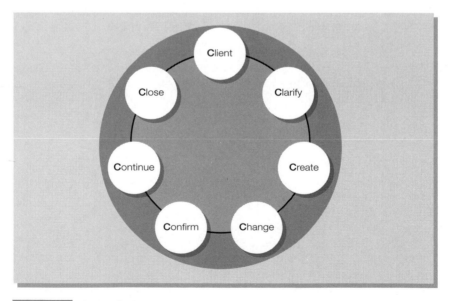

Figure 2.1   Seven Cs framework

1 **Client:** Define the client's orientation of the world, their perception of the situation, what goals they have regarding the final outcome and who has power to influence the outcome. Once this stage is concluded, you will have a clear agreement as to what value you will deliver to the client and what value they will offer in return. The essence of this stage is to understand the person and the problem.

2 **Clarify:** Determine the nature and detail of the problem to be addressed. Map the construction of the system under consideration, identify what and who is to be included and excluded from the change and determine what areas pose a risk for the assignment. The primary question to understand is 'What is going on?'.

3 **Create:** Use creative techniques to develop a sustainable solution. Critically develop a solution that is measured against clear success criteria, takes as divergent a view as possible to find potential options and then chooses the option that meets the defined criteria.

4 **Change:** Understand the fundamental aspects that drive and underpin the change process, and in particular the human factors that need to be managed.

5 **Confirm:** Ensure that change has taken place using quantitative and qualitative measures.

6 **Continue:** Ensure that the change will be sustained, using learning that emerges from the transition, the skills of the change agents and the sharing of new knowledge and skills.

7 **Close:** End the engagement process with the client, emphasizing the need to understand the final outcomes, the added value, new learning and what further action you might undertake.

> **❝ consulting projects are like life – they are unpredictable and will throw up new and different surprises around every**

Contained within each of these seven stages are tools and diagnostic models that are applied during the consulting process. These tools are not meant to be exclusive to the stage and can be used at any time within the life of the project. This reinforces the notion that the framework is meant as a guide for action, not a rigid process that needs to be followed slavishly.

It is important to emphasize that although the stages in the Seven Cs model are shown in a linear fashion, it is a rare consultancy project that would follow such a structured path. Consulting projects are like life – they are unpredictable and will throw up new and different surprises around every corner. The stages are symbolic rather than prescriptive, offering different actions and viewpoints to be applied depending on the needs of the client, consumer and consultant.

Rapid mapping

It is amazing to think about how many important things are decided in the first 10 minutes of any client consultant meeting. These include:

- the nature of the relationship and whether there is mutual respect in the professionalism of both players;

- whether the consultant wants to take the client's project on;

- whether the client wants to employ the consultant;

- whether the proposed project has life, will survive and can add value for the business;

- what level of risk both players are exposed to by entering into a partnership.

The problem is that both players need to ascertain this type of information before committing to any form of formal relationship, but this can be difficult when under time pressure. The client is being pressured to fix the problem fast because costs are rising and they are losing customers. The consultant is being (subtly) pressured to take on the client because they need to hit the utilization and revenue targets. As a consequence the first consulting date often looks like the first romantic encounter. Both players are eager to meet and get to know each other, while at the same time have a pre-arranged escape path just in case it does not feel right. The trouble is that a successful kiss on a first date is not a good predictor that a long-term relationship will develop. In the same way, the early coffee chat or beauty parade offers little chance for either side to really ascertain if the consulting partnership will enable both sides to create real value from the engagement.

The Seven Cs framework is quite deliberately not a complex model. This means that it can be used in a very short timeframe to produce a rich and robust understanding of the client's situation without attempting to look at the detail or resolve the problem too quickly. This allows the consultant to determine if they wish to pursue the project, the client to determine if they wish to work with the consultant and for both players rapidly to ascertain if the project is worth pursuing.

The rapid mapping technique allows you to spin the client around the Seven Cs in 10–15 minutes (*see* Figure 2.2). The goal is not to climb inside the situation or define a solution. It is simply to understand the client's perception of the problem and make a conscious choice about whether to proceed to the next stage of the engagement. It works in the same way as when buying a new car – you ascertain a number of key points about the person and the car over the telephone or e-mail; if at this stage you feel comfortable that the sale is viable and of value then you might be prepared to commit a few hours to drive to the seller's house to have a look in more detail. The consulting process is often no different. The potential client might call you up, meet you in a corridor, or simply pop in as they are passing the office. At that stage they may outline the problem they are trying to resolve. This stage is normally quite rushed as both client and consultant are in the middle of something else, so there is literally time just for a coffee and croissant. Hence all you might have time for is to ask the client the following questions:

■ **Client:**
 – What is the 'specific' change you require?
 – Is the change tangible or intangible?
 – Is the outcome under your control?
 – What value can I add?

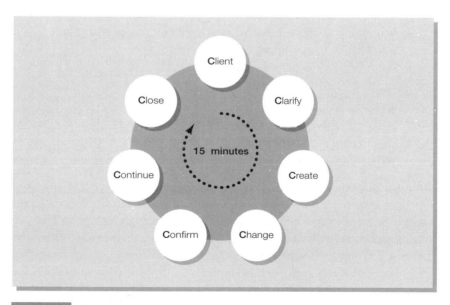

Figure 2.2   Rapid mapping

▇ **Clarify:**
- Is the change based on fact or intuition?
- What are the undiscussables?
- What/who will block the change?
- What are the risks of changing?

▇ **Create:**
- What is the criteria for a good solution?
- What solutions do you have at present?
- Do you want to be creative or practical?
- What role would we play in the creative process?

▇ **Change:**
- Will people let go of the past?
- What resistance will there be?
- What resources can you draw upon?
- What is the empathy – command balance?

▇ **Confirm:**
- How will you know that the change has worked?
- How will you feel when the change has worked?
- How will you know if the users like the change?
- How will you know if the users are using the change?

▇ **Continue:**
- Have previous change initiatives failed?
- How will you know if the change is not working at a later date?
- What might cause slippage or reversion?
- What factors will help the change last?

▇ **Close:**
- What can you learn from the change?
- Will you be dependent on anyone?
- What value will the change add?
- What will be the next action once the change is complete?

At this stage you have briefly spun the client around the Seven Cs framework and should have enough data to make a go or no-go decision. If you can get round the seven stages and come away both knowing and feeling that the engagement can be delivered, will add value and will be sustainable, then the chances are that it is worth progressing to the next stage. If, however, you touch some road blocks (explicit or implicit) then you still have the option to decline the invitation. Although you might not wish to reject potential client engagements, you might have cause for concern if the client offers any of the responses in Figure 2.3 as you progress round the rapid mapping process.

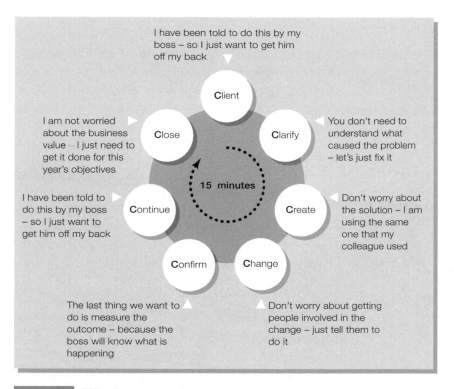

Figure 2.3 Difficult engagements

One of the most significant commercial benefits of the rapid mapping process is that the client cannot fail to be impressed with your professionalism. Within 15 minutes you will have demonstrated:

- that you understand what makes successful change work;

- the ability to use a process tool to investigate and understand a problem, even within a limited timeframe;

- that where necessary you can analyze with clarity and not bluster and bluff through the use of complex concepts that no-one can understand;

- any possible areas of risk that the client might not have considered or understood prior to the conversation.

More important, by sending signals of your integrity and professionalism the chances are that the client will be more than willing to move to the next stage of the engagement – which would be ask you to meet with their team for a full review to consider the project in more detail.

Spiral build

Once you have the confidence that the engagement is valid and has value then it makes sense to progress from the 15-minute spin to a two-hour meeting. Building the relationships and engagement over time allows the consultant to be sure that all aspects of the project are considered and thus reduce risk from the process. It also allows the client to gain a deeper appreciation of the change process being employed by the consultant – something that needs to happen more if the relationship is to be enhanced. With each spin of the wheel the client begins to appreciate what process the consultant is following and the importance of each of the seven stages to the delivery of sustainable value (*see* Figure 2.4).

> **building the relationships and engagement over time allows the consultant to be sure that all aspects of the project are considered**

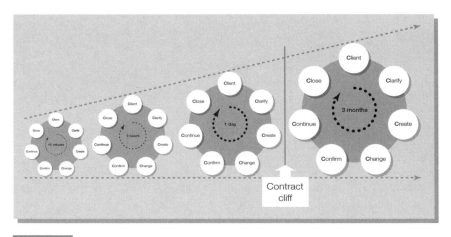

Figure 2.4   Spiral build

Although there is no defined or set process for the spiral build, the one objective that should underpin the process is that the questions used by the consultant at each stage should grow and build on the previous set. The questions will always vary with the context of the change being considered and the context in which it sits, but the following range of questions and issues are typical of those that might be considered over the life of the spiral build:

- **Client:**
    - What is the problem or reason for the project/change?
    - Why has the problem surfaced?
    - What are the implications of doing nothing?

- Who is the real/end client and what is their level of 'buy-in' to the proposed project?
- Who are the end consumers (people who will be affected) and what is their support for the project?
- What trade offs will have to be made to deliver the final change (what will have to be given up)?
- How will things be different or better once the project is complete?
- What concerns do you have about the project?
- What is the background – has it been tried before?
- How will you know when it has been successful?

■ **Clarify:**
- What is the reason for the current situation?
- What evidence do you have to indicate there is a problem?
- How sure are you as to the cause of the problem?
- Do you have any concerns about factors that might impact the project?
- What concerns would the consumers or users of the change voice about what will happen?
- Are there any side effects that could arise from undertaking the project?
- Who else is involved in the change – do they support it?
- Who will any change impact upon?
- Who can stop the change from being successful?
- What are the unspoken or shadow issues that might cause the change to fail?

■ **Create:**
- What constraints are there on any proposed solution?
- What are the criteria for a successful solution?
- Is there anything we cannot do?
- What is the budget and timescale?
- What have you thought of already?
- What has been tried before?
- What risks are you prepared to take?
- What flexibility is there in any proposed solution?
- How will you know when you see the right solution?

■ **Change:**
- Who will be impacted by the change?
- What will their response be?
- What methods will you be prepared to use to implement the change (controlled to empathetic)?

- Will we have the necessary power to effect a successful change?
- What other changes are taking place that will impact on our programme?
- Do you have a standard engagement/deployment process that will have to be followed?
- Are there any aspects of the change that we will not be managing?
- How brutal are you prepared to be to make the change happen?
- Where is the power to effect change held?
- Do you appreciate the full cost involved in effecting the change successfully?
- Have you segmented those people who will and will not resist and who the key influencers might be?

■ **Confirm:**
- How important is it for measurement to take place?
- Are you prepared to pay for the measurement to take place?
- Will you use quantitative or qualitative measures?
- How will you measure the consumer's buy-in to the change?
- Who will undertake the measurement?
- What measures have you used in the past?
- How will you measure our performance?
- For how long will measurements continue?

■ **Continue:**
- How long do you want the change to last?
- Have you tried this before – did it last – if not why?
- What can we do to help ensure that the change will last?
- Are you prepared to invest in things that will make it last?
- Do you have the resources in place to support any change?
- Are responsibilities defined to maintain the change once it is complete?
- Is there anyone who will try to eradicate the change once it is complete?

■ **Close:**
- What does 'good' look like?
- Once the change is complete what differentiated value will we have added?
- What can be learnt from the exercise?
- How can this learning be used elsewhere?
- What can we do to ensure that you are not dependent on us once the change is complete?

  – What would we have to do for you to recommend us to a colleague?
  – What else might we be able to help you with?

Once you have spun round the wheel a number of times then you and the client will have the confidence to commit to a full contract. At this point you have reached contract cliff – the point of no return where you both agree to commit to a change process. At this stage you can then enter into another Seven Cs cycle that will progress to the next stage of the engagement. For more on this, see the build model in Chapter 9 (Stage Seven: Close).

3

Stage one: Client

Trade is a social act.   John Stuart Mill

The consulting process begins and ends with the client. However, it is all too easy (when faced with pressing deadlines and the need to generate revenue) to place greater emphasis on the area of problem resolution. However, it is imperative you apply sufficient time and energy to understanding the person as well as the problem. The client is the voice of the organization, the paymaster and the confidant in times of trouble. It is important to establish a solid relationship that will hold together when unforeseen problems occur once the real – and often unseen – issues surrounding the problem start to surface and need to be dealt with.

One reason why so many consulting projects fail or get a bad name is because the commercial need subsumes the drive to manage an effective relationship. As a result, the client is treated as a thing, rather than a real person. Just like the Tom and Jerry cartoon films where Tom will look at Jerry and see the next meal rather than a mouse, in the same way, the client can feel like a large dollar sign – as a revenue stream rather than a valued individual. It is important that you never treat the client as a means to an end, where the end is a contract or money.

To this end, the Client stage consist of two distinct groups of tools: the first are designed to understand the nature of the social relationship with the client and the second focus more on the problem or opportunity.

Understand the person

The client–consultant relationship is the foundation stone that supports the entire assignment. Consulting is driven by the extent to which you can get close to the client – to arrive at a position where you become more of a confidant or trusted adviser than a supplier of services. How far you can build a sense of rapport with a client before the consulting process begins will affect your ability to deliver sustainable change.

Rapport is not something that occurs when you first meet the client. It is something that you must think through before the first contact. Your goal is to ensure that when you walk through the client's door for the first time you are totally tuned in and focused on their mindset and needs. By the time you take the last few steps into the client office, you must be clear and confident on the following four issues:

■ **(Three-legged) stool:** Who is the client, who are the end consumers of any change I might make and what is my primary role within the relationship?

■ **Head–heart negotiation:** – To what extent do they tend to take emotional decisions or are they more logical in outlook?

■ **Trust index:** To what extent do they trust me and how can I make it more likely they will before the first contact?

■ **Push–pull relationship:** Will I use a social style to build a relationship with the client or focus on the product pitch?

Consider one of the most common engagements that we all experience – the double glazing salesperson. Although the job is primarily viewed as a sales process, a successful sale will actually go through all seven stages in the Seven Cs framework. Now, the secret of a good sale is not in the techniques that the salesperson uses, it is in the mental framework that is in place before the client meeting take place. A good salesperson is not thinking about their products or what products the client might want. As they walk up the driveway they will be reflecting on the deeper emotional issues that will come into play: how does the customer feel about the visit? Have they any preconceptions about me or my company? Do I have any way to build an emotional connection with them early in the relationship? Who is the real decision maker in the family? Although the salesperson might not have the answer to these questions, they will be mentally focused on getting an answer to them in the first few minutes of the engagement.

In many cases the emotional decisions that people form in the first five minutes of a meeting will drive how they think and behave towards someone for the next five months. As a consultant you must be able to manage this window of opportunity to ensure that the client as a minimum warms to you as a person, and ideally starts to respect your professional capability. To achieve this you must quite consciously think through your opening approach and how you can influence the client's perception of you. This approach must be used whatever your situation. It might be that you are about to make the first telephone call to the client to arrange for a meeting; or you are about to meet for coffee and a bagel; or you are at the conference where you are about to present to 300 people; or you are simply making eye contact with an old client at a party. Before you utter the first word it is essential that you have thought through and appraised your relationship against the four issues listed above.

Understand the problem

There also needs to be a high level discipline and rigour built into the early stages of the client relationship so that you can fully understand the problem or opportunity being presented by the client. Although this seems obvious, in reality this stage is often dealt with superficially, causing problems to emerge later.

The steps outlined below help to address many of these issues by offering a simple but effective framework to ensure that all the key elements are dealt with at the start of the life cycle. They include:

- **MPH client mapping:** From the very beginning, seek to view the problem as the client sees it, not how you see it.
- **OUTCOME testing:** Through the use of questions, draw out the client's real wished-for outcome.
- **Change ladder:** Remove fog from the initial situation problem by focusing on the dominant area where the intervention might need to take place.
- **Compound contracting:** Agree a synergistic contract that will set out a framework for action, define the roles and responsibilities of each party and offer a tool by which the success or failure of the change process can be measured.

Three-legged stool

Consulting projects often fail because all the needs of the various stakeholders are not taken into consideration. This puts the whole project out of alignment because one group's needs are given priority over those of another. Like a three-legged stool, the consultancy process must always be in balance, and the needs of the client, consultant and consumer (end user) understood and maintained (*see* Figure 3.1). All three have deep motivational needs and if one is left partially dissatisfied, the project is likely to hit problems.

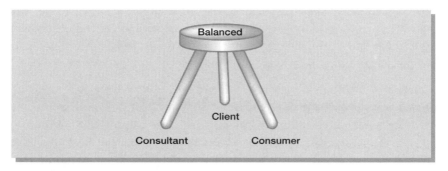

Figure 3.1   Three-legged stool

In any project that has failed this lack of alignment is likely to be a source of the problem:

■ You have developed a good sense of rapport with the client, agreed a contract and are ready to start the implementation phase. However, you discover that in reality the client has instigated the assignment for personal or political ambitions and has not taken the needs of the consumer into account. Therefore, the project will possibly fail because of resistance from the end user (consumer misalignment).

■ You contract with the regional director to implement a new customer service technique. However, as you start to roll the programme out, the client takes on a new set of operational responsibilities. Therefore the client offers figurehead support to the change but little else (client misalignment).

■ You meet a client who has gained significant support for a change process. Although you agree to manage the change, the client has beaten you down on price and you are running at a loss on the project. This is because you have only taken it on as a stopgap until a more lucrative contract comes along. Although you deliver the project to the letter of the contract, your heart is not in it, so valuable opportunities to improve the outcomes are missed (consultant misalignment).

In these three examples the imbalance shows as a lack of energy on the part of the client, consumer or consultant. This misalignment arises because each of the three agents has a different perception of the purpose of the project. In a change programme, all three agents may think they have a clear and shared understanding of the change. But, when viewed collectively, it turns out that they are all thinking in different ways. This results in one of two situations. In the first, the different parties go into fight mode, each battling to assert their model over the other group. In the second, the weaker party decides to take an apathetic stance and let the others win (although often only in the short term – their vengeance may come eventually in more subtle ways).

Imagine a traditional personnel project where you have contracted to install and develop a new appraisal system. The client's view is that the line managers have been ineffective in appraising their teams because they do not have the necessary feedback and counselling skills. The client views this as primarily a capability issue and has contracted you to improve the organization's ability to manage its people. However, although you are building a whole system for the company, you believe that the need for a new appraisal system is merely a symptom. You feel the key issue is the poor morale created by the fact that managers have little desire to follow the procedural guidelines laid down by the personnel department.

❝ it is essential that you check with the client and consumer that a shared appreciation of the issue is being addressed ❞

For their part, the line managers, or end consumers, think you have been employed simply to install another bureaucratic system, effectively changing the procedures that direct how the senior managers want the business to operate. The problem is that the operational managers will ignore the new procedure because they prefer their own local methods. They are convinced that managers should be allowed to manage their teams as they think fit and that it is unlikely that any top-down mechanistic system will help them to deal with the problems they face at the operational end of the business.

Unless any imbalance is brought out and resolved early on, it will fester away behind the scenes, only to explode later. It is essential that you take time out at all stages of the consulting cycle to review constantly and check with the client and consumer that a shared appreciation of the issue is being addressed. Unless this happens then problems will eventually arise – typically in the guise of political wrangling, deferred milestones, communication problems and even industrial action.

Head–heart negotiation

A human being is a complex system involving the interaction of behaviours, emotions and thoughts. There are three elements or domains (*see* Figure 3.2):

■ **Behavioural:** Having to do with activity and doing – the hand.

■ **Affective:** Having to do with feelings, emotions, values and motivation – the heart.

■ **Cognitive:** Having to do with thinking and believing – the head.

This model is not new or unique. It is the basic psychological view of humankind that goes back to the Greeks and probably the Egyptians. It views a human as composed of three interdependent processes. All are interdependent, and no one part can change without the other parts also changing.

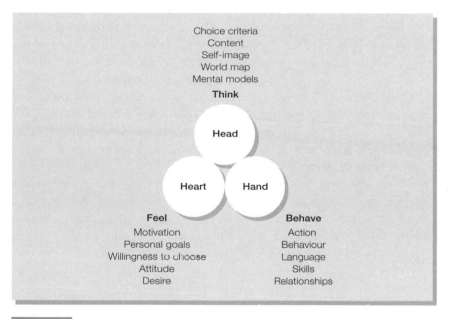

Figure 3.2   Three interdependent processes

Driver negotiation

Everything we say and do (hand) is driven by a combination of our cognitive (head) and affective (heart) dimensions (*see* Figure 3.3). Although everybody has head and heart dimensions that drives their behaviour, some pay more attention to their thoughts than to their feelings, while others pay more attention to their feelings than to their thoughts.

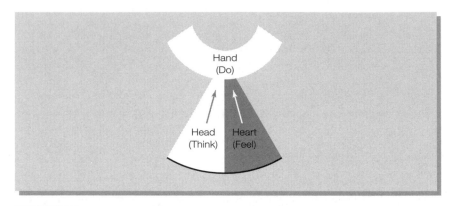

Figure 3.3 Driver negotiation

In Homer's *Odyssey* Ulysses is faced with a classic interpersonal conflict. He knows he will soon encounter the Sirens – the mythical female enchantresses who try to lure seafaring men to their island and to eventual death. These nymphs had the power of charming by their song all who heard them, so that mariners were impelled to cast themselves into the sea to destruction. Circe directed Ulysses to stop the ears of his seamen with wax, so that they should not hear the strain. She advised him to bind himself to the mast, and to enjoin his people, whatever he might say or do, by no means to release him until they had passed the Sirens' island. Ulysses obeyed these directions. As his ship approached the Sirens' island, the sea was calm, and over the waters came notes of music that caused Ulysses to struggle to get loose and cry out for his people to release him; but they, obedient to his previous orders, sprang forward and bound him still faster. They held on their course and the music grew fainter until it ceased to be heard. With joy, Ulysses gave his companions the signal to unseal their ears, and they relieved him from his bonds.

In this way Ulysses manages his competing preferences. He knows that his heart will pull him to listen to the music but his head says not to listen, since he will die. This internal contradiction or inconsistency is one he faced and was able to resolve. Unfortunately, it is a negotiation that so many people fail to resolve. The addict wants a drink but knows it is wrong; Eve wanted the apple but knew she should not eat it; I don't want to get up in the morning but know I have to make a living. These two conflicting dimensions can be seen as impulse (heart) and reason (head).

Every second of the day people are choosing between what they want to do and what they should do. Think of shopping – it is often a constant turmoil of want and should. Want the king prawns but should get the cheap prawns to save money, want the expensive cut of meat but should get the cheap cut so that it will go further. Often these 'want' and 'should' drivers are driven by short and long-term payback or discounting factors. People may want to act in a way that satisfies immediate needs but feel they should look for the long-term payback in order to be sensible.

Interestingly, this is just the internal conflict that salespeople often exploit. The car salesperson, double glazing salespeople, or even impulse purchase stands at the exit in a supermarket are using this internal conflict to trigger short-term impulsive purchases. They use every trick in the book to encourage people to focus on what they want rather than what they should have.

Dimensional drivers

Head-type people will use facts, reality or principles and in many ways may seem slightly formal in their behaviour. They use established concepts and perceptions as their guides to action. These people may have a preference to make decisions based on what appears to be logical or rational. They are very much fact decision makers and can be seen to be quite sensible in the way they make choices.

Heart people will use words like 'caring' or 'values' and seem to be quite personal and emotional in the way they talk. In contrast to head people, those who pay more attention to their feelings are said to follow their heart, which means that much of what they do is based on emotion or desire. These people will make decisions based against emotional criteria. They will focus on what feels right at that moment and effectively make a heart choice.

The behaviours and language associated with these dimensions can be seen in Table 3.1.

Table 3.1 **Personal choices**

Head	Heart
■ Principle based – i.e. this is the right thing to do	■ Values based – i.e. this feels like the right thing to do
■ The need for a right decision may take precedence over the success of the relationship	■ Decisions strive for effective relationships and consensus
■ Assesses pros and cons to put logical factors first	■ Sensitive to the needs and emotions of the person

When they can get past the stereotypes, these two orientations usually find they can complement each other quite well, with the head dimension providing a source of clarity and toughness, and the heart driver providing a source of compassion and personal consideration. Rather than being an either or choice, the dimensions might be seen as an arc. Some people will have a strong preference for the heart orientation, others for the head, while the rest will sit somewhere in the middle (*see* Figure 3.4).

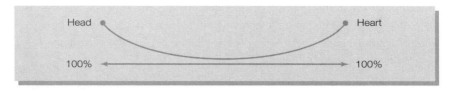

Figure 3.4   **Head and heart preferences**

It is interesting that, in the USA at least, about 67 per cent of all men define themselves as thinkers, while 67 per cent of females are feelers. It is this that might drive the stereotype that women are emotional while men are logical. Or perhaps this is the way we train our children, expecting boys to be more rational while allowing girls to vent their feelings. Again this preference is a continuum rather than two extremes: most people are probably able to use both logic and emotion in their decision making. Nevertheless, most of us will be more comfortable using one over the other.

As a consultant, the challenge you have to face is to understand that inside the client may be two people. There is the logical rational person with whom you would use language such as what you should do or what is the best way to manage. And there is the emotional person who needs you to ask how they feel and what they want. In addition, the consultant must be aware of the dual personality inside themselves and how the head and heart preference will drive how they behave. The key thing is that head and heart drivers will be manifest in the way the coach and client talk. Language is the primary bridge in a coaching situation and so the coach must be acutely tuned in to their internal drivers, the client's internal drivers and the language that occurs when the two meet.

The important action for any consultant is to:

- understand their preference (head or heart);
- listen to the client's language to map their preference;
- develop the ability to flex their own preferred style and adapt to that of the client.

The effective consultant will develop the capability to step into the client's world rather than forcing them to step into their own preference. If you have a head preference and meet a client who has a heart preference, then be emotional. Use affective language and make the client feel comfortable by entering their world. After a while you can then shift the language more towards a head style and adopt a more logical tone. Above all, try to migrate the client at a pace at which they feel comfortable – do not rush just because you want to get the facts on the table as quickly as possible.

Trust index

Trust is the cement that builds and sustains any client relationship. It provides the underlying bond to ensure that promises are kept, work is completed on time and knowledge shared. Even before this, it is what gives the client the confidence to seek your services in the first place. O'Shea and Madigan (1997) emphasize this point:

The decision to bring in management consultants is one that can place at stake the careers of the very people who hire them, the jobs of thousands of employees, millions upon millions of dollars invested by shareholders, and long-term relationships with customers. Indeed, the most valuable asset a corporation has, its reputation, can be put on the line. And all these risks are connected to the motivation of outsiders whose primary interest is in fattening the treasuries of their consulting partnerships.

Whenever a potential client thinks about employing you as a consultant, they are betting on the future. They need to make a rational decision (head) based on the premise that you will deliver an outcome. However this decision is often taken on little more than a guess or gut feel and much of this intuitive process depends on the extent to which they trust you (heart).

The choices you make about the babysitter, frozen food or new car are all influenced by the trust you have that the product or service will deliver an agreed conclusion. So when you purchase these products, what is it that gives you this sense of trust? Similarly, how do you engender this same confidence in a potential client? What do you need to do that will help them to choose your products and services over a competitor?

The problem with trust is that it is like a good partnership – you know it when you see it, but it is hard to define the individual contributory factors. As an example, think about someone whom you know well and trust implicitly. What is it that makes you think of that person? What do they and you do to maintain the relationship? Now think of another person you know just as well but do not trust. Consider what it is that each of you does to create a relationship lacking in substance and value. What is the impact of such a relationship and what overheads does it impose? If you ask that person to do a job or help you out, to what extent do you have to give up valuable personal time to check and oversee the work? Do you lose sleep because there is a fear in the back of your mind that they might not deliver on time?

The time that the client and coach spend with each other is an investment process, where each chooses to offer and invest their personal resources and capital to create social capital. If you end up spending a large chunk of your time with people who actually turn out to be untrustworthy, it feels awful. Consultancy partnerships are like savings accounts – you put time and energy into them in the hope of a return on investment: a resolution of the problem for the client and appropriate reward for the consultant.

Managing the investment

A simple definition of TRUST can be used to measure and manage the nature of a relationship:

- **Truthful:** The extent to which integrity, honesty and truthfulness are developed and maintained.
- **Responsive:** The openness, mental accessibility or willingness to share ideas and information freely.
- **Uniform:** The degree of consistency, reliability and predictability contained within the relationship.
- **Safe:** The loyalty, benevolence or willingness to protect, support and encourage each other.
- **Trained:** The competence, technical knowledge and capabilities of both parties.

Where these five attributes are soundly in place, the client relationship might be deemed to be in credit; where one or more of the factors is diminished or missing, it is possible the relationship is moving into a debit. For any relationship it is very easy to move the account sliders on the account into credit or debit – as seen in Figure 3.5. When working with a client you only have to give a false reason for being late one day to weaken the 'truthful' slider; ignore some of their requests for help for them to feel that you are not being 'responsive'; tell them different things at different times to upset the 'uniform' balance; be indiscrete about someone else to raise concerns about how 'safe' they feel sharing company issues; or appear not to be a competent in the questioning process to reduce the value in the 'trained' sub-account. Slippage in any one area of the trust fund erodes the value of the trust fund and – even worse – reduces any hope of delivering real sustainable value.

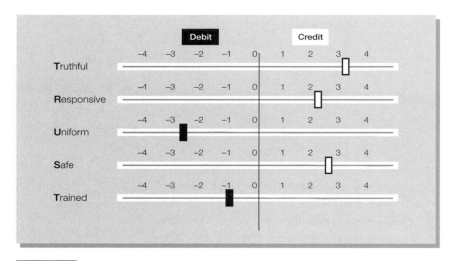

Figure 3.5   **Trust fund**

In a client relationship, the TRUST factors can be described as follows:

■ **Truthful:** Both the consultant and client have a responsibility to be truthful with each other. When entering into a commercial partnership it is very easy to tell the other person what they want to hear – for the consultant to give signals about the successes they have had in helping people to change or for the client to suggest that they have no worries about making the desired transformation. However, in most cases the truth will out. The obvious route for discovery is when information is received from a third party that indicates that a lie has been told or inferred. There can also be more subtle indications of a lie being told. This is where there is no congruence between the head, hand and heart. For example, the consultant says the right words and indicates that they want to support the client (hand); thinks the right thoughts and uses good diagnostic routines to manage the process (head); but deep inside they do not feel like working on this project, so there is little emotional buy-in (heart). People are very adept at measuring this lack of congruence. Once the client notices this in the consultant they will begin to question the value to be derived from the relationship; if the consultant notices such a lack of congruence in the client they should look deeper for the disconnect and more importantly question why the client feels the need to not be truthful with them.

- **Responsive:** This refers to the consultant's ability to focus on the client world and suspend their own maps and needs. By being responsive to the client the consultant is signalling a willingness and ability to affiliate and experience the whole situation the client is experiencing. In practice, demonstration of responsiveness can be verbal restatements of the client's emotions; facial expressions of acceptance, such as smiling; body posture that shows interest in the client's world, such as leaning forward and the use of eye contact; not taking direct notes when the client is talking; and nodding and using a soft tone of voice that does not seek to subdue or outdo the client's tonal volume or quality.

- **Uniform:** Much of the value from the consultant–client relationship comes from the repetition that resides in the relationship – the way that the players meet on a regular basis and are able to build on previous trust deposits and create a compound relationship. However, the moment that the consultant is not consistent then confusion will reign. The client might start to question which of the consultant's two responses is the most appropriate: if the consultant says one thing one day and another the following day, then which is the preferred option? If you are someone who changes your mind often or tends to retract decisions because you 'promised' before you knew you could deliver, you will lose an essential element of effective consulting – your client's trust.

- **Safe:** Establishing a safe environment for the client is paramount in the development of the other four trust levers. Unless the client really believes that the consultant will not cause them any misfortune then any interaction will be constrained and cloaked in a protective veil. However, it is difficult to define what factors will make the client feel 'safe' in the consulting partnership. For some, safety might be driven by working with a consultant who has shared the same experiences as they have; for others, it can be a formal contract of non-disclosure; in other cases it might be the use of someone who has no formal relationship with their current work area. At the end of the day the simplest way might be to ask the client what would help them feel safe in the relationship and then check this out on a regular basis to confirm that they feel secure.

■ **Trained:** Think about any life situation where you seek help or development from another person. One of the key prerequisites will be believing that they know what they are doing. Do they have the requisite knowledge to be able to help me out of my dilemma? In the same way, the client will seek to understand the consultant's level of competence. This might be in the content area – do they have the specialist knowledge to have a sensible conversation about the topic being addressed? – or it might be process competence – do they know how to coach?

The allocation and transfer of trust brings with it quite significant responsibilities. If I entrust my child with someone then I expect them to take responsibility for the child's emotional and physical well-being, and if I put my car into the garage then I expect the owner to take responsibility for its upkeep. In the same way, when developing a client relationship you must be acutely conscious of the extent to which you are asking the client to entrust their business and personal career to you. This entrustment carries responsibilities that are quite serious and demand due care and consideration. The trust fund is a precious commodity and not one to be frittered away.

> **❝ the trust fund is a precious commodity and not one to be frittered away ❞**

Push–pull relationship

Any consultant–client relationship will have an element of sales. In some cases it might be the opening pitch for a new tender, so the sales process will be very overt and understood by both parties. In other cases it might be more subtle, with a cup of coffee with someone who might be a client sometime in the future. Either way, there will be a sales element that needs to be consciously managed by the consultant.

When approaching a new client you are in a sense selling yourself. You are trying to promote yourself to this other person and ideally you would like them to buy you or the ideas you are offering. If this is the case, then you need to have a clear sales strategy.

Two key factors that impact on the success of the opening stage of a sales relationship are:

■ To what extent do I know the person (known or unknown)?

■ To what extent will they have an interest in what I am selling? Will I have to press them to take an interest or have they approached me (push or pull)?

By understanding where you sit against these dynamics it becomes easier to understand the nature of the sales relationship on which you are about to embark.

If we take the model in Figure 3.6 then our relationships will sit in one of the four quadrants:

- **Cold chill:** This is the tough one. You do not know the other person (unknown) and the pressure is on you to sell you or your idea (push).

- **Warm feeling:** Life gets a bit easier here because you already have some form of relationship with the person (known) but they will not have an obvious interest in the idea you want to put to them (push).

- **Warm front:** This is the alternative position. In this quadrant you to know that the person is really keen on an idea similar to yours (pull), but unfortunately you do not know them personally (unknown).

- **Hot Spot:** This is the jackpot. You have a relationship with them already (known) and they have an interest in the field you want to discuss (pull)

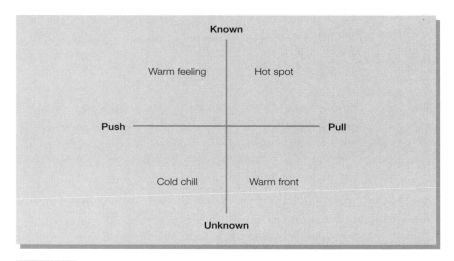

Figure 3.6   Relationship dynamics

Although there are clearly many ways to open up a bridging process, it often comes down to a choice of two core entry strategies, socialization or specialization (*see* Figure 3.7).

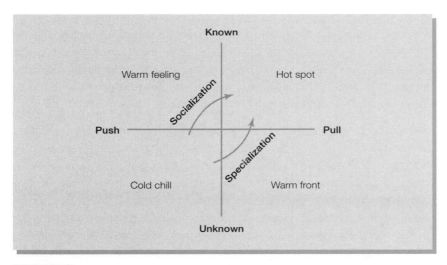

Figure 3.7   Specialization or Socialization strategy

For example, as you pop in to see a current client you suddenly see someone with whom you have been dying to touch base. You understand that she has terrific contacts in an organization where you would like to develop some work. You are at one end of the room and she is on the other. Somehow or another you need to build a bridge across the chasm.

If you decide to use the socialization style then the approach will be to promote yourself by focusing on the relationship rather than the idea being sold. So you decide to create conversations focused on the person and not what she does for a living. Clearly in this contact an opening conversation around work issues, who you both know and even just chewing the fat about hobbies are ideal reference points. The idea is to create a flow of conversation that allows you to understand the person and to give her a chance to get to know you. Once this opening bridge is built then you will have an opportunity to introduce your pitch.

The alternative strategy is the specialization approach. Here your opening gambit is to build on her interest in the topic that you want to talk about. Again, in this case if you know that the person is quite open about her contacts and is always happy to broker relationships then entry through the specialization route will seem quite natural. Once you have been able to talk about your shared interests then the social relationship can develop over time.

Ultimately there is no right sales strategy because people are people and they can react unpredictably. However, by taking time to understand the context before making the introduction, then the odds might be in your favour to pick a strategy that has some chance of success. At worst, if it is all going wrong, then maybe try a shift from a socialization to a specialization or vice versa – what can you lose?

Your ability to switch between the strategies will be critical. In Figure 3.8 the route taken from the cold chill to the hot spot is quite a complicated one. The first move is socialization; this might be the time you meet someone for a coffee to catch up on things. After this you send them a copy of a paper you have written on a new product that gets you to point (b). From this they are suitably impressed with your ideas and you arrange to meet for lunch one day to talk over the suggestion (c). You then send a proposition on how your new idea fits with the work they are doing (d). You meet again for dinner and really start to focus on what areas of commercial interest you share (e) and then you reach point (f) where you agree to try some of the ideas out in their team.

This framework attempts to demystify the sales strategy that we all follow from the age of five, as we seek to win friends and favour with children in the school playground with a combination of rude jokes and jelly beans. There is no rocket science with this approach, but it might help to make clear or codify much of what you already do. Once understood, it allows you to manage the process more consciously and then enhance the sales strategies you already employ.

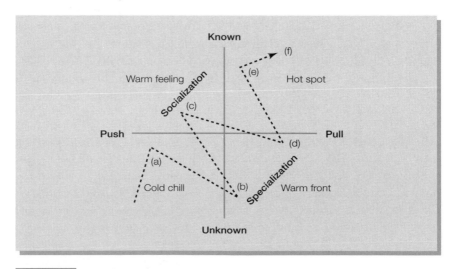

Figure 3.8   Bridging strategies

MPH client mapping

Think of clients with whom you have worked recently. There might be some with whom you are able to work really well – you have an effective working relationship. There might be others you get along with – generally you have a satisfactory relationship. And then there are the clients who are a struggle. You try to work closely with them but nothing seems to click. The easy way out is just to assume that these people are difficult and that the best solution is to move them into someone else's area as soon as possible. But just maybe the problem is that you see the world different from them. Just maybe you both think, feel and act in different ways and the conflict is more a result of differing views rather than any real desire to upset you.

For example, imagine two people, one an avid vegetarian and the other a passionate meat eater, cooking a meal together. If their personal viewpoints are understood, then it will be possible to cook a meal that satisfies both their needs. However, if their views remain unspoken, then at best the preparation of the meal will turn into a fiasco. At worst there will be a fight as they both strive to assert their frame of reference.

This misalignment happens because people often do not understand how they map the world, let alone how other people build their own maps. All people filter the world according to their experiences, values and beliefs. These perceptual filters are invisible to the owner and are only made visible by a process of comparison, feedback or reflection. We use filters because we need to sift out certain elements of information that hit us from the environment because we can only physically process so much data.

MPH filters

Three of the more common filters we use to make sense of the world are:

■ **Magnitude:** This is how we use information to make sense of life – some people will prefer to spend time looking at the detail of a situation whereas others will seek to climb up to a conceptual or strategic level.

■ **Periodicity:** Some people will start to consider a situation using the question 'What has happened?' and tend to start from the past or history as a basis to understand something. Others will want to consider what is going to happen and work from a future perspective.

■ **Holistic dimension:** We all tend to have a base preference for dealing with the world in relationship to the heart, head or hand model (*see*

Figure 3.2). Some people take the emotional angle, others will look for the logic in the situation and others will want to deal with the pragmatic issues.

No one filter is right or wrong. They are just indications of the preferences that people have in the way they make sense of things. If we are to build a bridge with someone it is important that we understand their preference and have a clear strategy or process or approach to help us across the bridge to see their worldview.

For each of the three filters (magnitude, periodicity and holistic) there are three possible biases or favoured preferences that an individual might use.

Magnitude filters

Meta	Macro	Micro

This filter describes how people take information in from the outside world. It defines what size of information they like to take in. Do they chunk up to look at the big picture, or do they chunk down to consider the detail of a situation?

- **Meta:** This person will tend to look at high-level information. Rather than focus on the detail, they will chunk up to look for the high-level view. So imagine you have just met someone at a conference and you are talking about the last speaker. Their conversation will be focused on how the speaker's ideas might fit with the industry view or they might be relating it to a general economic or academic theory.

- **Macro:** This filter is more focused on the mid-point view of the world. The macro person does not want to climb into the stratosphere of concept and does not want to get into the detail of a problem. They might be pragmatic and look for just enough information to form a view but not too much to get bogged down in the detail. If you were talking with someone at a conference they might talk about the general aspects of the last speaker, not the grand concepts or the specific detail, but just a view of the whole presentation at the level it was offered.

- **Micro:** The micro person is more concerned with the detail of a situation – they will seek out the particular item within a situation because they want to really understand what is going on. If you were to meet someone at a conference with this filter they might reflect on the previous speaker and examine one core aspect of the presentation. They would focus on the detail from one slide and really want to question and build an opinion based on the fine detail.

Periodicity filters

The time filter indicates where people initially go to gather data or present a view of the world:

- **Past:** This person will prefer to focus initially on what has happened previously and then move into what is happening and might then ask what is going to happen. They are more comfortable talking about the things that have occurred, bringing in their learning from previous experiences, possibly because they believe the past is a good predictor of the future.
- **Present:** People with a present filter will have a preference to focus on what is going on at the moment. What is happening here and now will be their primary concern. They might be happy to talk about what has happened and where they are going, but these are not as interesting for them as what is going on now.
- **Projected:** This is very much a vision or futures person. They will try to link what is being talked about with their projections for the next stage in their life. While they are happy to look at past and present actions, they tend to measure them against how they fit into the future view.

Holistic filters

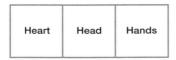

It can be quite easy to look at people and identify if they have a preference for a certain way of talking and behaving. This filter uses the heart, head and hand dimensions as a way to understand how people orientate themselves in the world.

■ **Heart:** The heart dimension includes our emotions, beliefs, values and general sense of what we are here for and is the emotional nucleus of our personal style. It is the belief system that helps us make vocational choices that affect the rest of our lives. People who prefer this dimension will tend to focus on how people feel, what their motivation is or the softer aspects of a situation.

■ **Head:** The head dimension offers a rational view of the world and is the guiding voice of calm and reason. People who have a preference for this dimension will tend to look for the facts of a situation rather than getting tied up in emotional factors. This is not to say that they cannot be emotional, just that they will tend to be practical about an emotional situation and use good common sense.

■ **Hand:** The hand dimension is concerned with doing or action. When talking about a situation a person with this preference will talk about doing things, asking what is going to happen and who will be involved, They want to focus on the pragmatic and action-based issues and are less worried about the emotions or logic of a situation – just what needs to happen.

MPH framework

If we put these three filters together we end up with the MPH framework. This is a nine-block matrix that represents all the possible variations that one person can use to frame their world (*see* Figure 3.9).

Like the ramblers setting out on a Sunday afternoon walk, each person uses a frame to pick their own route. One rambler might have certain preferences

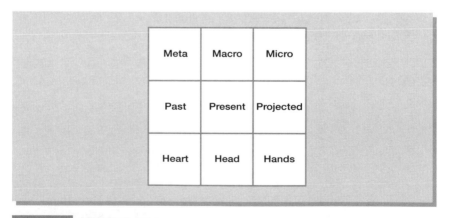

Figure 3.9   MPH framework

that mean they do not want to plan any specific route (meta), want to take the choice of routes as they come to the options (present) and like to ramble for the emotional buzz it gives them (heart). Their partner might want to plan the specific route in detail (micro), want to talk about previous routes they have taken to pick the best one (past) and is concerned with the equipment they are going to take (hand). If both ramblers are used to the differences then they will probably have a great afternoon. However, if they are meeting for the first time, then watch out – because an argument is about to explode as they each try to manage the event according to their frame preference.

By using the MPH model you can start to understand the client's world view. For example you meet with someone who has a preference for 'meta-past-head'. Their conversation will be centred on the logic of what has happened in their background. They will talk about the programme they ran, the strategic benefit it offered and the general background to their business and where it came from. What you might find difficult to find out is how they felt about what happened (heart), what they actually did (hand), what they are doing now (present), what they what to do (projected) or the specific detail of what they do (micro). Without these other factors you are seeing only a small window on their life and as such it is difficult to find any hooks on which to build a relationship with them.

> **the art of effective consulting is accept that people see the world using their favoured frames and filters**

Hence the art of effective consulting is first to accept that people see the world using their favoured frames and filters. Second, be prepared to step outside your favoured approach and see the world from the client's perspective. Once you understand and can manage both perspectives then it becomes possible to understand how the client interprets or makes sense of the world. Only once you can step inside out – to step inside their world view – can you truly begin to understand how you can help them on their journey.

Use every technique you have ever been taught to tune into what people are saying and try to assign it to one of the MPH frames. For example, if someone tends always to ask for the big picture, talk about concepts, use sentences with few details or they get bored when you ask detailed questions, then the suspicion is that they have a meta preference. If, however, they always get to the point quickly, use a lot of descriptive language or use words like 'detail' or 'list', then you might guess that they come from a micro perspective. If they seem to look for operational examples and focus on the practical aspects, then maybe they have a macro preference.

Understand the current position

Once you have used the MPH framework to understand how the other person makes sense of the world, you can then use it to help gather data about the issue they wish to address. The MPH framework offers a powerful tool to understand what the client is telling you, but more importantly what they are not telling you.

For example, if you have a client who has a 'meta, projected, heart' preference, they will spend all their time exposing where they are going with great passion and verve. What you might get very little of is what has happened (past) and what they are doing now (present) about the issue. You may not get any operational example of what needs to happen (macro) and have little chance of understanding what specifically this change will mean in any detail (micro). Finally, although they are giving you passion about the change, you may struggle to find the logic behind it (head) and what they will need to do (hand).

By the end of the Client stage the MPH nine-box model should be populated with data (*see* Figure 3.10). This data should give you nine key sets of information:

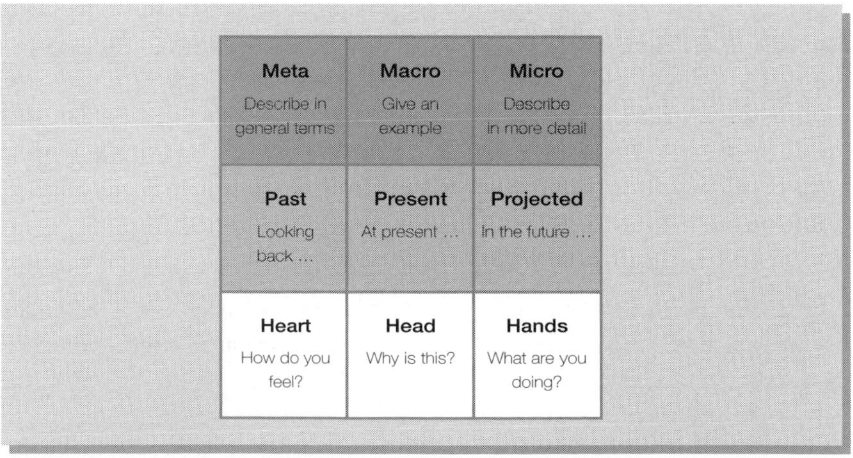

Meta	Macro	Micro
Describe in general terms	Give an example	Describe in more detail
Past	**Present**	**Projected**
Looking back ...	At present ...	In the future ...
Heart	**Head**	**Hands**
How do you feel?	Why is this?	What are you doing?

Figure 3.10 Gathering data

- the broad or high-level issues for the client (meta);
- the operational or practical factors that need to be considered (macro);
- important specific or detailed issues (micro);
- what has happened to client and how they got the current position (past);
- the client's current position is (present);
- what the client wishes to achieve in the future as part of the engagement (projected);
- the client's feelings about the engagement (heart);
- what the client thinks is important (head);
- what needs to be done as part of the engagement (hand).

The important issue here is that the consultant has explicitly not attempted to:

- climb inside the client's position to understand what has caused the problem (that comes later);
- offer a solution or even hinted at things that might help the client;
- talked about what will need to be 'done'.

What the consultant needs to do is to understand the person and the problem – not to resolve the situation before understanding what caused the situation.

The 'Are you serious?' test

One really important aspect of the Client stage is to test the seriousness of the person and their desire for change. Like any blooming holiday relationship, both sides will swear undying love for each other, profess that they would jump from the cliff if ever separated and swear never to be parted. Then the holiday is over and they come down to earth with a big bump. Reality bites, in-tray's overflow, the fact you live 200 miles apart starts to irritate and eventually the relationship withers away – just like most holiday flings.

The danger is that consulting can fall into the same trap. Clients will swear blind that they want to (change the company culture, install a radical new process or fix all the problems overnight – delete as appropriate), but it is very easy to be blinded by their passion. Once the engagement begins they start to cancel appointments, fail to complete agreed tasks and eventually fade from view. The problem is that your brand value as a consultant has been eroded because you are tainted with the brush of a failed engagement. Although the client wants a successful personal outcome, you want a successful outcome to protect your brand integrity.

Hence you need to look for triggers and indicators that might suggest that the engagement could fail to be successful for either party. The MPH framework cannot guarantee to identify these factors, but there are certain subtle clues that can be spotted in the early stages that provide an indicator of areas that need to be challenged and investigated before proceeding with the engagement.

Magnitude: Sweat the small stuff

Dreams are very easy to create: I am going to sail across the Atlantic single-handed; I am going to lose five stone; I am not going to drink alcohol for three months. They are easy to say and even easier to proclaim. However, they are harder to back up when you ask the person 'How many miles will that mean you have to row?' or 'So what will you stop eating?'. The devil is in the detail because only once you challenge people to go to the micro level – to explain what they specifically mean, what the outcome will actually look like, or what they specifically will have to do differently – do you get a real understanding of their seriousness. When you start to ask these questions, does the client start to find other things to talk about, fiddle nervously or shrug them off by saying 'that is stuff to sort our later'? In most cases it is probably stuff to sort out during the course of the engagement, and if the client has not taken at least some thinking time to reflect on the consequences of their action in some detail they might not be serious about making the change.

Periodicty: The past predicts the future

Further questions to ask someone who is proclaiming their desire to do something are 'Have you tried it before?', 'Did it work?', and 'Why not?'. The reality is that behaviour change (personal and organizational) is very difficult and something that most people will struggle with. There are few people who have not taken a vow on New Year's Eve to make a big change in their life, only to see it fade and wither after a few days or weeks. Past behaviour will often predict future performance. If people did something in the past, are doing it now, then there is a good chance that they will carry on doing it. This is because we are all creatures of habit and this is the one thing that most change processes seeks to modify – getting people to do something different on the Monday morning to what they did on the

Friday. We do what we do because we like to do it. We might say that we do not want to smoke, drink or eat – but there is always part of us that really does want to do it.

Maybe we have to start to understand what it is that makes people develop habits and why they are loath to give them up. One way to do this it to explore the idea of addictive behavior. Addictions are everywhere. Some of us are addicted to our spouses, our work and our hobbies. Some of us are addicted to working out, ham radios, reading in bed, chocolate, helicopter skiing, sex. The brain mechanism that reinforces such dependencies is the same one that mediates more compelling drug addictions. At work is a cluster of cells, called the dopamine neuron, that evolved over millions of years to reward activities we find pleasing. The primary role of this central circuit is to reinforce behaviours – like mating, gathering food, pounding a rival – that will propel our genes into the next generation. Often the role of the consultant is to determine the extent to which the client (or the client's organization) seeks to break an addictive behaviour and if they are really prepared to go through with the change – even to the point of going cold turkey.

Holistic: Ensure authentic alignment

There are often three types of change that people embark upon that end up in failure. First is to know what to do and have a passion for it but don't do anything (high heart and head, low hand). Failure here is often because of environmental constraints like business dependencies or debt restriction. Second, there is the passion for it and actual behaviour, but don't know what to do (high heart and hand but low head). This is often where people don't think through the consequences of the change they are making and fail because of practical problems. Finally there is the know what to do and start to do it, but have no real passion (high head and hand but low heart). This is often where someone is being coerced into a situation for which they have no personal passion. The trouble is that even clients sometimes know deep down that something is missing but still proclaim loudly how much they want to make the change. The result is that we see 'faking it' behaviours, where the client tries to convince the consultant that they are serious about the transformation but is compensating for the gaps in one of the three dimensions. Unless the consultant is able to ferret out such 'faking it' behaviours then things may go wrong downstream.

Exit stage right

One rule of thumb is the notion of 'exit stage right'. You know when a client engagement has gone well when the right-hand column of the MPH matrix is all covered off (micro, projected and hand). In addressing these three areas the client will be able to answer the question 'What can we do tomorrow?'.

It is important to stress with all three tests that the goal is not to find reasons to reject the client. It is more about ensuring that a culture of integrity and genuineness is created at the start of the engagement so that both parties are aware of the difficulties they might face and can then develop the necessary energy and strategies to ensure that the engagement adds value through sustainable change.

OUTCOME testing

Building on the idea of seriousness and the need to exit stage right – knowing that something will happen after the first meeting – you need to help the client achieve two things. First, to be clear on what they believe to be the source of the problem and, second, to be clear on how they think it might be resolved. Although there is every chance that both ideas will be modified as the project matures, it is important to help the client gain clarity in the early stage of the change. To achieve this, you need to take them through two ways of thinking. The first is to funnel down and understand what they believe to be the real source of the issue, and the second is to help them focus on what they believe to be a valid and productive outcome.

In clarifying the course of the problem, you need to be clear about the symptoms, then understand the setting – where specifically is it happening – and, lastly, to drag from this the source of the issue under consideration.

Take as an example your young daughter arriving home from school and complaining that no one likes her. At this level she might be seen to be talking about the symptoms of the problem but with little clarity as to what is really happening. Your role as a parent is to get below this to understand what is causing the problem. Your first step might be to ask her to describe the problem as she sees is – to list out loud all the symptoms that are causing her to be upset. At this stage it is important not to argue or criticize, as she will probably believe that these factors are the source of the problem rather than just the symptoms. Next, it can help to understand the setting where the problem has occurred. This will be based on the typical, who, where, what and when type questions. By the end of this stage you should have a good view of what is happening. Last, your role is to act as a mirror and play back what she has told you. By doing this she will start to take a more objective view of the situation and can start to question some of her earlier assumptions. You can then work through the problem to understand the core source of the issue, which in the vast majority of cases will be attributable to one root cause. So for the daughter, the source of the problem is probably that she has had an argument with one of her friends and believes the whole world is against her.

Taking someone through this process can be like climbing down a funnel of barbed wire (*see* Figure 3.11). At every step of the journey you can hit a potential prickly spot – one that triggers a negative response, often aimed back at you. Clearly, there is no simple solution to managing this tenuous process. It is generally down to you to make decisions based upon your experience, the client's problem and the context in which the funnelling is taking place. However, it is important to emphasize this step in the process. Unless the client is challenged to explore the root source of the problem, you can end up wasting everybody's time, including your own.

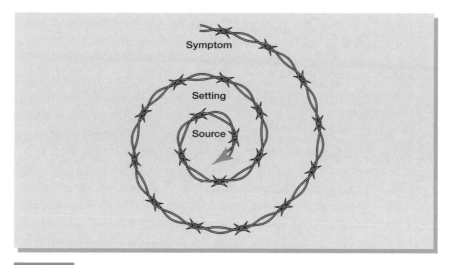

Figure 3.11 Barbed-wire funnel

Once the source of the problem has been unearthed, you can start to consider how the problem might be resolved. At this point, it can be easy to offer a potential solution based on your expertise in other areas. Unless you have been explicitly called in to offer such knowledge and service, this will be a disastrous idea. If the client is not able to build a solution that they own, love and cherish, then the engagement is likely to have the rug pulled out at any stage from that point on.

The goal is for the client to develop an outcome or solution that they feel will 'really' resolve the source problem. Forcing them to consider both sides of the equation can be a powerful and catalytic process. Often the client will have a good idea of what is wrong but be unable to describe clearly how the situation should be resolved. Alternatively, they might come to you with a great idea but not really understand what it is they are trying to resolve. Even where they have an idea of what the end goal is, in many cases it is vague and blurred – almost a 'just make things better' statement. Your role is to act as an investigator and catalyst, to help draw out a realistic, tangible and measurable solution for the client, consumer and consultancy team. You can help achieve this by asking seven simple questions in the OUTCOME framework:

> **unless the client is challenged to explore the root source of the problem, you can end up wasting everybody's time**

- **Owns:** Who owns the outcome and is it self-maintained? Ultimately, at the end of the project you will move on and the client will be expected to maintain the change. The question is, do they have the desire and capability to hold the gains or will other external forces be able to erode any movement forward?

- **Unease:** What triggered the need for change? Ask why the issue is really important at a deep, rather than superficial, level. Why has the issue surfaced now and what priority does it hold over other issues?

- **Trade-off:** What will have to be given up to achieve the change? One often forgotten fact is that people or organizations adopt certain policies or behaviours because there is a payback. Effecting a change within an organization means that something will have to change and something will have to be lost. The client must think through and appreciate the potential loss before they can confirm what outcome is required.

- **Changed:** How will life be different when the change is made? At this point the client has clarified the desired outcome and you can help to solidify the changes. One way of doing this is by asking the client to take a mental step forward in time – to consider how life will be different at the end of the project. They can imagine what language will be used, what the environment will look like, what the productivity figures will be – anything that helps them actually 'be' in the future.

■ **Others:** What impact will the change have on others (losers, winners and neutral)? In effecting a change, one of the dangers is that short-term and urgent forces are responded to and little attention is paid to the impact that any change will have on other parties or groups. It is important to consider all the people that are affected by any change and possibly to consider them in terms of winners, losers or neutral. From this the client should be able to offer a realistic picture of who will be affected by the proposed change and, more importantly, what reaction can be anticipated.

■ **Measure:** How will outcomes be measured? How will the client know if the change has been successful? To be sure that the outcome is one that the client really wants and can achieve they should be able to describe in simple terms how they will 'know' that a successful change has been delivered.

■ **Engage:** What value can this engagement add? You must always ask 'Why me?' Why has the client chosen to use an external resource as opposed to drawing upon their own resources? Building on this question, the next step is to understand what is stopping them from rectifying the issue at present and what are the restraining forces that any engagement must overcome.

Once the outcomes are clearly defined from the client's perspective, you need to focus on what the change will be and your role within it. You need to develop a much firmer picture of the type of change that you will be asked to make. More importantly, ensure the client has the necessary resolve and stamina to manage the transition through to its completion and not be waylaid by diversionary forces.

Change ladder

Before finalizing what the problem really is, it will help if you determine what type of change the client believes is needed, what the 'real' problem is and the likelihood of being able to effect a sustainable change within the given confines. However it can be difficult to gauge the issue being addressed in the early stage of the change programme because of the vagueness that surrounds the problem. Since the client is often influenced by subjective needs, the views of other political players and the vagaries of history, the issue offered to you might well consist of a hotch-potch of different stories and concerns. Consequently, when the relationship first begins, the client will implicitly be looking for you to help take away some of the surrounding fog. As Schein (1994) suggests:

In reality the manager often does not know what he is looking for and indeed should not be expected to know. All he knows is that something is not working right and he needs some kind of help. An important part of any consultation process, then, must be to help the manager or organization to figure out what the problem is, and only then decide what further kind of help is needed.

The change ladder is a simple but effective tool that will allow the client to chart and assess the issue under consideration and in particular the extent to which sustainable change will be delivered. It does this by considering a number of factors:

- the input side of the consultancy process (or what will be done) as well as the anticipated output;

- the nature of the intangible as well as the tangible elements within the system being changed;

- the different types of interventions that are used to effect a sustainable change.

In addition, different types of change ladder profiles can illustrate how change programmes may fail. By using the change ladder chart, the consultant can highlight many of the shadow factors that cause problems later in an engagement.

Input–output relationship

The first step is to separate out the change being made from the anticipated outcome. All too often these factors get mixed up and talked about in the same breath. In the same way that you must separate out cause and effect, it is important to separate out the consultant's input effort from the resulting output or business benefit. This is because there might not always be a direct causal relationship between what the consultant does and the end result.

Look in any Sunday paper and it will be full of miracle cures. The latest gizmo or gadget that will cure back pains, ease arthritis, help you find a true love or win the lottery. However, how many of these wonder cures deliver the change they promise, how many give value and to what extent is the value really sustainable? The advertisers are very clever in their sales pitch because they confuse the reader by intermingling the product with the supposed solution that it will deliver. They subtly infer direct and causal linkage between the use of their product or service and the benefits you will receive. In one sentence you will get 'by using product x you will achieve benefit y'. What they rarely do is to break down this causal relationship and explain just how it is that this product can achieve such miraculous benefits.

Too often advertising focuses on the predicted outcomes rather than what the product will specifically do to achieve the outcome (*see* Table 3.2). The problem is that many agents will use a range of well-used phrases and statements that are designed to make their products and services sound somewhat more impressive than they might be when considered from an input perspective.

Table 3.2 **Advertising outputs and inputs**

The output: what they deliver	The input: what they do
We offer advanced network-based calling services'	We are a phone company
We are a leader in container transportation and flexible logistics services	We organize and move stuff
We manage your network resources to deliver customer-focused competitive advantage	We help you do computer stuff
We offer comprehensive data warehouse strategies	We tell you how to file stuff
We offer customer-focused mailing systems	We mail stuff
We offer global delivery services	We mail stuff around the world

In the short term these techniques can create client interest and generate revenue, but in the long run they feed the increasing concerns about the consulting and change industry. This is because we often use similar promotional processes as the charlatans in the press! For example, 'This is a quality process and your organization will be transformed into a quality-focused business'; 'Adopt this new customer service software and your customers will come flocking back'; or 'Upgrade your software and all the operational glitches and problems will be sorted'. However, when you look at the small print the firms do not explain just how this will happen. There is a real act of faith on the part of the client to accept that by using product x then improvement y will occur (see Figure 3.12).

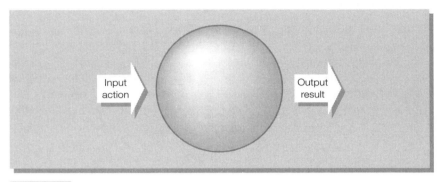

Figure 3.12 Ideal consultancy process

The problem is that six months after the project is complete the client starts to wonder just why their new customer service system is not delivering improved satisfaction ratings; why quality has not improved even after the new statistical process control programme has been implemented; or why costs are still rising even after the reorganization. Often the client has focused purely on the output of the change process or the anticipated benefits and has been less than rigorous in really testing out what will be 'done' rather than what will be delivered.

Tangible and intangible factors

The next factor to consider in any change process is the balance between the tangible and intangible elements involved in the transformation. The tangible factors are the fixed assets, hard processes, policies or manuals. These are the touchable, sustainable and concrete things you know exist and can readily verify both before the change and once it is complete. It might be the provision of new pieces of hardware, the construction of a building, writing new procedures or the development of a training programme.

However, with all these tangible changes there will be intangible factors that also need to be understood and managed (*see* Figure 3.13). These indefinable factors are the innate and latest skills that people have, their motivation and willingness to make a change and finally the deep internal sense of purpose that drives the choices people make.

Virtually all change actions will impact both the tangible and intangible factors. There is little point in providing a new piece of computer kit if the

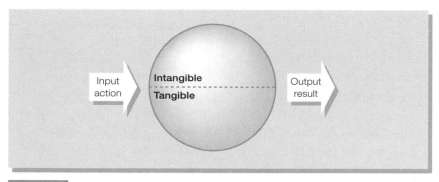

Figure 3.13 Tangible and intangible factors

user cannot be bothered to use it or if they do not have the necessary skills; there is no point in developing new training or operating procedures if people do not understand what value they will receive from using them; and there is little point in setting up a new building if customers or employees do not like it and prefer to use the old one.

The consultant must understand what tangible and intangible factors will impact upon the change and use this knowledge to challenge the client about the viability of the project. For example, imagine a client who wants to install a new computer system that will enhance the customer service process. It can be quite easy as a consultant to take the order and implement the system. However, history and experience suggests that the simple act of dropping in a new system will not result in sustainable benefits. For any new system to deliver the anticipated benefits the client must be prepared to invest in other processes, specific training for the users, coaching for people who might have difficulties with specific aspects of the system, motivational packages to encourage people to use the system, and processes to aid any behavioural changes required to support the new system.

The factors shown in Table 3.3 suggest why so much change is managed at the tangible level. Because of their ease of management and reliability, it is simpler to spend time talking about and dealing with the tangible factors. However, it should also be easy to see why a failure to address the intangible factors associated with the process will result in non-sustainable change being delivered.

Table 3.3   Tangible and intangible factors

Tangible	Intangible
▪ Easy to change	▪ Difficult to change how people feel
▪ Can be changed quickly	▪ Can take time to change people's intrinsic factors
▪ Can be easily measured	▪ Cannot always be directly measured – often needs to be inferred
▪ Change is visible	▪ Change is always inside the person so difficult to see
▪ Easy to raise invoice because of visibility	▪ Hard to justify payment because change is intangible
▪ Once change is made it tends to remain locked in place	▪ Once change is made can be modified by the individual
▪ Can be easily replicated and transported between environments	▪ Hard to replicate and transport because change is centred on thoughts and feelings

Industry reports often suggest that change programmes are not delivering the anticipated benefits. In many cases the rate of failure of change sits between 60 and 90 per cent. One industry review suggested that £25 billion is wasted each year on change management errors. The Challenge of Change 2002 study found that UK businesses undertake at least three major change projects a year – costing companies £52 billion in management charges alone – and around half are a waste of time and money. This study of more than 100 directors also revealed that UK company boards devote 35 per cent of their time to managing change but only half of this is well spent. The Change Management Online study found that many mergers, restructures, acquisitions and downsizing operations are ill-conceived and poorly managed. Shining through this study is the realization that real organizational transformation is a people issue.

❝ real organizational transformation is a people issue ❞

Unless you as the consultant are prepared to challenge the client on the intangible people issues then the likelihood is that all your effort will result in a non-sustainable intervention. What is needed is a set of questions that will help to challenge the client without appearing confrontational. One of the most powerful ways that the consultant can challenge the client around their readiness to effect change at the intangible level is by educating them as to the problems that will arise downstream if they fail to address the softer issues. However, to do this it can help to open out the tangible–intangible model into a more structured series of intervention levels that indicate what specific actions can be taken to effect sustainable change.

Change levels

One way to make the tangible and intangible factors easier to understand and change is by overlaying the two areas with a graduated set of change levels. These change levels are the core aspects that need to be addressed when managing any sustainable intervention (*see* Figure 3.14).

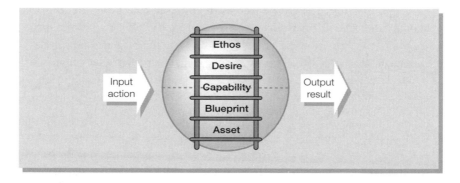

Figure 3.14 Change levels

The vast majority of change actions will fall into one of these categories (A–E):

- **Asset**: An asset is the tool, plant or piece of equipment used to deliver a product or service. For the company this is land, building and production equipment; for the racing driver it is the Formula One car; and for the pop musician it is an electric guitar. In the case of a professional services firm or the Rolling Stones, people are the primary asset, because they deliver the final product and services. However, once the assets are in place it is normal to develop the necessary policies and procedures that define how the assets are to be managed.

- **Blueprint**: This is the method by which a system is managed. For the large organization it is the strategic and tactical plans, processes, quality systems and personnel procedures. For a theatre company it is the script, lighting schedule and backstage directions. For the financial trading group it is the standard internal procedures and the external regulations that control the trading operations. However, before these procedures can be adhered to, people will need to attain the necessary skills and competencies.

- **Capability:** These are the skills and competencies that people have. With a football team it is the players' tacit ability, the manager's knowledge and experience, and the capability of the ground staff to maintain a quality pitch. For the racing driver, it is the driver's ability to outperform competitors on the racetrack and the team's ability to maintain the car at top performance. However, although people might have the capability to do something, they will need to want to take the action.

- **Desire:** This is the motivation that drives people to take action. Within an organization it might be seen as the mission that drives the business goals and, in the individual, the personal motivation that stimulates people to take action on a daily basis. For the neighbourhood watch organization it is the desire for people to protect themselves against burglary. For the racing driver it is the single-minded determination to win. However, although desire will drive behaviour in the short term, long-term behaviour is normally driven by what is really important at the ethos level.

- **Ethos:** This is the core reason why a person, team or organization exists. For the organization it is the real (as opposed to the stated) values and culture. At an international level it is the way that countries will go to war over what might be seen as minor issues. At a micro level it is the charity to which an individual will give or where they decide to allocate their time. It is ethos that drives behaviour. It is a person's faith that drives behaviour in support of their religion; it is a belief in a particular football team that means the supporter will turn out rain or shine for them; and it is a belief in a just cause that results in protesters taking action. It is even the reason why a smoker smokes, even if they say they want to give up; although the espoused or stated ethos might be one of 'I don't want to smoke' – the actual or shadow ethos might be 'I will smoke because I like it'. So the ethos level can be a difficult area to manage because there is a high difference between the choices someone says they want to make and the ones they actually make.

These five factors can be seen in Figure 3.15 as the change ladder. However, the importance of the change ladder is less about these aspects, but more around the deeper issues within each level.

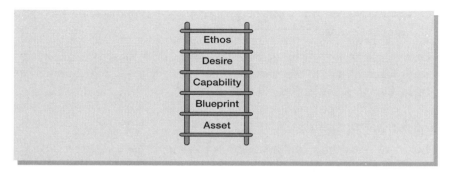

Figure 3.15 Change ladder

Change drivers

For each of the five levels there are further drivers that have a significant impact on the nature and likelihood of success for the change you and the client are embarking on:

■ **Associated assets:** The management of simple assets might appear to be a simple process, but in reality can be complex and troublesome. An asset to one person might seem mundane and functional but to another act as emotional symbolic representations of something important.

■ **Blueprint blockage:** Process changes are intriguing because they appear to be so easy to deliver but can end up in horrendous failures, simply because the psychological preferences of the client and consumers are not taken into account.

■ **Cocktail capability:** The creation of new skills in a team or organization is not simply a case of sending someone on the latest training course and hoping that they will come back sorted and ready to do their job. A person's skills are a complex cocktail mix of explicit and tacit talent – the trick is to understand what mix is appropriate for the particular change.

■ **Double desire:** This is the motivation to achieve. Although we might clearly describe what we wish to achieve in life, often we fail to achieve it. This is because inside everyone is complex combination of a desire 'to be' coupled with a deeper or secondary desire to keep things as they are.

■ **Elusive ethos:** Often someone will present one set of beliefs and principles by which they want the organization to abide, only to act in a way that is contrary to these stated beliefs. For example, the MD who sends a memo that says we must save money – issued on a fax from the company jet. Often this conflict is because we have a public or espoused set of beliefs and a deeper set of beliefs that actually drive the choices we make.

Only by understanding the drivers that reside within these five levels can we truly begin to chart the problem that faces the client and develop solutions that will deliver sustainable value.

Associated assets

I used to work for a communications company that serviced a large car design centre. This place was huge, with hundreds of people all involved in the design and development of the next-generation car. For me the amazing thing about the place was the design centre. This was a huge room full of design engineers, laid out row after row all with their individual workspace, desk and telephone. At the edge of the room was the manager's office. He too had his workspace, but in his case an office rather than a desk.

As a field engineer I used to visit the office to repair the phones and do general maintenance on the system. One late afternoon I was called out on a call because one of the design engineers had a telephone fault. It was late in the afternoon and I wanted to get off home to see the family. Rather than trying the fix the telephone I simply gave him a new one. The following morning I had an urgent message to go back to the design centre because all sorts of complaints were being hurled about. I rushed back to see what the problem was, only to find that it was about the telephone I had changed.

Since I was very new to the subtleties and politics of work life I had missed a key factor that underpinned the managerial structure in offices. In the same way that the size of the company car, office or expenses budget will indicate the level of superiority of an employee, so in this place the colour of the telephone indicated the rank of the user. The design engineers all had grey telephones, whereas the managers had white telephones. In my rush to get away I had given the design engineer a white telephone and this caused all sorts of problems. Other engineers were surreptitiously destroying their telephones in the hope of getting a new white one and the managers were grumbling over their coffee about the waste of spending budget on quality telephones for the workers.

The root of the problem was that I regarded the telephone as an asset – a functional tool used for making telephone calls – and did not tacitly make the association with power within a complex hierarchy. By treating the telephone as an asset without understanding the associative symbolic meaning, my change failed to deliver the sustainable benefit required by the client.

We see this time and time again with so many change programmes, where the client and consultant believe they are simply changing a functional asset, but the end result is problems because of the associated symbolic meaning attached to the object (*see* Figure 3.16). Take, for example, moving people from one location to another. The new office offers great facilities and the client see all the benefits, but to the staff the move signifies that the company is losing its home-grown family values and becoming more of a corporate giant. Similarly, a new plant may be computer operated and offer functional and cost savings, but it is viewed by the teams as a sign that management is reducing their personal skills set.

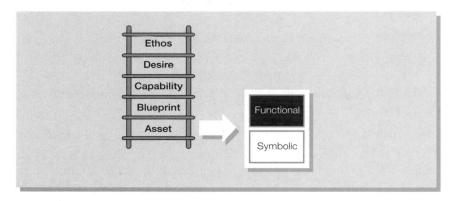

Figure 3.16 Associated assets

The challenge for the consultant in the Client stage of the engagement is to be clear about the level of association with the asset. If the plant, equipment or fixed asset has a low level of symbolic association then the change is likely to proceed with little resistance. However, if the asset is highly associated then there is a real chance that the change process will be fraught with risk (*see* Figure 3.17). It is important that this associative assesment is undertaken not just with the client, but also with the end consumers. It might be that their association with the object might be strong enough to trigger a wave of resistance that would cause the change to fail to deliver sustainable value.

Blueprint blockage

Take any generic industry problem that has surfaced over the past 30 years and there is always a simple solution that promises to fix the process. Time and time again consultants have offered blueprint solutions that notionally seem to resolve the problem in the short term but fail to deliver limited

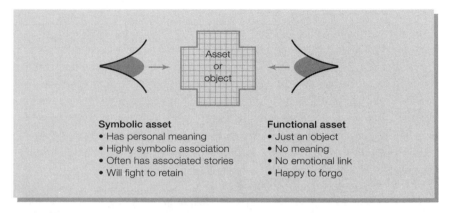

Figure 3.17 Symbolic and functional meaning

value in the long run – and in some cases can be detrimental because they add fixed cost to the business.

The usual suspects seem to be tools like quality standards, changes to organization design and structure, process redesign, knowledge management, training standards, policies updates, benchmarking, etc. These are all practical solutions that in the short term can offer an answer to a problem but in the long term may only offer limited value. The reason why these types of solution do not always deliver a sustainable answer can be quite complex, but one common reason can be found in the differing psychological types of people who work in organizations.

In simple terms the human population can found to consist of a mix of two types of people. There are those who like to operate in a tight structured environment and operate best with plans, policies and procedures. The other type is those who prefer to operate in a loose environment. They will work best when the process allows them the desired freedom and flexibility (*see* Figure 3.18). Characteristics of the two can be seen as:

- **Structured:** These people are decisive, self-regimented and like to make quick decisions. They focus on completing the task, only want to know the essentials and like to know what is ahead. They plan their work and work their plan. Deadlines are sacred and their motto is 'just do it'. They tend to dislike surprises and see time as a finite resource that is best managed.

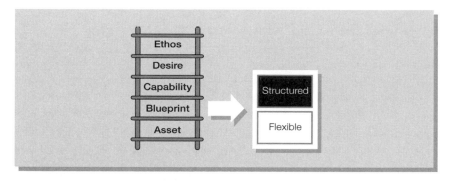

Figure 3.18 Blueprint preferences

- **Flexible:** These people are curious, adaptable, and spontaneous. They start many tasks, want to know everything about each task and often find it difficult to complete a task. Deadlines are meant to be stretched. Their maxim might be 'On the other hand . . .'. They will often put off doing a task until the very last minute, not because they are lazy, but because they see time as a renewable resource and see deadlines as elastic.

The challenge at this stage of the change process is to determine a number of things:

- What is the consultant's psychological preference and does this favour a tendency towards a more planned or flexible change process?
- What is the client's psychological preference and what will be their preferred implementation style – controlled or elastic?
- What is the natural preference of the consumers and how will they react if the blueprint pattern acts against this natural style?

Once these three factors are understood it will become easier to understand the true nature of the blueprint change and calculate the chances of it failing to deliver the anticipated benefits. If, for example, the client and consultant have a structured preference but the consumers have a flexible preference then the change will incur problems as the users start to react against the perceived high level of control. Alternatively, I have been in a situation where the client has requested a flexible intervention, but the consumers were desperate for a more structured approach and felt the need for guidance and direction. There is clearly no right model – the answer will sit between two options. As a consultant you need to chart the various preferences and create a solution that will fit with them, or, if the new blueprint style does not fit the current preferences, make sure that the change programme has sufficient time and resources to help people adapt to something that sits outside their comfort zone.

Cocktail capability

It is not enough to say that by training people a problem will be resolved. So often this is the quick-fix solution offered by consultants and coaches and lapped up by the client. For example, the customer service staff are not achieving high enough customer satisfaction figures, so let's put them through a customer care workshop. All might be great in the short term as people get the quick fix of fun, a few skills and more frequent visits by the senior team with a rousing speech, but what happens two months later once the programme is over? If the training is not 'sticky' and has not embedded itself deeply into how people think, feel and behave then little long-term benefit will be delivered.

It is important to test and understand the type of knowledge that the client group should end up with once the assignment is complete. Knowledge is typically seen in two forms, explicit and tacit (*see* Figure 3.19):

▨ **Explicit:** This is knowledge that can be expressed in words and
   numbers and can be easily communicated and shared in the form of
   hard data, scientific formulae, procedures, policies or universal
   principles (Nonaka and Takeuchi, 1995). It is the hard and tangible
   knowledge that can be codified, replicated and readily transferred

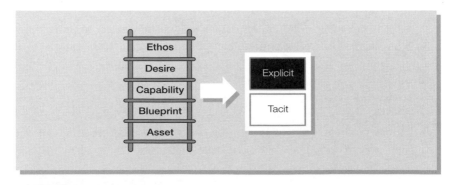

Figure 3.19 Capability types

across an organization. It is the stuff we find in books, reports, newspapers and safety instructions that are announced on the railway. One area where this often surfaces (and fails) is in the notion of best practice. While the idea that we should learn from the experience of others is valid and of immense benefit, I can only explicitly see and observe what you learnt; I cannot feel what you felt and therefore it is difficult for me to absorb the deep and rich experience that you went through. So often the explicit knowledge is grounded in a tacit experience and hence cannot be readily transferred.

■ **Tacit:** This is the informal, hard-to-pin down capability. It is a fingertips or muscle capability – where you can perform a task but find it difficult to explain. It can be the knowledge that you do not recognize that you have, for example, how to open a door may not seem like 'knowledge' until you meet somebody who has never seen a door. A simple way to describe tacit knowledge is in the phrase 'We can know more than we can tell' or 'The answer to questions that haven't been asked yet' (Smith, 2000). It is fundamentally about that which we apply and use, but have yet to codify in a way such that we can describe how we perform that action.

Tacit knowledge is the form of knowledge that has received a great deal of attention because it is recognized as valuable to both the individual and organization. However, because of its nature it is difficult to codify or store. Ask any individual to describe what they do and how they do it. The guarantee is that you will only gain a partial appreciation of their unique skills and knowledge. The tacit element is that knowledge that they are probably unable to describe. Ask any musician to explain how they get a unique sound, the sportsperson how they get that extra inch, or the police detective how they catch criminals. All these elements are buried deep within the individual and it can be difficult to transform this deep knowledge into a codified form.

It is for this very reason that tacit knowledge is highly prized by many companies. By building a competitive position around its tacit knowledge base, a company ensures that any competitor will find it difficult to replicate the market offering. As such, tacit knowledge is likely to be more a source of competitive advantage than the articulated or non-tacit knowledge (Sanchez, 1997, p. 166). However, the moment we make our tacit capability explicit, it can be replicated by another person or firm and offered in the market. Hence in many cases it might be to the firm's disadvantage to codify its tacit knowledge because, in the process of making it explicit, it can be copied by the competitors. Tacit knowledge is vital to the organization because organizations can only learn and innovate by somehow leveraging the implicit knowledge of its members. The most advanced computer-based information systems on their own do not generate new knowledge – only the human beings led by tacit knowledge have the capability to do so (Choo, 1998, p. 111).

The issue for any consultant working with a capability intervention is what type of capability the client group requires. Does the client want a simple shift in explicit capability, such as a new set of procedures, operational routines or machine instructions? Alternatively, does the client organization need the capability to be made at a deeper level, such as the skills to manage client relationships, leadership style or influencing techniques?

Failure to understand and address the differences can lead to costly mistakes and change interventions that fail to deliver sustainable value. So often change programmes are managed at the capability level that fails to address the fundamental difference between these two types of engagement. This can be seen in the following examples:

- The client who needs deep tacit capability such as customer management techniques but pushes the consultant to cut costs and install cheap and quick explicit processes such as e-learning programmes or short lunchtime sessions. People may get to know the ideas but there is little chance that there will be any real behavioural shift as a result of this cost-cutting exercise.

- The company who wants to change an explicit operating process but decides to over-invest by giving people too much training. It sends people away for long courses, brings in expensive agents and over-eggs the process – all for something that can be managed at a process level.

Although there are many ways to address the idea of explicit and tacit learning, it is useful to use the following simplification:

- **Explicit capability:** This can be delivered quickly and remotely, using codified structures, and as a result can be low cost.

- **Tacit capability:** This is routed in context and is transferred over time, through close association, and as a result costs can be higher.

This is why e-learning is so often sold as a low-cost option and the costs of training processes like coaching and mentoring can be seen as expensive in comparison. However, such a comparison is meaningless, because they address fundamentally different capability changes – and this must be understood and carefully managed at the very outset of the engagement.

Double desire

We can also see two competing forces interacting and competing at the desire level of the change ladder (*see* Figure 3.20). The first is the stated, overt or primary desire. This is the action that the client suggests they 'wish' to take. Over a coffee they will spend an hour convincing you just how serious their problem is and how much they want to effect a change that will resolve the issue. The second force is the secondary desire, which is the unspoken motivation to do something that might actually negate or act against the primary desire. It is the resisting force that causes people to not take action, even if they say they want to.

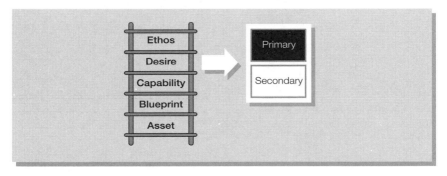

Figure 3.20 **Double desire**

For example, over coffee someone tells you that they are determined to give up smoking. However, you know the person of old, and as you take another sip of the cappuccino you hit a déjà vu moment and realize that they are telling you exactly the same thing they have told you three or four times before. They always have this really passionate desire to fix the problem but somehow it just never seems to get better. This is a common pattern that can be seen every Sunday morning as someone decides (yet again) to give up smoking, drinking or sweets.

Imagine someone whose espoused desire is to give up smoking. This makes sense, will save money, is ecologically sound and benefits those around her. But she continues, even though her biggest desire and goal in life is to stop. It turns out that smoking fills several useful roles in her life. Among other things, her husband cannot stand the thought of her quitting while he still smokes, so it ensures that this relationship is maintained. She smokes in the morning to 'wake up'; during the day to 'reduce stress', 'concentrate', and, paradoxically, at night to 'relax'. Smoking also helps her to maintain the group of friends who also smoke. A cigarette relaxes her at times of stress and gives her something to fiddle with. While her primary desire is to stop smoking, the secondary one is to hold on to these other factors that actually give her immense value in life. The net result is that the espoused desire is acting as a future force – hopefully pulling her into the required or 'to be' state. At the same time, the actual desire is acting as a rubber band or brake keeping her at the current state (*see* Figure 3.21).

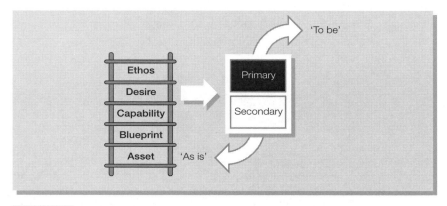

Figure 3.21   Opposite desires

The gap between the espoused and actual desire can emerge because people will have different parts of themselves. One aspect of a person may believe something is important while another part may believe it is unnecessary. As a result, an individual may have different parts with different intentions. These intentions may come into conflict with one another, or lead to behaviours that seem bizarre and irrational to others and even to part of a person's own consciousness. As a parent I will fight for the right to install cameras in the high street to make the town a safer place for my children; as an adult I will fight not to have cameras in the high street because they affect my civil liberties.

The goal is to determine if the client has a secondary desire that will hinder or block their capability to change as requested by the primary desire. For example if you are speaking with a client who has been doing all the 'right' things – planning, organizing, preparing and implementing – and the situation is still not getting better, then maybe they have a secondary desire holding them back. Dealing with this may not be as easy as it looks. Many clients do not want to admit that they have been preventing themselves from improving. Often, the secondary desire issue is subconscious because, consciously, they consider it to be undiscussable.

However, even when the actual desire is quite obvious to the consultant it is not always something that they can point out to the client. It is entirely natural to protect oneself from the truth – especially if it hurts. When the consultant tries to tell the client what the restraining desire might be, the client will often reject the proposition and in some cases reject the consultant. Clients will often 'fight for' their belief in their cause because they do not want to think that anything is wrong with their desire to change. Try telling someone who is dieting that they don't really want to lose weight!

In many cases, it is only once the client begins to fight that you might find the secondary desire. When they get emotional or resistant you may find the blockage that is causing them not to want to let go of the past. For example, if you challenge the smoker about the fact that they like to smoke because it helps them to make friends, their response might be one of emotional indignation and anger. However, the simple fact that the emotional trigger has been pulled may give a clue as to its importance.

When trying to understand the actual desire, the objective is to find out the real motivational drivers that cause someone to behave the way they do – not the way they will do it. So although you will need to ask questions about where the client want's to go, it is also important to ask questions about current behaviour: 'Why do you do this at the moment?', 'What is important to you about this?', 'What does that give you?'. Listen to your client's exact words, including their 'needs' 'wants' and 'likes' for each criteria, and try to tune in to the emotional moments and spot when they become emotionally engaged in describing the great things about the current situation. Compare this level of engagement with how they describe the future or 'to be' state. Is there a gap between the two and is the current or 'as is' state likely to give a stronger hold over their desire than the future state? If so, then you might need seriously to challenge the client about their level of conviction about the change process they are describing. In the same way, if the smoker describes with great passion the pleasure they get from a drag on the cigarette and then mundanely describe why they will not smoke in the future, my suggestion would be not to bet on the chances that they will overcome the addiction in the short term.

> **❝ the objective is to find out the real motivational drivers that cause someone to behave the way they do ❞**

Elusive ethos

The ethos level can be quite a complex area to understand. So often a client will present one set of beliefs and principles that they and the organization abide by, only to reveal later another set of principles that might run counter to those offered in the first instance. We have all worked for a company that espouses its values/mission/purpose by emblazing them in large letters across the company brochure and coffee cups. But the real killer question is whether someone would be challenged if they failed to fulfil the stated ethos. If they persisted in the counter behaviour, would they be disciplined? And if they still failed to align with the company wishes, would they be asked to leave, even if they were the biggest revenue earners in the division?

There is nearly always a gap between the espoused ethos and the actual ethos (*see* Figure 3.22). Although we see this in organizations across the world, it is also a trait that people demonstrate on a fairly consistent basis: someone's espoused ethos may be that addiction is wrong, yet they tuck into a bottle of wine every night; or they have an espoused ethos that it is wrong to break the law, but they slow down just for the speeding camera; or they tell the kids that it is wrong to eat sugar while finishing off their third croissant.

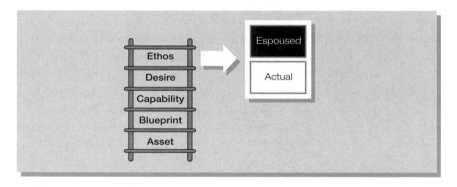

Figure 3.22   Elusive ethos

For any person, team, organization or even country there will generally be an espoused ethos – the stated criteria used to make choices – and the actual ethos – the choices that are really taken. The consultant must be prepared and able to take a number of actions:

- accept that both factors will nearly always exist;
- take time to understand and map the two criteria;
- identify the degree of separation between the two and determine if the gap is large enough to cause a problem;
- determine the extent of the problem and be prepared to challenge the client about what might happen if the gap is not addressed;
- educate the client as to the implications of the gap and what action needs to be taken to address the issue.

You must manage the degree of separation seen in Figure 3.23 and to bring this gap to the surface so that it can be dealt with in the Client stage (and not quietly swept under the carpet!). The trouble is that when these things are hidden from view they always pop out in the Change and Confirm stage – typically when it is too late to do anything about them.

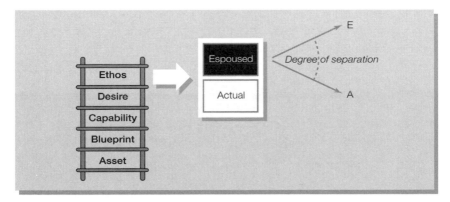

Figure 3.23 Degree of ethos separation

The end result is that the five-rung change ladder actually has two steps within each rung, which give it ten aspects to be considered when developing the opening picture with the client (*see* Figure 3.24).

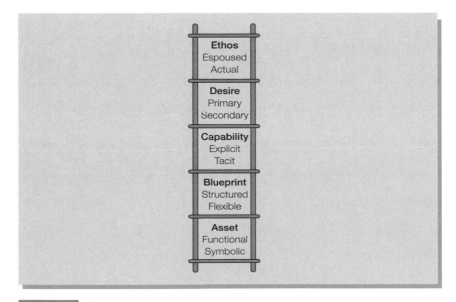

Figure 3.24 Steps on the change ladder

Change ladder profiles

The change ladder can be used to diagnose the nature of the problem and to forecast whether the change is likely to provide a sustainable solution. The five stages on the ladder allow for a simple analysis and mapping of what can be very complex problems. By understanding the different combinations on each of the ladder's rungs it is possible to begin to benchmark common transformation patterns and the results they will deliver. Six different change patterns that can be found to have taken place in most organizations:

The fix

This is the common solution to any organizational problem (*see* Figure 3.25). If performance is down then put some new kit in, set up some revised processes that will fix the problem. The trouble is that the stream of different consultancy interventions that have taken place over the past 25 years tends to prove that this is not the case. Just putting a new quality system in place does not give a quality ethos; implementing a new pay programme for the sales force will not automatically deliver a sustainable improvement in revenue; and the implementation of a new customer relationship management system will not guarantee improved customer service or sales. Simply putting these changes in place without paying any attention to the training and motivation factors will not deliver a certain solution. And installing any change that does not match the ethos of the consumers will only result in short-term 'faking-it' behaviour.

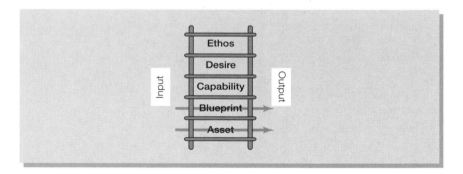

Figure 3.25 The fix

The miracle

In this instance, the consultant or client has resolved that by making a process change then a transformation will occur at the ethos and motivation level of the consumers (*see* Figure 3.26). This miracle cure is a common problem that

I see time and time again. The sales pitch is 'Buy this new enhanced process and your people will take quality decisions/be more customer focused/strive to cut costs (delete as appropriate)'. The hard reality is that a new diet will not help the dieter lose weight, a pill does not cure depression (in the long run) and hiding the bottles will not stop the alcoholic. People make choices at the ethos level and a new process or blueprint very rarely achieves a sustainable change at this level.

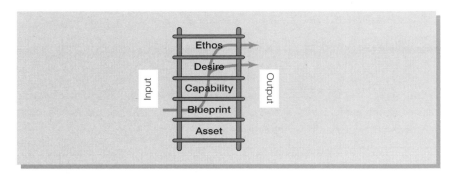

Figure 3.26   The miracle

The waterfall

This is the change intervention that we have all experienced. The new MD enters the firm with big ideas, new dreams and a strong desire to change how the business operates. The problem is that MDs are often hired for their really strong ethos around a particular area. It might be a customer focus, quality orientation, or a belief in the need to reduce costs. It is so important to them that it drives all the choices they make on a daily basis. Like someone who has a faith, their personal philosophy drives their behaviour unquestioningly. But what do new MDs do when they enter organizations as a visionary. They begin to implement change programmes that strive to change the ethos of people in the organization. They do this by issuing badges and banners with great new slogans and maybe setting up some new processes and software to drive the changes they wish to see (*see* Figure 3.27).

Now, just think – when is the last time that a free badge really changed your deep-seated belief or philosophy? In most cases direct personal association with someone will help you understand why things need to change. This is the role of the preacher, coach or mentor. These people will help change your ethos – not a pretty badge with a slogan on it. In most cases the leader

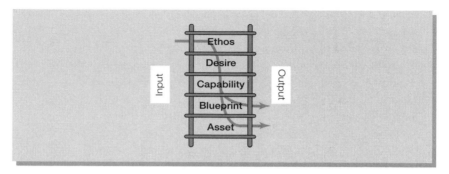

Figure 3.27 The waterfall

who wishes to effect a change in the deep ethos or beliefs of the organization will need to find ways to get close to people and not just try to effect change with corporate bangles and baubles.

The cult

With this model, new MDs accept the idea that they cannot simply change the business by doing things at the asset and blueprint level. They make a conscious choice to meet the teams and share their personal beliefs and dreams. All goes well, with people understanding why the MD wants to make the change and appreciating that the MD is serious. The employees begin to develop the capability to make the changes and also start to grow some personal desire to support the change process. Although they have not modified their belief system (ethos level), it is too early to expect such a deep change (*see* Figure 3.28). The cult process is such that the people and teams are beginning to buy into the belief system offered by the MD.

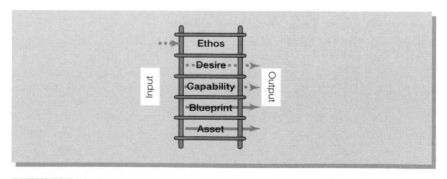

Figure 3.28 The cult

However, after a while the MD moves to a new position. The end result is that people are left high and dry. New equipment processes, training and motivation sometime surround them, but the cult leader has left. After a while the cult decays and all that is left are the tangible artefacts of the change. It is often possible to spot the legacy of precious transformation in organizations (much like an archaeological dig), with evidence of how previous incumbents have attempted to make big changes in the corporate system. The trouble is that all cults will die if the leader is not able to transfer the new belief system to groups of disciples before they move on, up or out.

The wall

The wall is often encountered by consultants, coaches and trainers. This is the situation where you are faced with a client who has asked for some development but for some reason nothing seems to stick. You might invest time developing their capability and helping to motivate them through the change, but the end result is that nothing changes. This is because the ethos is fundamentally different to that being offered by the consultant (*see* Figure 3.29). This is similar to a rugby fan trying to convince a die-hard American football fan to change sports. At a deep level each prefers a particular type of sport because they have received years of social conditioning. Even though the other person teaches them the rules of the games and encourages them to see how exciting it can be, in their heart they still prefer their sport.

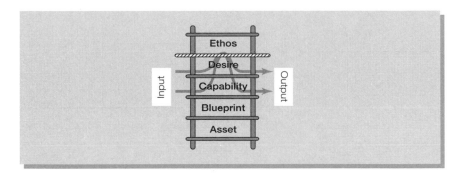

Figure 3.29 The wall

This is the wall that all consultant face at one time or another – when someone with whom they are working simply cannot accept the new way of operating. When faced with the wall there are a number of choices, but often they fall into two camps. The first is to spend more time and money helping the person understand why they need to change their belief systems. The second is to offer them redundancy. The latter is an option often favoured by companies that need to effect a cultural change and do not have the time to wait for all the employees to internalize the new ways of thinking, feeling and behaving.

The grip

The grip might be seen as the change that has a good chance of delivering sustainable value. Whatever level of the change ladder is being addressed (asset, blueprint, capability or desire), it is being supported by the espoused and actual ethos of this system (*see* Figure 3.30). This can be illustrated by the difference between a sustainable and non-sustainable diet. The non-sustainable diet is often driven by a blueprint change (maybe a new diet plan) but unsupported by an actual ethos that supports the desire to lose weight. The espoused ethos is to lose weight but the actual ethos is to enjoy chocolate. However, where the espoused and actual ethos are aligned around the choices not to eat chocolate, then this robust philosophy will grip and reinforce the change actions and so enhance the chance of sustainable success. If you have a client who wants to enhance the customer management processes in the organization and is prepared to spend two days a week working with the teams and meeting real clients, then the chances are that this is a change that will work.

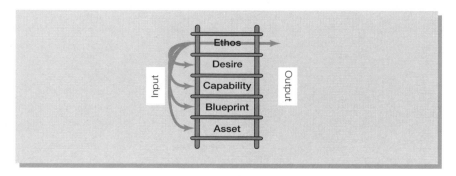

Figure 3.30 The grip

Recognizing profiles

These six profiles can be found anywhere that change is being managed on a regular basis. The fix is sold as a short-term organizational solution; the miracle cure can be seen in countless magazines, and the cult takes place every time a senior-level reorganization occurs and the leading light moves on. The trick is to be able to recognize the patterns before they take place and build compensatory action to prevent your consulting assignment from being another short-term success but long-term failure.

Change ladder chart

Building on the idea of the grip profile, the primary construct with the
change ladder is that successful change must always be delivered by
managing across all five levels. No matter what the change being managed,
these five factors must be understood and considered with care by both the
client and consultant. The goal is to ensure that reinforcing forces are acting
across all five levels on the change ladder (*see* Figure 3.31).

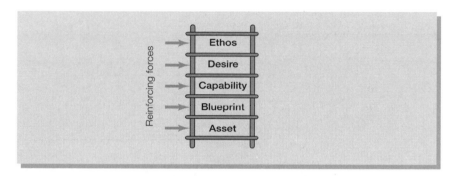

Figure 3.31 **Change ladder reinforcing forces**

For example, in a situation where a new customer relationship management
computer system is being implemented, consider the following reinforcing
aspects on each level:

▦ **Ethos:**
  – values mapping and matching processes;
  – open-door debates with MD about customer-focused strategy;
  – opt-out strategies for people who do not want to follow the new
    company ethos.

▦ **Desire:**
  – motivational processes;
  – segmentation and support of people who are opposed to change.

▦ **Capability:**
  – new system skills;
  – new customer interaction skills.

▦ **Blueprint:**
  – training procedures;
  – customer service process mapping and redesign;
  – office reorganization.

■ **Asset:**
  - computer system purchase and deployment;
  - people recruitment;
  - budget build.

As with Newtonian law, for any force there will be an opposite and equal reaction that will oppose the action. In effecting a change on the organization the client and consultant have a responsibility to understand the forces being used and what opposing force will arise from the consumers. As in Figure 3.32, in most cases a blueprint intervention like a company reorganization will provoke a range of opposing forces on the other levels.

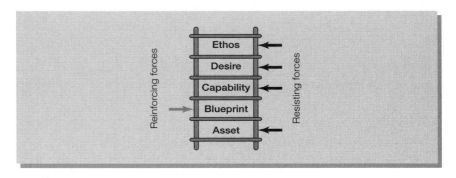

Figure 3.32 Force analysis

Teams resisting change may voice a number of objections:

■ **Ethos:**
  - This doesn't fit with what is important for me.

■ **Desire:**
  - Why should I do this?
  - What is in it for me?

■ **Capability:**
  - I don't have the skills for this.
  - My skills are not suitable for this change.

■ **Blueprint:**
  - We have a process already.

■ **Asset:**
  - My computer doesn't work.

The effective consultant will be able to take any change engagement and develop a change ladder chart. This map will indicate what actions need to

take place on each level of the change ladder, what resistance will be encountered from the recipients of the change, and what corresponding action
must be taken to manage any resistance. These maps will correlate with the
particular specialism or industry operated by the consultant. The IT consultant will understand what factors need to be addressed on the change
ladder for a system implementation, where the resistance will arise on each
of the five levels, and what action will need to be taken to address them. The
same will be true for a HR consultant, mergers expert or financial adviser. No
matter what your specialism, you should be able to build a structural representation of your engagement using the map shown in Figure 3.33.

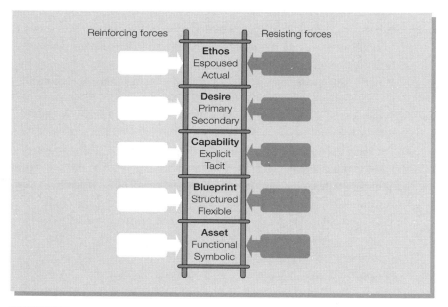

Figure 3.33 Change ladder chart

The change ladder chart is as an extremely powerful tool that can highlight
potential project failures early on for both the client and consultant. For
each of the five levels the consultant should be able to analyze the current
situation, even from a remote perspective. To gain some degree of confidence that the project will run without too many problems it is wise to
ensure that you have a clear response to the following questions:

▨ **Ethos (espoused and actual):**
  – What is the espoused ethos offered by the client? (Check mission
    and values etc.)

- What is the espoused ethos presented by the consumers? (Use focus groups.)
- What is the client's actual ethos? (Look at the diary, talk with their PA.)
- What is the consumer's actual ethos? (Listen at coffee breaks and team meetings.)
- What is the degree of separation between actual and espoused and what is the impact of this gap? (Listen for gossip about managerial inconsistencies between what they say and what they do.)

■ **Desire (primary and secondary):**
  - What is the client's primary desire – what is it they say they want to achieve with the project? (Check company brochures and promotional material.)
  - What is the client's secondary desire – what do you think they want to hold on to or retain? (Check their current diary and budget – see how they spend their time and money.)
  - What is the consumer's stated or primary desire? (Talk with field representatives.)
  - What is it that the consumers want to hold on to? (Listen to coffee-break chats.)
  - For both the client and consumers – which desire is stronger and what is the likely implication for the change process?
  - Will this opposing secondary desire show up as overt or covert resistance?
  - If the secondary desire is stronger than the primary desire, what is the cost to address this and transform it into the focus of the primary desire?

■ **Capability (explicit and tacit):**
  - Does the change require explicit or tacit knowledge and what is the balance?
  - What current explicit capability does the system have? (Look at training records.)
  - What new explicit capability is required to support the change process?
  - What tacit capability exists? (Watch what people do and what they say.)
  - What new tacit capability is required?
  - Are their sufficient time and funds to support the acquisition of the tacit capability?

■ **Blueprint (structured and flexible):**
  - To what extent does the process need to be structured or

unstructured to support the intervention? (Check the level of control required.)
- What is the client's structured/flexible preference – are they aware of it? (Check how have they deployed previous change processes.)
- What is the consumer's structured/flexible preference? (Refer back to previous change programmes and their response.)
- How will the consumers respond to the proposed blueprint style – will there be any latent resistance? (Test using a pilot or talk with staff associations.)
- Are there funds and support to manage any potential resistance? *(Assume it will cost more than budgeted for.)*

■ **Asset (functional and symbolic):**
- What assets need to be changed to support the intervention?
- What are the functional requirements?
- Will the project require any significant change to the existing assets?
- Do the client or consumers have any associative connection with the existing assets? (Listen to people language in relation to the asset.)
- Will they resist change to the current assets?

The change ladder chart offers the consultant a tool that will rapidly pull out the factors that could cause the project to fail to deliver sustainable change. However, it also offers a useful instrument with which to build an effective relationship with the client. As well as everything else in the Client stage, the two underlying process that the consultant must focus on are the ability to challenge and educate. The client must be seriously challenged to think about the consequences of their action and be sure that they have the resources and stamina to take the engagement through to the end. However, it is also fair to expect that the client may not be as well versed in the process of change as the consultant. So it may be incumbent on the consultant to help educate the client as to why change so often fails to deliver sustainable benefits and in particular why their project may not work in the long run. The change ladder chart can help the client understand some of these fundamental issues.

Compound contracting

The initial contract that you form with your client will set out a framework for action and offers a tool by which the success or failure of the engagement can be measured. There are many models that outline a basic structural framework that the document and process can follow and it would be foolish here to try to offer a definitive answer. The danger is that in offering a potential structure of the contract process, 99 per cent of practising consultants will say 'Yes, but you missed this item'. Hence the content offered in the contract model in Table 3.4 is meant to be indicative and is not offered as a definitive model. For example, it does not include any of the financial and legal aspects that will be found in many contracts.

Table 3.4 Contract model

Heading	Sub-heading
Background	▓ Outline description of client area
	▓ Situation under consideration
	▓ Business context
Outcome	▓ High-levels goals
	▓ Specific objectives
	▓ Measurement content
	▓ Measurement process
Engagement plan	▓ Timeframe
	▓ Methodology
	▓ Resource allocation
	▓ Key milestones and breakpoints
	▓ Initial known data requirements
Responsibilities	▓ Client
	▓ Client representative
	▓ Stakeholders
	▓ Consultancy team
	▓ Sub-contractors
Boundaries and scope	▓ Areas for inclusion
	▓ Areas for exclusion
	▓ Potential risks
Specifics	▓ Payment
	▓ Terms and conditions

Heading	Sub-heading
	▨ Termination process
	▨ Liability
Confidentiality	▨ Confidentiality ring
	▨ Disclosure policy
Review process	▨ Review process
	▨ Review goals
	▨ Deviation management
Closure	▨ Closure reviews dates
	▨ Closure process

Remember that the contract should never include anything that will surprise the client. If the client observes a new clause, proposition or assumption, trust will be eroded. If you or the client cannot be trusted at the opening stages of the relationship, what chance is there that integrity will be maintained once the project gets into turbulent waters?

When developing the contract, it is important to remember that it is a framework for the delivery of a service or product. It is not being written as a stick for either party to beat the other. If the contract reads like a 'screw-down' document then there is every chance that the relationship will operate according to that principle. If it is written with the intention that it will not see the light of day until the process is complete, there will be a greater chance that the relationship will operate with a collaborative spirit. However, before the contract is written, many of the details contained within the document must be negotiated, and this is where problems can surface.

As the old adage goes: 'Measure twice, cut once'. The goal at the contract stage must be to take extra care in the specification of the desired outcomes. This must be in the criteria specified in the document and more especially in the allocation of roles and responsibilities between you, the client and the consumer. One of the biggest causes of downstream problems can be disagreement over who owns what action or who is responsible for a particular aspect of the change. Simply by locking in clarity at this early stage it is possible to minimize any problems that might occur at a later date.

Contract negotiation

The negotiation phase is difficult because it is often the point when the undiscussable has to be discussed. When you first meet with a new client much of the emphasis is on the pleasant aspects of the business – the future benefits, change methodology or who will be involved at various stages. However, as you get closer to signing the contract, the more difficult issues need to be aired and resolved. This is where you must move your client out of the comfort zone and into the reality zone, discussing issues such as responsibilities, remuneration, risks and results. However, in dealing with such difficult issues, there can often be a tendency to go for fight or flight. Fight means that you go into battle with the client, battling to leverage every bean out of the situation. Flight means avoiding dealing with the difficult issues and sticking with a basic contract that does not offer any beneficial agreements.

Always go for a balanced outcome – one where both parties are genuinely happy with the result and where, even better, there is a sense of collaboration rather than compromise. In this type of agreement, you and the client are not people staring at a problem from different sides of the street. You are standing together trying to reach an equitable, aligned and mutually beneficial solution. If this happens then there is less chance that either side will see itself as a winner or loser. The moment one person agrees to a contract with a voice in their head telling them that they have lost the negotiating game then the relationship is doomed. In driving for an aligned negotiation process the goal is to avoid the fight or flight syndrome and to come to a position where the outcome is win/win.

Although the model suggests that the negotiation phase is at the end of the client phase, in reality it starts from the point when you first meet the client. Negotiation is a fact of life. Children negotiate for sweets, partners negotiate for wardrobe space in the bedroom and you will negotiate throughout the life cycle of the change process.

Shared success

Consulting contracts that are focused on selfish outcomes may deliver short-term gain but will offer little opportunity to create a long-term relationship. Effective contracting is founded on the notion of achieving shared and sustainable outcomes. The key to this choice is the absolute focus on mutual benefit and the generation of shared success through the delivery of sustainable value.

However, you can only really achieve shared success if you understand what success means for yourself and others. Many people want to achieve a successful contract but do not take the time to understand what the other person wants to achieve. They are focused on achieving their goal and pay little attention to the other person's needs and desires. The end result teeters between a battle of wills as each person struggles to assert their view of success, or lacklustre output because no one has really said what is important for them. Only by understanding what real success is for the people with whom we work and live can we hope to achieve sustainable success with them.

> **effective contracting is founded on the notion of achieving shared and sustainable outcomes**

The way to do this is to keep two ideas in mind. First is the need for constant inquiry – to understand what success means for the client. Second is the need for advocacy – to make sure that the client knows what you want and need by having the courage to tell them. Once you understand these two dimensions you can appreciate how your needs and their needs interrelate and where you can start to find synergies in the abundance. The balance and relationship between these two processes can be seen in Figure 3.34. There are four dimensions to the model:

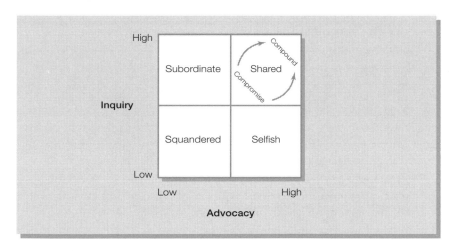

Figure 3.34 Shared success

■ **Squandered:** In this contracting process little is happening. You might have a formal process in place, but it only represents what you will both deliver to ensure that the engagement meets the minimum needed to deliver a success. There is no real inquiry or advocacy on the part of either the client or consultant, so neither understands what benefit could accrue from the relationship.

- **Subordinate:** In this relationship value is being created, but you are not receiving any of it. The emphasis is on giving benefit to the client without any focus on what you, the consultant, will gain from the contract. This type of contract will often emerge if the consultant is being pressured to grow revenue or if the consulant is new and inexperienced. In this situation the consultant feels under pressure not to voice their needs and consequently satisfy only the client's needs.

- **Selfish:** This is the inverse of the subordinate level, where you do the taking, without giving anything back. Your revenue will grow, but it is not renewable and sustainable because the client will eventually have enough of your demands and exploitation. (Unless they, too, are doormat wannabes.)

- **Shared:** At this level, you are both gaining value from the relationship, but there is little or no synergy between you. This might be the case in the bricklayer and carpenter who work together. They do not offer new products or special discount schemes or differentiate themselves in the market because of the joint proposition. In a consulting environment this might be the contract where both client and consultant have been through the hoops many times before and so simply jump to a standard routine when they agree the contract. They have forgotten to delve deeper to understand what additional success the other person might be able to achieve from the relationship.

- **Synergistic:** This is shared success at a compound level. This type of relationship is where two people spend time together and in doing so create something that exceeds the sum of their two parts. Thus it is the interaction of two or more agents or forces so that their combined effect is greater than the sum of their individual effects. With this contracting process both client and consultant take time to understand the engagement, what the other person can really gain form the process and what synergistic benefits they might gain. For example, the consultant might wish to promote a new software tool overseas and the client wants to leave a few hooks in the system for future internal enhancement. By careful advocacy and inquiry, they start to realize that the consultant's willingness to leave such embedded memory hooks for no charge means that the client would be willing to help promote the consultant's company in its overseas offices.

The synergistic or compound relationship is an important factor in the contracting stage. It is easy to invest in a client relationship that produces nothing more than the sum of the parts. If you choose to spend time with someone on a project, you are using valuable time, energy and ideas and you cannot afford to waste good opportunities. By spending more time on advocacy and inquiry, the net result is a compound contract – in which the sum of the parts is greater than the whole.

Compound contract development

Compound contracting is founded on two principles:

▓ **Exposed advocacy:** The consultant is prepared to expose their success criteria with the client.

▓ **Empathic inquiry:** The goal is to use a questioning structure that enables the client to expose personal success criteria.

Where both principles are employed a shift is made from compromise to compound success.

The key features of exposed advocacy are that you:

▓ **Expose private wins:** You have a clear and focused understanding of what good means to you. How would you define success from your perspective and how can you make it clear enough for the client to understand?

▓ **Discuss undiscussables:** The essence of exposed advocacy is to bring to the surface the shadow desires – to feel comfortable enough to expose and explain the deep personal successes that really would make this engagement of personal value.

▓ **Welcome debate:** You offer others the chance to explore, challenge and understand your success factors. Unless the client feels able to explore the success factors for which you are aiming, there is a chance they will not fully understand what the aims are and how they can be achieved.

The key features of empathic inquiry are that you:

▓ **Choose to listen:** This is the conscious desire to put the tacit receptors into gear and to listen with your heart. This is a very specific and conscious process, not something that might automatically happen as you are walking along the corridor chatting with someone. As any parent knows, it is easy to give superficial yes and no answers when a child is constantly raising issues and questions. This can also happen at work where we switch into autopilot and just talk with people on a surface level while processing our important issues internally. Sometimes we have to turn the inner voice off and listen with our whole self. When the client is describing what success would be like for them, try to really listen to what they are inferring.

■ **Minimize internal distractions:** As we listen to the client describe their objectives it is easy for the inner voice to jump in and challenge or disagree with the statement being made. Your inner voice must be tightly managed to ensure it does not corrupt the inflow of thoughts and feelings from the other person. The next time you are listening to someone who is presenting you with a case or argument to do something with which you disagree listen to your inner voice. There is every chance that the moment you 'know' what they are about to say you will begin to formulate your answer, then you move into a holding position ready to launch your packaged solution before they have a chance to pause for breath. The problem is that you have missed over 50 per cent of what they are saying – and this might be the most important element. The trick is to turn this inner voice off so that it no longer presents a distraction.

■ **Love paradox:** You must be able to agree with the client's wish to achieve a set of goals – even if you disagree with the actual goals. This is the art of listening without prejudice and accepting other people's wishes without acting as critic.

■ **Manage air space:** You must stay conscious to the balance between listening and telling, since there is always competition for air space. Try to ensure that the balance is appropriate for the outcome you wish to achieve. Don't formulate an answer in your head before the person has finished speaking. Wherever possible, leave space in the conversation to allow the other person room to play with an idea *that has just exposed*.

The shift from a compromise contract to a compound one is based on your ability and desire to take the advocacy and inquiry dimensions to the limit. If the relationship is not reaching its full potential, are you really using the full power of exposed advocacy and empathic inquiry? Is all your energy and passion focused on extracting the client's personal success criteria and helping them understand your own? By investing energy and focus into the relationship and the contract design, both sides can really share in the successful outcomes of the project.

Stage two: Clarify

The wise man doesn't give the right answers;
he poses the right questions.

Claude Lévi-Strauss

Once your client has been emotionally and contractually engaged, you need to move beyond what is a relatively narrow field of vision. The goal is to take away some of the haze – to understand the real source of the problem. Only then can you make a firm proposal as to how the situation can be resolved.

It is at this stage that the first dilemma can occur. Often a client will employ you because they have a problem that is urgent and pressing. When the wolves are at the door, it is difficult to suggest that your client should set aside time for detailed diagnostics. With a client in panic mode you may be expected to be in the same frame of mind. The expectation is that you will be able to walk in, fix the problem, take the 50 pieces of silver and then let the organization carry on with its affairs.

If you are being paid on a daily rate and employed solely to deliver a focused outcome, your client may well regard activities such as investigation, research and diagnosis as wasteful (and unnecessarily expensive). This is because they (often) think they know what the cause of the problem is already; you are just expected to fix it. But even when time is of the essence, the same underlying disciplines and rigour need to be applied so that errors are not made. Rushing in and attempting a quick fix is as dangerous as a doctor prescribing an operation based on the patient's own diagnosis.

You have a legal responsibility to deliver an agreed outcome and you also have an ethical responsibility to deliver the 'appropriate' one. Prescribing a solution without correctly diagnosing the cause of the problem may offer short-term income but leads to long-term erosion in your market credibility. If clients realize that a consultant's solutions do not result in a true resolution of their problem, then the jokes about consultants become perpetuated.

The process offered in this stage of the Seven Cs model follows this pattern:

- **Diagnosis:** Gather information that will help determine the real source of the issue and not just tackle the symptoms.
- **Phase Mapping:** Determine the extent to which known and unknown factors within the change process will affect its potential for success.
- **Shadow dancing:** Determine the extent to which unspoken activities and arrangements affect the situation.
- **Culture:** Understand the cultural factors that affect the change process.
- **Decision makers:** Be clear about who is actually making the decisions as opposed to who says they are.
- **System construction:** Understand the structure of the organizational system and how it is likely to react to any changes.
- **Stakeholders:** Develop a map that indicates who can influence the outcome of the change and to what extent they have the capability and desire to wield their power.
- **Life-cycle risk:** Gauge the level of risk associated with the project.

If we follow the components in the Clarify stage, it becomes possible to ensure that the Create and Change stages actually resolve the source of the problems rather than simply eradicate the evidence.

Diagnosis

At this stage our primary objective is to discover timely, robust and accurate data. However, before you can start to collect data you must make a methodological decision on the approach you are going to use. There are many schools of thought behind the process of data gathering and research but the two common models are the outside-in and inside-out models.

Outside-in model

The outside-in model is based on the idea of prior hypotheses. Data is collected against a predetermined model or mental framework. You will be trying to prove or disprove a specific argument or develop a test bed for future expansion. A strategist might use Porter's five forces model as a tool to understand a company's strengths in the market; an organizational development consultant will use Lewin's force-field tool to map and understand what negative and positive forces are operating in the organization; the marketing consultant might analyze the company's product positioning against the portfolio positioning tool. You are working on the assumption that a predefined model or paradigm can help to identify a clear solution to a problem. This type of research is driven by the following assumptions:

■ **Hypothesis:** A pre-defined model is used as a guiding framework to drive the data-gathering process.

■ **Independence:** There is no subjective bias. The data sits on the table and is manipulated without being clouded by your personal views.

■ **Value-freedom:** Objective criteria rather than human beliefs and interests determine the choice of what to study and how to study it.

■ **Operationalism:** Concepts need to be operationalized in a way that enables facts to be measured quantitatively.

■ **Reductionism:** Problems are better understood if they are reduced to their simplest elements.

■ **Generalism:** In order to generalize about regularities it is necessary to select sizeable samples. Once a statistically sound sample is used then any conclusion drawn from the process is applied across the entire population.

Inside-out model

The alternative approach is built around an inside-out, or grounded, model. With this model the research process is open-ended and uncluttered by the mental framework of the consultant. Any output will be guided purely by the content of the data. This model uses a set of principles that are quite different to the outside-in model:

■ **Natural setting:** Realities cannot be understood in isolation from the context in which the study is undertaken. So although Porter's five forces model is suitable for the areas Porter studied, it might not be applicable in all contexts.

■ **Human instrument:** Only humans are capable of grasping the variety of realities that will be encountered. Rigid and structured data-gathering processes will be unable to pick up the minor nuances of inflection that can indicate so much, for example during an interview.

■ **Use of tacit knowledge:** Intuitive/felt knowledge is used to appreciate the existence of multiple realities and because it mirrors the value patterns of the investigator.

■ **Qualitative methods:** The use of words rather than numbers makes the data more adaptable when dealing with multiple realities and patterns and influences.

■ **Emergent design:** It is impracticable to assume you know enough ahead of time to build a research design that could capture all the necessary data – the research process must emerge with the findings from the data.

This approach operates on the basis that discovery and diagnosis is not a black and white process. Since most data gathering will involve people, there is a good chance that the process will be full of uncertainty, emotion and confusion. The gathering process needs to be built around an emergent rather than fixed design.

Diagnostic process

When you visit the doctor, take a car to the mechanic or attend counselling, it involves some form of diagnostic exercise. Does the doctor warm the stethoscope before applying it to your chest? Did the mechanic clean their hands before touching the upholstery? Did the counsellor find a comfortable seat for you? These issues might seem minor, but they are significant because they indicate a person's process capability – their ability to appreciate all the factors that will affect an effective diagnostic process.

❝ the gathering process needs to be built around an emergent rather than fixed design ❞

In the same way, your diagnostic process is likely to be the client's first experience of your professional capability. You need to ensure that you have a clear map of the process. Even more important will be your capability to explain the process to the client. If your client likes to take an interest in the process then you must have a clear and concise model that will explain how you will define, gather and analyze the data.

Although there are many diagnostic styles and frameworks used in the consulting cycle, they all fall within three basic actions (*see* Figure 4.1):

■ define what data is required;

■ gather the data;

■ analyze the data and draw conclusions about the source of the problem.

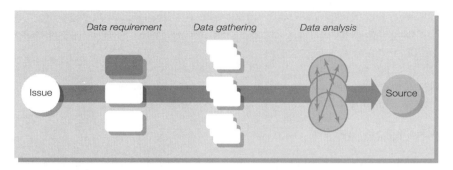

Figure 4.1 Diagnostic process

A range of different tools and techniques has augmented these three steps but in essence they form the backbone of a typical diagnostic project. Two additional factors that must be stressed are the need to ensure clarity about the actual issues being researched and the importance of taking a reality check to ensure that the diagnosis has not drifted off track.

Issues

As you start on the data-gathering process, it really does pay to stop, sit down and think about the issues being addressed. Once the data collection phase begins you often find out that the world has moved on since the contract was signed. People leave, new team members join, organizations merge or split. In many cases the client who initiated the contract might no longer be around to clarify what is required. So, while the contract process within the Client stage does focus on outcomes and deliverables, it pays to spend time at this stage to confirm that the issue is still current and active.

One of the best ways to frame and clarify the issue is to ensure that it is built around a statement of 'We can't', 'We are unable to', or 'X isn't doing Y'. Once this is defined then it becomes quite easy to map what data is required. We need a negative focus because a positive one can lead to misdirected outcomes. For example, saying 'We want a new sales bonus scheme' can lead to a range of outcomes, many of which do not address the real issue causing the problem. What we should say is 'The present bonus scheme does not encourage a collective style of working between the account managers'. Then the options for resolution are not linked into the provision of a new bonus scheme. The statement offers the problem and goal without presenting a prescriptive outcome.

Using a negative issue statement challenges the client to question what area of the concern is being dealt with and what value will be added by any change. For example, as a consultant you will often be employed simply as an excuse to delay or defer action. The introduction of an external agent can offer convenient breathing space for the client if they are in a battle with others in the company. In forcing the research issue to be framed in this way, both you and the client will have a clear understanding of what is not happening and what information you will need to retrieve.

Data requirements

Once the issue has been clarified and a shared model is held by each member of the data-gathering team, the next step is to make sure you know what data is required. One way to do this is by breaking down the total data load into sets that define a unique package of information to be discovered. The set description will indicate the data type, source, owner, purpose, etc. Only by taking this type of structured approach can you ensure that you do not spend valuable time and money gathering redundant information. However, although this helps to clarify how the data gathering is managed, it does not resolve the issue of how to identify what data needs to be gathered.

Gathering framework

The content and context of whatever problem you are dealing with will drive the actual data sets. But in many cases it can be difficult to take the first step. Modern organizations hold millions and millions of units of data they use to run their business. Once you start to delve into the archives the amount of data will explode. Financial reports, customer complaints, supplier receipts, memos, staff surveys, etc., all come together to form this mountain of information. So in deciding where to start, the framework set out in Figure 4.2 will help to focus on what data needs to be gathered.

In any situation where a change has to be made, there are five sets of data that need to be understood:

- **Root:** Is it possible to carry out an audit to identify the original source of the problem? In the case of industrial action in a small manufacturing company, it might be changes in pay rates, poor industrial relations or a change in government policy.

- **Result:** What is the true impact of the issue? Is it something that affects the whole organization, one particular group, or is it something that causes a problem for one product area? Whatever the breakdown, you have to collect firm and valid data that describes the impact the issue is having. The data must indicate what is really happening rather than what the client or consumer believes is happening.

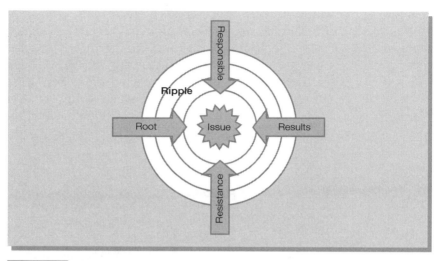

Figure 4.2 Data-gathering drivers

■ **Responsible:** Whatever the problem, someone somewhere must have allowed it to happen. This 'permission' might have been given explicitly – the managing director deciding to reduce the organization's cost base by running a re-engineering programme. Alternatively, it may have been given implicitly – a parent leaving too many sweets around the house, thus tempting a child.

■ **Resistance:** There is often a temptation to ignore an issue in the hope that it will disappear once the problem has been resolved. However, there can be data elements within this area that might be of interest to you. Consider the resistance that might arise if a company announces plans to change its policy on using company telephones for private calls. The level of any opposition to such a change can indicate a number of important factors, such as the strength of the culture, the extent to which people are prepared to accept centralized decisions or the capability of the people to form co-ordinated counterattacks to any imposed change.

■ **Ripple effect:** The first four data areas are visible and can readily be measured and mapped. But with any issue there will be an intangible radiation, or energy, emitted as change 'ripples' through the organization. This is the anger and emotion that surround a downsizing exercise or the excitement released by an impending global merger. This radiated energy must be understood, since it will often contain the power to amplify or attenuate the change process associated with any consultancy project.

The ease with which these five factors can be translated into data sets is shown in Figure 4.3. The example shows a consultancy project looking at the issue of falling product sales. For each of the five data drivers, a range of hard, focused and relevant data sets are shown. Each of these data sets has a purpose within the analytical framework and is seen to add value to the total picture. Although the ripple factors are perceived as 'vague', they can add valuable qualitative data that will help to make sense of the quantitative data emerging in the other four areas.

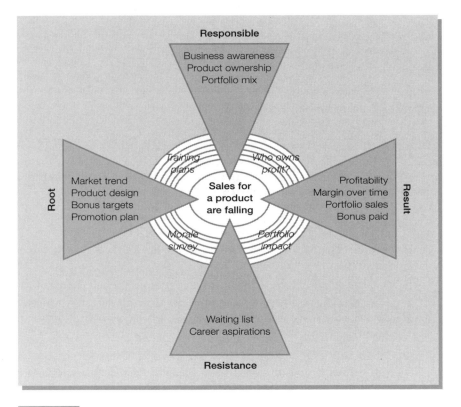

Figure 4.3   Data map example

Although the data you capture in these five areas might not offer the total picture, it does help to build a robust and rigorous data map that is less clouded by an intuitive and emotional decision-making process. It also offers a simple but effective tool that will help your client and the consumer to understand your data-gathering strategy. As such they will be able to look quickly at the map and point out data sets that are obsolete and other areas where data sets are needed to highlight a certain issue.

Data richness

When planning how to gather data, it can help to take a slightly different approach in setting the boundaries. Data gathering often pushes for hard, tangible and actionable facts, whereas the actual problem may lie in the soft, intangible areas of the business. If you take a clinical view of the problem, the resulting data will offer a robust story about the situation but will have little heart. If, however, it is possible to get data sets that reflect some of the softer issues, it becomes possible to enrich the picture so that it tells the real story of what is happening.

Using the model offered in Figure 4.2, far greater value could be mined by using the full depth and breadth of our capability to gather data. This gathering information can be categorized at the cognitive (head), behavioural (hand) and emotional (heart) level. Just consider the examples below and see if you have had a similar experience:

■ Your son starts to keep his bedroom tidy after receiving the fifth warning that it must never happen again. Although there is a short-term change in behaviour, he soon drifts back again because he does not understand the reason why a bedroom must be kept tidy and feels that it is not as important as playing with his friends (high hand, but low head and heart).

■ A manager listens to a passionate call from the chairman for a reduction in costs and goes back to the office fired up to deliver an improvement. However, although he believes in the need for change, he does not really understand what can be done and what he can deliver personally. The change ends up as something that other people will have to deliver (high heart, low head and hand).

■ An organization decides to put its people through customer care training. The goal is to help people to understand why customer service is important and what they can do to make a difference. People leave the course knowing the process they have to follow when dealing with a customer, but the change is short-lived and the old routines soon return because they are unable to translate what they know into what they do (high head, but low heart and hand).

For each of the five factors identified in the model in Figure 4.2, always try to gather data that represents the head, hand and heart factors. For example, if you are trying to get information about high staff turnover in a call centre, Table 4.1 identifies questions that might help to determine what data is required.

Table 4.1   Data needs example

	Head	Hand	Heart
Root What caused the problem?	How did people perceive their remuneration in comparison to other companies in the region?	What training did people receive?	Is there a system that tracks morale within the call centre?
Responsible Who allowed it to happen?	What level of staff turnover did the senior team want to aim for?	How has the company been seen to respond when people leave?	Does the senior team really care about the turnover, or is short-term the profit real driver?
Result What has happened as a result?	Do people think that the competition will offer a better career alternative?	How has the situation affected business performance?	Do the call operators believe that this is a problem and are they thinking about leaving?
Resistance What forces are trying to stop the problem from happening?	What plans do the local managers have in place to stop the problem from getting worse?	What action have the team managers taken to stem the flow?	Who are the leaders that really want to fix the problem as opposed to those who see it as a minor issue?
Ripple What are the side issues?		Is this problem impacting upon how people behave in other parts of the company?	

Data gathering

Once the data sets are clearly mapped, the next stage is to start the gathering process. You must determine where the data is held and how it can be accessed. This stage of the diagnostic process is well documented so what follows is a simple overview of some of the more common forms of data gathering.

Questionnaire survey

This is one of the more common methods used to elicit data from a large population. It offers a 'quick and dirty' way to gather information about the views of your customers, staff, suppliers, etc., in a comparatively cost-effective manner. The basic steps are:

- decide what you need to know;
- code it into a series of questions;
- send the questionnaires to the target population;
- draw general conclusions from the questionnaires once they are returned.

The major problem with this method is the typically low rate of return. A good result will be a 50 per cent return but it can fall as low as 10 per cent. In this case it is important to ensure that a good statistical model is used to ensure that any conclusion can be generalized as representative of the entire population.

Sampling people at random is relatively simple, but it is difficult to ensure that an accurate representation is drawn from the total population. Although a true random selection might offer a fair selection, it might be that your population does not have an even distribution and there may be heavy clusters of responses from a particular area. You can deal with this possible bias by stratifying your sample. This resolves a problem where a particular tendency exists in the population, such as a localized ethnic group, focused skill set or age profile. For the sample to be representative, random samples should be taken from these particular sub-groups or strata. Another alternative is the quota sample, where the sample is based on a prescribed quota criterion. There is no pre-set make-up of the sample; the criterion is simply to gather sufficient information to meet the sample requirements. For example, the target may be to interview the first 30 people that walk into a shop.

Face-to-face interview

The face-to-face interview has the advantage that it is flexible, probing and sensitive to changing moods in the population. It allows you to get a first-hand feel for the intangible problems associated with the project. Furthermore, meeting people reduces some of the anxiety caused by your presence. The downside is that it can be prone to bias by the interviewer and it can be difficult to compile the information into a meaningful form. These problems can be partially eliminated by carefully structuring the interview. The options are a predefined question structure, limited questions and prompted responses. However, with these options you start to eliminate some of the richness associated with this approach.

Focus group

This takes the idea of the single interview and expands it to a wider group of participants. A focus group might consist of between five and 20 people and in some cases even more. The initial benefit of this approach is that it brings disparate people together and so saves time. Another important benefit is that it offers the opportunity to extract a sense of synergistic spontaneity from the group. As people interact and share knowledge, so a vein of new knowledge can be elicited that might not have been uncovered by other methods. This data can be used as information to feed into the analysis stage or as foundation data to help construct a questionnaire.

Observing people

In some cases you might want to find out what people do rather than what they say they do. In this case it can be useful to gather data by observing people in their normal setting. This process is sometimes used in process re-engineering. Although you might gather data as to the effectiveness of a particular process, you might also choose to watch how people operate over a longer period. Often this will highlight valuable data that would have been unavailable by other means. The short cuts that people take to save time or the way that a team interacts can only be identified by observation at close quarters.

Personal logs

Another method is to ask people to observe themselves and to record what actions they take, to whom they talk and what they think about certain issues, noting it in a personal log or diary. Although diaries are often used for social science research, they are less frequently used in consultancy. However, they are a wonderful tool for gathering specific information at local and specific levels within an organization. Diaries record both quali-tative and quantitative information and can be constructed to include some pre-analysis coding. The advantage is that they offer the perspective of the employees, rather than the consultants, of what is happening. They also allow the use of comparative analysis, possibly to compare how different people feel about the same issue. One final advantage is that diaries operate in the background, freeing the researcher to do other activities.

Customer database

Not all data analysis is concerned with understanding what people think, feel or do. One of the most important assets of any business is the database of financial, operational and customer information. It is also one of the most underused assets in many consultancy projects, partly because it is an erratic process fraught with bias and error. However, there are tools on the market that might help to extract some of the necessary data from company archives. These are divided into two types:

■ **Predictive modelling:** This method is used to determine the relationship between data and the desired outcomes. The most common statistical tools used in this type of analysis include stepwise multiple regression, logistic regression, discriminant analysis and neural network modelling. These models all share the same basic idea – to predict the future, for example how customers will respond to a direct mail campaign.

■ **Descriptive statistics:** These are used to describe and summarize what the existing data sets are indicating and what is in the database and how it is organized. Some common types of descriptive tools are frequency distributions, cross tabulations, employee age profiles, customer profiles, penetration analysis, factor analysis and cluster analysis. While this type of analysis does not predict a future event, it does describe past events very accurately.

Data validity

Although data-gathering methods differ, there are common rules that ensure that the data is of value.

■ Be relevant. The process must gather knowledge about the subject area and not just cloud the issue.

■ Always take the process for a test run. Use a sample population from the targeted areas or use a group of volunteers. Ask them to test drive the process and take it to breaking point so that it will be robust when applied in the field.

■ Trying to save money at this stage can severely limit the whole process. As the adage goes, 'Garbage in – garbage out'. If the gathering process fails to deliver data of any real value then the rest of the consultancy process will suffer.

■ Market yourself in the data-gathering process. If people receive a dirty envelope with a questionnaire full of typing mistakes, they will form an immediate (poor) opinion about you and the whole process.

■ When gathering the data, ensure that people are told why it is wanted and how it will be used. Just because people are performing mundane jobs, it does not mean that they have mundane thoughts. Treat the data donors with the same respect accorded the client.

■ Be aware of timing. The classic mistake is to come up with wonderful project plans only to find that the data research phase falls smack in the middle of August when everyone is on holiday.

■ Above all else, ethics are crucial. Unless people believe that their information will be held in confidence then the process and content will end up being corrupted. If the process cannot be trusted then people will only put down what they think the researchers want to hear.

The construction of the survey will often be driven by practical constraints. Although you must take an idealistic stance when you define the methodology for gathering data, at the end of the day the client's hand is on the tiller. They will have to bear the cost of the process so you must ensure that they are fully aware of the process being used, the associated costs and the potential benefits of each methodology. Make sure you are able to defend each strand in your diagnostic phase. Otherwise your client might start arguing for cuts, with the risk that the whole assignment is put in jeopardy because of insufficient or inaccurate data.

> **❝ treat the data donors with the same respect accorded the client ❞**

Data analysis

Towards the end of the diagnostic phase you will start to find yourself awash with data. This increases the chance that critical aspects may be missed through data overload. The data analysis phase needs to ensure that the data:

■ has been reduced to a manageable size;

■ has been synthesized to provide an indication of the root issue to be addressed;

■ is prepared in a form that will help to develop a compelling argument for action.

The two views that drive the analysis phases, the outside-in (pre-determined analytical model) or the inside-out (emergent analytical model), were described earlier. In the first, you use a degree of scientific rigour to analyze the data and understand how it matches the initial proposition. In the second approach, an inductive framework is used, where you draw upon some form of emergent cognitive framework to tease out patterns and themes in the data.

Outside-in

With this method, your task is to take the data and find out if it proves or disproves the hypothesis offered at the outset of the diagnostic phase. This is a relatively simple process and can be facilitated by the use of a comparative matrix.

Table 4.2 Data matrix example

Hypothesis test	Data set 1 Morale survey	Data set 2 Focus groups	Data set 3 Readiness survey	Data set 4 Previous programmes
Proposition 1 Change needs the support of the top managers	Senior managers are only partially trusted: pocket of good and bad	Support is fragmented	Certain key managers are sending out the right signals	Have had problems: stalling in the areas of difficult change.
Proposition 2 People must be able to express their concerns about the change	Good sense of openness across total population	People concerned about impact to change on their personal lives	In general, but some project groups have concerns	Some have failed because of industrial relation problems
Proposition 3 The new order must be appealing to the population	No data	People do not understand what is expected of them	Willing to change, but not sure what they have to do	No data

Table 4.2 offers an example of such a process. For example, you might have identified three core propositions that you believe are true. These propositions are then tested against the data collected during the research phase. The result is a number of summary statements, each indicating how the data stands up against the core propositions. Your first proposition may be that senior managers must actively support the change for the transition to be effective. However, data from the morale survey suggests there are doubts about trusting the senior team. The implication is that even if the senior team offers support for the transition, staff might not believe it. This offers both evidence that a problem might exist and a compelling argument that the senior team needs to take immediate action.

As an analytical tool, this method is powerful, simple and cost effective. However, the downside is that it limits your level of flexibility. Since the whole emphasis is on the original hypothesis, this limits the opportunity to pick up on some of the more spurious or complex indicators. At the end of the day, you are simply getting an answer to the question posed at the outset of the diagnosis phase. However, you are unable to say confidently that the questions were correct.

Inside-out

Rather than using a fixed argument at the outset, this approach uses an emergent model where the continuous analysis of the data will drive the questions and processes used. This is often driven by a desire to discover how things 'are' within an organization or to come up with an innovative solution that has not been tried before. This search for innovative and creative solutions means that you will be breaking new ground every time the process is used.

The outside-in model is like building a house according to a prescribed architect's design; the inside-out approach, on the other hand, is like building a house according to the materials available (*see* Figure 4.4).

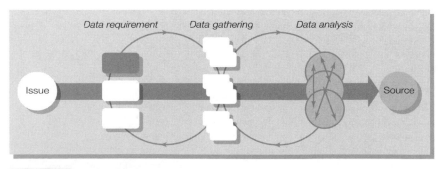

Figure 4.4 Inside-out data analysis

Source check

One of the biggest mistakes people make in data collection is to draw conclusions regarding the source or root of the problem, only to forget the original issue under investigation. The danger is that after weeks or months of frantic data gathering, followed by torturous days of data reduction, the consulting team finally let out a eureka scream, and brings forth their view of the source issue that needs to be addressed. However, in this euphoric moment, no one thinks to go back to the source problem, undertake a reality check and ensure that a resolution of the problem identified by the data analysis would actually address the issue first raised by the client.

For example, a consultancy team is investigating why sales are falling on a particular product line. After weeks of data gathering, it comes to the conclusion that the problem lies in the method used to manage the sales team's bonuses. Although this diagnosis is sound on a superficial level, before the team progresses to the Create stage of the consultancy model, it would pay to undertake a 'quick and dirty' reality check. Only when it checks with the original problem raised by the client does it realize that the bonus scheme operates across all product lines but the problem only exists in one area. This indicates that the problem cannot lie solely with the bonus and that a more local problem must be at work.

The tendency to drift in the diagnosis stage is a common occurrence. After labouring away at the data definition, gathering and analysis, it is easy to lose sight of your goal and slowly slip into another frame of reference.

Phase mapping

The second point to consider in the Clarify stage is is how the different components within the system relate to each other. Most engagements act on sub-systems of other systems, such as teams within a unit, a unit within a division, a division within a business and so on. As such there will always be external factors that can suddenly affect the engagement. These might include inward investment, changing personnel policies, corporate expansion schemes, downsizing, etc.

Imagine a product development team that needs to recruit new people to complete a market review. Unfortunately, the division within which it sits has budget constraints from head office resulting in headcount restrictions. Additionally, at a group level, there may be plans for downsizing. The decisions taken at each level make sense in isolation but, when taken as a whole, result in discontinuities across the organization.

It can help to view these variations at each level as waveforms with differing amplitudes and frequency. There will be times when the waves complement each other and times when they are in conflict. You need to be able to map these energy waves and determine if the change is timely, taking into account any wave conflicts. For example, at times investment will be green-flagged and capital will be readily available. At other times capital might be rationed and teams will struggle to fund their projects. Given the complex structures that exist within many organizations, this change in state will not always be common or clear to everyone. Thus different levels of the organization will have opposite views as to the availability of capital.

In Figure 4.5 the consulting window suggests that the team is about to progress with a capital investment programme that is tacitly supported at divisional level. However, once the business case reaches organization level it is likely to be rescinded as the organization is on a downward cycle. Although the organization has advance knowledge of the impending scarcity of capital at an industry level, this is invisible to the team.

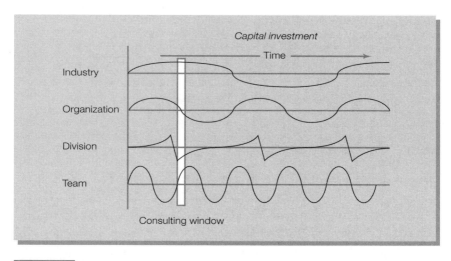

Figure 4.5   Organizational waveforms

The danger is that if you are unaware of this phase misalignment, then time and money can be spent developing a proposal that is rejected once it reaches another part of the system. Although the investment project might make sense to the team based on its local view of the world, if it is unable to appreciate how the world looks to the other systems then it will be frustrated in its change process.

One way to avoid this trap is by networking. If you consider the client system in isolation there is a risk that phase problems will occur. Obviously you must focus on your project area but it is also important to cultivate relationships across other systems within the organization, both vertically and laterally. Only by creating a network of 'informants' will you be able to understand the total picture. For example, a police detective will not focus on the criminal in isolation. Shrewd detectives will draw upon an entire network of informants and contacts to understand what is happening in other parts of the criminal world. By doing this, they are able to manage both the immediate crime investigation and the bigger picture.

Once you have a clear view of the problem, the nature of the change and the viability for success, you must identify those people with power over any proposed changes. Although your client is often the person that has the power to take decisions on the progress of the project, in the majority of cases many of the real decision makers only come out of the woodwork once the project has progressed beyond the contracting stage.

Shadow dancing

Whenever the client and consultant come together, there are two sides to the association:

■ **Surface issues:** These are things that both are happy to share.

■ **Shadow issues:** These are the hidden behaviours, thoughts and feelings that they are less comfortable about sharing.

Shadow issues are important because they often drive the force and direction of any change. You probably know people who are scared of spiders or have a particular aversion to a type of food. Although these fears are seemingly silly, they can significantly influence the decisions people take and how they manage their lives.

> **❝ shadow issues are important because they often drive the force and direction of any change ❞**

In organizations the shadow factors might be all the important information that does not get identified, discussed and managed in the open. The shadow side deals with the covert, the undiscussed, the undiscussible and the unmentionable (Egan, 1994, p. 35). These sit in the shade of the person and only appear when a light is deliberately shone upon them (*see* Figure 4.6).

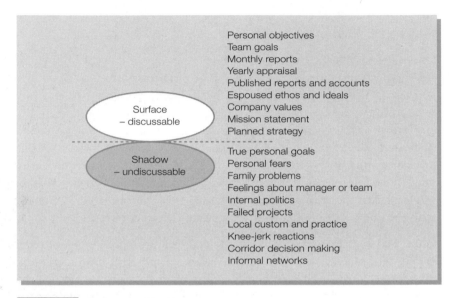

Surface
– discussable

Shadow
– undiscussable

Personal objectives
Team goals
Monthly reports
Yearly appraisal
Published reports and accounts
Espoused ethos and ideals
Company values
Mission statement
Planned strategy

True personal goals
Personal fears
Family problems
Feelings about manager or team
Internal politics
Failed projects
Local custom and practice
Knee-jerk reactions
Corridor decision making
Informal networks

Figure 4.6 Surface–shadow spilt

We might see this with the smile of a clown. The public sees the fool who entertains the children. But the smiling face often conceals a sadder person on the inside. They might see themselves as old and weary and not having achieved the goal of running their own circus. Finally, who are they really? Do they know what is deep inside and are they prepared to share that with others?

Although you might be fortunate enough to know your client well, in the early stage of the engagement you are unlikely to be emotionally connected with them. This can be like the first fumbling teenage date, where both kids are trying to second guess and satisfy the goals of the other person without compromising their personal values and integrity. In the same way, the early meetings with a client can end up as a series of fumbling encounters, where both people are trying to understand the needs and goals of the other. Part of the reason why this dilemma occurs is because we all operate on these two levels of interaction, the surface and the shadow. The surface issues are considered on an open and level playing field and the shadow issues are the factors that both sides choose to hide from each other.

In a typical consulting project you might offer what appears to be a practical and sensible change proposition, which the client may rebuff with arguments and concerns about its feasibility. But are these rebuttals coming from the reasoned head of the client or are shadow concerns forcing unrelated and often irrelevant issues to the surface? For example, a re-engineering proposal has been turned down because it involves head office relocation. On the surface the proposal offers a number of financial and operational improvements for the client. However, the unseen shadow implication is that the client's children's education will be interrupted and their partner's work and social life hampered. This type of personal prejudice can swing the balance against a rational solution, thus destroying (for an unknown, or at least unstated, reason) your proposal.

Crucially, when developing a relationship with the client, you must listen to what they say and, more importantly, watch what they do. The pained facial expression as your client talks about the business goals or the involuntary eye movement as the topic of relocation emerges are valuable indicators that highlight a shadow problem. They will not automatically tell you about the deeper issues at play but they certainly offer signals that the topic could be explored further to pull out any shadow factors.

Argyris (1992) suggests that there is a fundamental set of behavioural rules that drives shadow behaviour and they cross all nations and cultures. People keep these rules in their heads to help them deal with embarrassment or threat:

■ bypass embarrassment or threat whenever possible;

■ act as if you are not bypassing them;

■ do not discuss this bypassing while it is happening;

■ do not discuss the undiscussability of the undiscussable.

In tacitly following these four rules, people will inherently lock themselves into a 'I know it's true because I say so' style of behaviour. The problem surfaces when you attempt to tackle any of these four rules head-on – asking people to clarify what the problem is and trying to discuss some of the deeper issues as part of the diagnosis process. All of these are likely to trigger some form of defensive reaction that in turn drive up the shadows.

Suspicion often surrounds the diagnostic stage. People are likely to ignore anyone who tries to delve deeply into the shadows. You must be able mentally to climb inside the person under investigation, to take on board their beliefs and goals and feel what they are feeling, no matter how alien or bizarre it might seem. By doing this, it becomes possible to understand what their personal needs are and why they are operating from the shadow side of their personality. To do this it helps to map the nature of the shadows that both you and the client have.

Shadow map

The shadow map is a simple tool that allows you to understand what shadows might reside in you and the client (or consumer) and then determine how to take remedial action to bring to the surface the factors that need to be addressed.

In Figure 4.7 the consultant must be able to reflect on any shadow issues that you have in relation to the client and the project. At a surface level you might be prepared to talk about the project plan, fees, your skills set and other clients with whom you have worked on similar projects. However, shadows for the consultant might be the fact that the project was sold because of pressure from the senior partner to drive up revenue, a concern that the technology is not proven, and maybe that you have contracted to deliver another project at the same time and so will need to split your time across two key clients.

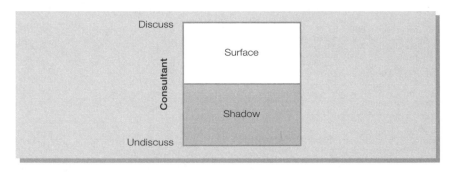

Figure 4.7   Consultant shadow map

In Figure 4.8 the client's surface issues may be the company strategy and business processes, the current budget and the personal goals that are associated with the success of the project. The client's shadow issues might be the fact that they know the budget will be cut in the near future, that the project has been tried a number of times before and failed and that the managing director sees the change as very low on the list of business priorities.

Once the consultant and client come together then we end up with a combination of four constructs (*see* Figure 4.9): the things neither wants to discuss; the things the client will discuss and the consultant will not; the things the consultant will discuss and the client will not; and the things that both will happily discuss. The resulting four segments are not fixed elements, since

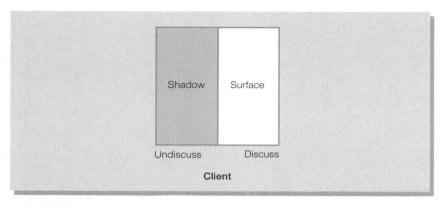

Figure 4.8   Client shadow map

they change in size depending upon the level of disclosure and willingness to share undiscussables by the client and consultant. As both players flex their degree of discussables, so the shape of the shadow map will vary.

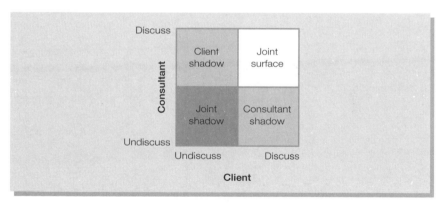

Figure 4.9   Consultant and client shadow map

When the shadow map is like Figure 4.10 both client and consultant are open in their interaction. The surface area offers plenty of space for both to share the discussable items and so effect a robust clarification stage. The one risk with this shape is being lulled into a false sense of security. It is like the married couple who proudly proclaim their openness to the world, only to find out that one of them has a deep secret that blows the whole relationship apart. Although the bottom left box is only small, it can contain dangerous viral spores that can kill a relationship.

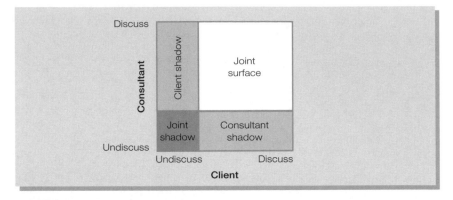

Figure 4.10   Open interaction

In Figure 4.11 the client is happy to disclose and share many things but the consultant is closing down and is not happy to share what they are thinking and feeling. The first question to ask is why – what is causing them to hold back and create undiscussables in the relationship? Second, what does this large shadow box contain and are there elements in there that can be destructive for the engagement?

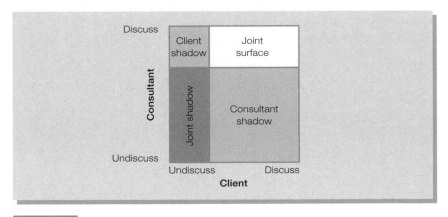

Figure 4.11   Consultant withdrawal

Figure 4.12 is the killer shape. Both the client and consultant are limiting their level of disclosure. Now, if this is the start of the relationship then it is a shape that might be expected and possibly makes sense as both sides might have commercial sensitivities to protect. However, if this shape exists part-way through the engagement then this is a dangerous sign since neither party is prepared to open up and share their thoughts and feelings.

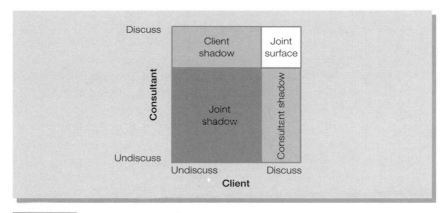

Figure 4.12   Limited interaction

An example of this shape can be found in large bureaucratic companies that are near to shut-down as all the players in the internal market fight to protect their patch and cover their backs. It is also a style of day-to-day management that can still be found in certain companies.

Effective clarification can only really take place when the (necessary) shadow has been brought to the surface and you are free to understand what is going on. The art of shadow dancing comes in your ability to move two key lines within the shadow map, as shown in Figure 4.13. Although there will always be a variety of strategies that can be used to open up the surface area and shrink the shadow area, they will be primary dependent upon the ability to move the two lines in the direction shown by the arrows. The

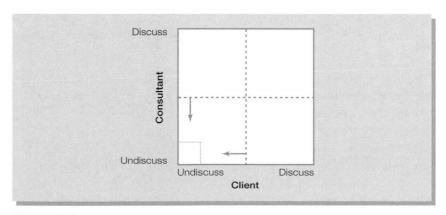

Figure 4.13   Redrawing the shadow map

consultant must be able to move their line from top to bottom to make more things discussable and the client must be helped to move the line from right to left and do the same.

A caution with this model. Your goal is to attain the necessary information to facilitate the clarification of the problem or issue being raised by the client. The key word is 'necessary'. The danger in surfacing shadows is that all of a sudden you are faced with the undiscussable that you don't want to deal with and has little to do with the project on which you are working. This is a real danger no matter what the change being managed. For example, when analyzing processes in readiness for a new computer system the analysts might uncover deep organizational rifts between departments that lead to the axing of a senior manager; the quality auditor may surface the fact that faulty items are actually being sold on the sly by local managers; and penetrating questions the independent financial adviser may uncover deep rifts in a marriage that trigger a divorce.

Very few consultants or coaches are trained to deal with deep cognitive, emotional or behavioural problems that may surface when they try to clarify a client's needs. It is therefore vital that, if faced with a situation you are not equipped to deal with, you act responsibly and advise the client to seek the appropriate, professional help. Unless you are trained, however well intentioned your actions, you may well do more harm than good. In some circumstances it can pay to agree this with the client when agreeing a contract for the engagement.

Sabotage secrets

Beware also the sabotage factors that have the potential to destroy a relationship and client engagement. The sabotage secrets are those shadow factors that sit deep in the bottom left-hand corner of the shadow map (*see* Figure 4.14).

The problem with sabotage secrets is that they are buried so deep that neither the client nor consultant really wants them to be surfaced. This might be the case on the morning after the office Christmas party. When people walk into the room in the morning a certain number of people probably know that something awful happened and that they were part of the awfulness. However, they choose not to go there and stick with the maxim of 'Let sleeping dogs lie'. All will be fine so long as the dog stays asleep and does not get woken. The problem comes when the deep shadow issue does finally get surfaced – maybe by someone inadvertently sharing some photos from the party. Then it becomes destructive and sabotages

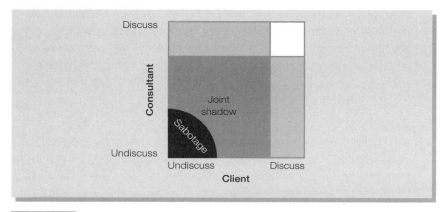

Figure 4.14 Sabotage secrets

the office relationships that had managed to tick along nicely in blind ignorance.

People often believe that by keeping these potentially destructive acts at a deep shadow level they can be forgotten. Unfortunately, too often there will be leakage. This leakage might be nervousness when around certain people, potential panic when dealing with certain information and the constant fear of disclosure that leads to sleepless nights. The paradox is that although the secrets can be destructive when hidden, the process of bringing them to the surface can also be destructive. There is no right answer; the trick is to be aware that secrets can exist for many people and organizations and be prepared to deal with them if you believe that they are causing a potential problem.

Surfacing strategies

If you really want the client relationship to be open and free of destructive shadows then you will need to develop strategies that will allow you to unearth and expose areas of potential liability. Although the emotional act of making the undiscussable discussable can be difficult, there are simple strategies that you can employ to help manage this process.

■ **Disclosure:** This is possibly one of the most powerful and effective ways to open up the shadow area. If you are with someone who really does not want to open up (and we all generally know this when it is happening to us), be brave and open up to them. Find things that maybe you were not going to share with them and explain that it is quite a deep feeling but that you want to share it with them so as to help the relationship develop. The up side is that by sharing this and demonstrating that you trust them they might reciprocate and begin to open up. The down side is that they may simply soak up all you shadow information and give nothing back. Only you can decide how far to go with this, but if you feel that nothing is being reciprocated then in many cases it might be prudent to pull back for a while and try an alternative strategy.

- **Deflection:** This is a displacement process that is often used in marketing. Imagine you are walking down the street and a market researcher inquires whether they can ask some questions. They want to test out a new perfume to see whether people believe it will make them smell sexier. Now if someone sprays this on you and asks, 'Do you feel sexier?' – the chances are that it can be really awkward to answer truthfully because you feel embarrassed. However, if the researcher lets you smell the perfume and then shows a picture of a woman who is wearing the scent, you are more likely to answer the question, 'Do you think that this scent will make her smell sexier?'. This is because the focus of attention has been displaced. It has created a safe haven where you feel that you can answer truthfully without being embarrassed. In the same way, if you are with someone who is showing signs of shadows, then talk about another friend of yours that has a problem they will not share with anyone. Talk about this and say that you really want to help this person but are not sure of the best way to do it. Alternatively, maybe talk about a TV show or film that you saw recently where the characters caused all kinds of problems for themselves simply because they did not open up when it was important. By making the shadows discussable you may create a safe house for your friend to start to surface some of their issues.

- **Direct:** If your relationship is strong enough then sometimes you just have to tell it as you see it. Maybe there is no time to pussyfoot around or someone else is being hurt or damaged because of the shadow games, so you just have to go for it. A friend of mine had a drink problem and we both spent years avoiding the issue and just finding ways not to talk about it, until one day I just surfaced the issue and said how I felt. It did not resolve the issue directly, but it has certainly put it on the table so that we can now raise it again without having to play too many games.

- **Drink:** Liberal amounts of alcohol certainly break down barriers – it happens every night in most city centres after work. However, the downside is obviously that maybe too many shadows can surface, which leads to even more shadows the following morning when you meet the person and realize that you said things that should not have been said – or even worse you passed other people's private shadows that were shared with you in confidence. In summary: big gain – but big risk.

■ **Diversion:** Sometimes it helps to talk about something that takes the other person's mind off the shadow area; once the rapport is developed you can gently ease back into the area without appearing confrontational. This way the bond and trust is put in place to ensure that when the shadows are surfaced the other person will not feel too uncomfortable.

■ **Delay:** Some issues are best not dealt with it there and then. Just wait and bide your time until a convenient moment surfaces when it is appropriate. However, be sure that this is a conscious strategy and not a natural tendency to avoid talking about something that may provoke an emotional response from the other person.

> **❝ always be open about the use of the strategy and never try to use it in a covert or duplicitous way ❞**

With all surfacing strategies the objective is to create an emotional connection that will in turn allow you to clarify what is really going on. The danger with these strategies is that they can be viewed and used as manipulative tools. This is a dangerous game to play and one that is diametrically opposite to the shared success outlined in the Client stage. My advice is to use the strategies if they help to build effective relationships, but always be open about the use of the strategy and never try to use it in a covert or duplicitous way.

When using the shadow map there are a number of rules of thumb that are useful to remember:

■ **Shadow dancing:** We often expend more energy avoiding the shadow issues than we do dealing with them. Sometimes it is better in the long run to stop dancing and start delving into the undiscussable areas.

■ **Shadow management takes courage:** In the same way that it is difficult to go home and talk about the unspoken problems that have been dogging you for the past week, surfacing shadow issues with the client or consumer takes immense courage. Never underestimate just how hard it is going to be to dive into the shadow area and how painful it can be once the issues are out in the open.

■ **Pandora's box:** There are always shadow factors that you need to know because they impact on your change programme. However, there will always be shadow factors that have no bearing whatsoever on your programme and surfacing them may cause you a problem.

- **Professional–personal switch:** The danger is that once you have entered the shadow arena the client regards you as their friend. At this point all their problems might start to surface. In this situation you might take that difficult step from a professional relationship to a personal one. Once in this area it can be difficult to move back into the professional one. The consequence is that you gain a new friend but lose a client.

- **Terms of trade:** Often, shadows are managed by trading – being prepared to advocate and expose a shadow area or secret that you have in the hope that the client will be prepared to expose one of their secrets. You need to understand the trading process and decide how much you are prepared to trade away before pulling up the protective drawbridge.

- **Complex shadows grids:** Don't forget that you will always have a myriad of shadow grids in operation – with your client, the various consumers, different stakeholders and even with your family after you have spent the third week away from home.

Culture

When clarifying how change is undertaken, the culture of an organization needs to be understood. Culture can stall and kill a project with hardly the blink of an eye. All the professional and passionate planning initiated by a consultant will be ruined if the change and outcomes do not align with the culture. You must clarify three things:

- What is the cultural make-up of the target audience?
- What personal cultural bias do you have?
- What is the degree of cultural diversity within the group?

Culture audit

A culture audit is designed to give a clearer view of the culture with which you are dealing. This knowledge is used to aid the diagnostics process, ensure that an appropriate change methodology is applied and test the viability of any solutions. This is clearly an art as opposed to a science. An organization's culture is simply an approximate description of the preferred style that the people choose to use. As you deconstruct the organization, so the approximation becomes less accurate because individual personalities and tendencies will emerge. At best, the outcome of any audit must be treated with some scepticism and at worse treated on a par with a horoscope. However, generally, it is possible to get a feel for a culture even if it cannot be specifically calibrated. A simple test is to walk into the foyer of three different hotels. There is every chance that within a few minutes you will have an intuitive grasp of the culture of the organization. You will be able to guess what is acceptable to the staff, who wields the power and the extent to which the hotel has verve and energy. Although you would not invest your money on the strength of this, it can offer enough data on which to make a number of broad suppositions about an organization's operating style.

It can help to think of an organization as an empty canvas that has been painted with a varied mix of paints and colours. Like the artist who slowly builds up a picture, often not knowing quite how it will end up, so as an organization grows it adopts a range of different cultural attributes. When investigating the make-up of the picture, the consultant's role is to deconstruct the colour base and understand how the way the colours have been mixed contributes to the end picture. Just consider what a varied mix of pictures an artist can create from a simple range of colours. In the same way, although each organization will be unique, it is essentially made up from the same set of cultural attributes (A–G):

■ **Artefacts:** They can include tools for company rituals, common business definitions, reward systems, logos and office design.

■ **Beliefs:** What does the organization value and regard as being important? This is seen in the moral and ethical codes offered by the business. The difficulty is that beliefs are deeply personal things, so trying to define them at a global level will lead to averaging or levelling will occur and some degree of compromise.

■ **Control:** Is power based around the structure of the organization or capability of the individual? To what extent does this leverage affect political action?

■ **Discourse:** What is the balance between the open and hidden elements within the business? To what extent will people open up and talk about issues in a shared environment and to what extent are issues held for debate in private, closed and secure groups? This gap between the open and hidden levels of discourse can be used to understand the difference between the espoused and actual cultural factors.

▨ **Energy:** Where is the energy expended? Is it on issues that are concerned with internal processes or is it externally orientated, where the primary focus is on the customers, suppliers and stakeholders?

▨ **Flow:** How do people move in, out and within the organization? What is the accepted staff turnover rate, what is the balance between formal and informal recruitment processes and why do people leave the business?

▨ **Generative:** To what extent does the organization understand and drive its capability to innovate and learn? Do individuals feel that they are empowered to develop themselves? To what extent is knowledge shared between individuals and what infrastructure exists to facilitate the sharing of knowledge?

One danger with this type of culture model is that it might be viewed as a prescriptive paradigm. Yet culture is dynamic and unpredictable, so dissecting an organization at any time, region or level will produce a range of varying ideas and themes, some of which align while others conflict. Any culture analysis can only offer a subjective snapshot and should never be treated as the definitive model of an organization's style of interaction. However, the purpose of the analysis is not only to understand the culture but to also develop a multi-perspective map and to understand how the culture is perceived by the various elements within a business.

Table 4.3 shows the culture model mapped against the hierarchical levels within an organization. In this case, the matrix might highlight potential issues:

▨ Is there culture blindness between the various layers within the business? Does one layer believe that certain behaviours are natural while another group feels that an alternative set of norms is in place? One example might be that the directors and seniors managers believe that learning is encouraged at all levels while line managers and process operators feel they do not get the opportunity to develop their competencies.

▨ Is there is a cultural paradox? For example, directors might advocate cross-team migration to encourage knowledge-flow across the business. However, from a control perspective, the directors still operate a highly centralized system where all internal transfer must be signed off at senior management level. This creates a 'gate' that inhibits internal movement because people are wary of requesting a transfer in case their current manager sees it as a reflection on their ability to retain staff.

Table 4.3	Culture audit

Cultural factor	Directors	Senior managers	Line managers	Process operators
Artefacts				
Beliefs				
Control				
Discourse				
Energy				
Flow				
Generative				

Trying to gather information on culture is difficult because it is intangible and subjective. If the goal is to gather descriptive information then that is relatively easy. All the respondent needs to do is outline the world as they see it. You can then undertake a comparative analysis to identify potential mismatches or inconsistencies. However, it becomes harder if you are trying to encourage participants to offer an evaluative comment on the culture. It will be difficult for people to say if anything is good or bad because the response will be biased by the culture in which they exist. And they will often be the least able to diagnose the culture in which they operate. It may be possible to draw objective data from a subjective position through comparative measures. For example, it is difficult to ask someone to describe a sound or picture, but asking them to describe it in relation to another sound or colour will make life easier.

Personal bias

As part of any diagnosis process, it is important to map your own cultural bias. All people have schema, or maps, that drive both the thoughts they have and the actions they take. To understand this, you might try to calibrate your own cultural schema. You do this by calibrating your schematic view against a range of alternative views. For example, you might ask yourself the question: 'When are organizations most effective?'. Choose an answer between: (a) when financial control is held at the most senior level; (b) when financial control is devolved to the lowest level.

Once your cultural bias has been mapped (*see* Figure 4.15), then you can take it into account when developing the client's map. For example, if you naturally orientated towards the individualistic style of control then some organizations might appear to be excessively autocratic and vice versa. This can never be calibrated in a truly scientific way since it is built upon a subjective precept. However, if you have a clear view of your own schematic map, then it can help to temper how your opinions are formed about the client organization.

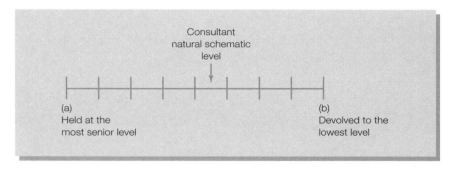

Figure 4.15 Personal bias indicator

Cultural diversity

In any change process, the level of cultural diversity within an organization will be significant. What seems natural to a white Anglo-Saxon male might appear as rude to an Asian female; what might appear to be a natural action for a Japanese businessman might feel uncomfortable to an American. Cultural diversity is an everyday issue since cultural differences are found in coffee rooms around the world. Whereas culture was once broken simply into blue or white-collar, now no two cultures will be the same because all organizations are made up from a complex mix of people from different backgrounds. This can emerge as a significant problem when companies try to effect large-scale change. Consider the following example of problems associated with a global merger:

> **❝ cultural diversity can cause major problems within a company that has an inherent and embedded dislike for change and variety ❞**

A potentially damaging clash of cultures is brewing among executives at the newly merged oil giant BP Amoco just a month after the deal was approved. British executives fear their new US counterparts do not share their concern about corporate expenses, according to a senior source at the conglomerate. Attention has focused on the retention of a corporate jet by the American chairman, the costs of last month's board meeting in London, and the use of Concorde by US executives. There is increasing irritation at every level in the company and a feeling that this is totally inconsistent with the culture of BP. (Cracknell, 1999)

Cultural diversity can cause major problems within a company that has an inherent and embedded dislike for change and variety. However, an organization that welcomes the richness of diversity can build on this variety to enhance its ability to sell and operate in diverse global markets.

Your challenge is first to understand the make-up of the cultural mix within the client organization and second to manage the engagement within this bias. There are two main areas to consider: the intra and inter-cultural factors.

■ **Intra-cultural mix:** This is where an organization is constructed using people from different geographical, religious or ethnic backgrounds. As this internal mix changes, so the overt and covert rules that drive and underpin the organization are constantly being challenged, sometimes in horrific ways. Consider the case of the US oil company that set up a drilling operation on an island in the Pacific using local labour. Within a week all the foremen were found lined up on the floor with their throats cut. It turned out that hiring younger people as foremen to supervise older workers was not acceptable in a society where age indicated status (*The Economist*, 1984). The absorption of people from different cultural backgrounds is fraught with problems and you must be alert to two things: the mix ratio and the extent to which the diversity is openly accepted. If the mix ratio is one where there is a predominance of one cultural group and the others are in the minority then there are issues held in check by the majority group. This leads to the second point, the extent to which the diversity of cultural drivers is discussable within the business. Is it OK to talk about the different cultural beliefs and ideas or are they repressed by the dominant cultural force? Unless you are able to map and manage the intra-cultural dynamics, there is a risk that they will be wasting both your and your client's time and money.

■ **Inter-cultural mix:** This affects the point of interconnection between the business units. It may be in a long-term international relationship, the development of a joint venture or teams within the same company operating from different continents. When two culturally diverse groups meet and work together, the difference in values, beliefs and accepted work practices can cause chaos and in some cases result in the cancellation of a multi-million-pound contract. Consider the case of the American firm that purchased a textile machinery company in the UK as a bridgehead into Europe. The American management team was unhappy with the idea that tea breaks in the UK could take up to half an hour as each worker brewed their own tea. To cut down the waste time, the American team installed a tea machine. As a result, the local workers boycotted the company and it finally went out of business (Stessin, 1979). This highlights the problem of one group attempting to work with another. Although the ideal approach is always focused on a collaborative model, often the relationship becomes embedded in competitive game playing as each side tries to assert its own cultural schema over the other.

The inter and intra-cultural mix and degree of openness must be mapped before attempting any type of change. Since all change involves people and all people are critically influenced by their cultural upbringing, then clearly the 'total' cultural source of the target audience must be understood in relation to the desired outcome and the delivery process. So when using the cultural audit outlined above it might make sense also to undertake the same diagnostic process using the cultural groups in the analysis. The first step will be to identify the major cultural groups that make up the organization. This might be by gender, religion, race, etc. Once understood, each of these groups can be mapped against the six cultural factors (artefacts, beliefs, control, discourse, flow and generative). The result will start to indicate what cultural disruption might occur as a result of the change and where any barriers might surface.

Only the foolish consultant ignores the impact of culture. Just consider the spate of corporate mergers that go through trauma or indeed fail simply because different cultures are deemed to be incompatible; the way that an entrenched culture will resist any form of action by people from outside the organization; and the significant differences that exist between profit and not-for-profit sectors. As the consultant managing any type of change, you must ensure that you take sufficient time and space to understand your client's culture.

Decision makers

The person that you meet, greet and contract with is often not the true decision maker. He or she may hold the title, reserved parking space and corner office but in reality may just be a puppet that the organization presents to the world. Sitting behind this person will be a range of hidden power brokers. These are the people who can green-light your proposal with the blink of an eye. Alternatively, they can consign it to the bottom of an in-tray to collect dust for months. Unless you are able to root out and map the genuine decision makers it is likely that your efforts will be frustrated before the change starts.

This mapping process is like playing a game of poker with a group of strangers in a strange town with a strange pack of cards. You have to develop intuition and blind sight – the ability to look beyond the words and external factors and understand the interplay that takes place between people. The person dealing the cards may be the perceived leader at the table, but in reality there are subtle messages that indicate who really wields the power to take decisions.

Consider the following decision-making types that are found in most organizations:

■ **Kingmaker:** This is the person who prefers to hold and wield control through another individual. Just as Rasputin influenced the Russian monarchy in its last years, the kingmaker will find people who are pliable and can be presented to the public as a passable face for the organization. The best way to tackle this person is by offering yourself as an ally rather than an aggressor. There is every chance that they might perceive you are entering their kingdom to do damage. Take the time to understand their power base and why they prefer to be kingmaker rather than king and decide how you might be able to help them in their goals.

■ **Queen of hearts:** One individual might have the formal power to agree a contract with you but another 'queen of hearts' may hold a greater degree of influence over people in the organization. There is every chance that this person is operating from a values-based rather than a logical standpoint as their power is likely to be at the desire level on the change ladder. You need to understand why this person appeals to the consumers. Once you have done that you can appreciate how best to gain their confidence. The one danger with this type of power broker is that they can go quickly from being in favour to being ostracized by the crowd. You must always watch which way the wind is blowing to ensure that you do not fall from grace with the queen.

■ **Knave:** The knave is the common individual that sits at the bottom of the organization pile – deemed to be of little consequence by the senior people within it. However, it can often be the 'little people' that have the greatest influence over a business. Think of the gatekeepers that can make your life hell in a client organization – the car park attendant or the director's PA. Although these people might not block the high-level processes within a change programme, they can cause significant problems once the project is rolling if they are not brought into alignment.

■ **Joker:** This is the unexpected wildcard – the person who appears to be invisible most of the time, only to pop up with a solution or problem that completely throws the whole change proposition. Although by their very nature these people are difficult to spot, one ruse is to talk to people in the organization to find out what problems beset earlier change initiatives. It might well be that one person's name starts to crop up again and again.

■ **Ace:** When working with the ace in the pack you will be dealing with the person that has the true power to agree and effect a decision. Like an ace up the sleeve, you might need to pull this person out when facing real problems, when blockages occur at a certain layer in the organization or funds start to run dry part-way through a training session. However, the danger may be in exposing the person too soon in a conflict and effectively giving the game away.

It is a rare and privileged person that has the right and ability to take one single all-embracing decision and see it completed in full. People have to lobby, cajole, bribe and influence others to initiate and complete a decision. Presidents, prime ministers, CEOs, dentists and doctors all have paymasters who can influence the decisions they take. You must take the time to consider any organization critically and really understand who holds the reigns of power before signing a contract. Failure to do this can result in wasted time and resources being expended on a project that has little chance of being delivered.

System construction

Whether you are trying to implement a culture change programme, build a new marketing strategy or implement a financial management system, you must be able to develop a real feel for the system under consideration. You must be able to predict with a fair degree of accuracy how the system will react to changes. Will it take the hedgehog approach and curl up into a ball at the first sign of danger, or does it become like a Labrador dog and actively welcome strangers?

In the same way that an architect will diagnose and map the stresses and strains that hold a building together before knocking down a wall, you must be intimately aware of the factors that bind together an organization and allow it to be effective. Taking this analogy, you might consider the client organization in terms of its structure: What holds it together? Where are the stresses in the system? What prevents it from collapsing at the first sign of subsidence? It can help to examine the following areas:

■ **Stress:** The extent to which the organization feels pressured by external forces.

■ **Strain:** The tension that exists within the organization, pulling people between different choices.

■ **Strength:** The capacity of the organization to resist external force.

■ **Surface tension:** The ability of the organization's skin to prevent intruders from entering.

■ **Stretch:** How far the organization can expand when an external force is applied.

By understanding and mapping these factors, you will gain better clarity and start to develop a feel for the way that the organization might respond when the change is made.

Stress

Stress is a measure of how hard the atoms within a material are being pushed together as a result of external forces. The stress at any given point is the force in a given direction divided by the area over which the force acts. (Gordon, 1978)

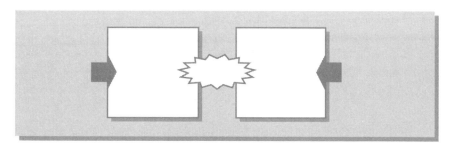

With a little effort you will be able to see how external forces can create stress for a person, team or organization. Examples include the individual being pressured by an excessive workload, the team that feels pressured by an unremitting manager, or the company that has to operate in a shrinking market. Alternatively, working with an organization that does not feel stressed can also be quite apparent: the simple fact that equipment is readily available, first-class travel is accepted as standard, or that there is time and space in which to be creative – all these signs indicate that time or money is not in short supply.

Neither situation is good or bad. But internal pressure of any type will affect your ability to manage change. Imagine trying to implement a new empowerment model in a company that has recently introduced a cost-reduction programme. The stress caused by this type of action will have a significant impact on the engagement – perhaps so much so that you might decide to withdraw until the issue has been removed from the system. Alternatively, consider a stress-free company operating in an expanding market. Senior management recognizes that their fortunes are likely to change in the near future so they employ you to deliver a new productivity programme. What chance of success will you have in convincing people of the need to cut costs and focus on raising quality?

When clarifying the system construction, you must develop the capability to tune in to stress points. A builder adding an extension to a house will walk the job and test out different stress points in the infrastructure before taking any action. The builder needs to separate the supporting walls from those that can be modified without disrupting the stability of the building. In the same way, you must be able to walk the job and determine the areas that are highly stressed. Only then can you decide how best to ensure that problems do not occur as a result of the change. Unless you develop the capability to calibrate stress levels, then there is a chance that your project will trigger problems that disrupt any benefit associated with the change.

Strain

Strain indicates how 'hard' and far the atoms at any point are being pulled apart – that is, by what proportion the bonds between the atoms are being stretched. It is measured at a particular point in the cross-section of a piece of material. (Gordon, 1978)

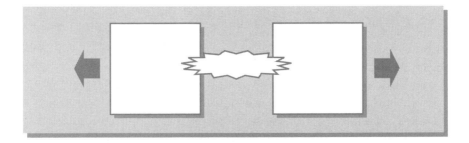

Strain differs from stress because it looks at the extent to which people are being pulled in different directions. So whereas stress might be having to deal with too much work, strain might be the problem associated with managing a home and work life. Unless the level and location of the strain are fully appreciated, any change will potentially exacerbate the tension that people are experiencing.

Within an organization, strain can be seen in a number of ways:

■ the tension that surfaces as people are pressured to follow top-level procedures while being compelled by their line manager to deliver increased customer service by breaking the rules;

■ the anxiety that emerges from internal company politics as people are forced to choose between two different powerbrokers;

■ the frustration that people can feel when asked to attend a workshop when they believe that it is better to stay at their post to deal with their in-tray.

The issue of strain is important because it helps determine how far you can push your client's organization before it becomes damaged. This might be at a senior level where the general manager is forced to adopt new business principles or methods that they believe are inappropriate. Alternatively, it might be at a line level, where the cleaner is unhappy with the imposed reduction in time they can spend in certain areas. Any action that pulls people away from their normal work pattern will cause some form of strain – your role is to understand the risks associated with this pull.

When a change proposition is offered to a client, you need to ask two questions:

■ How hard am I pushing the client or consumer with this change proposition? Will it be too much for the system to sustain and will it spring back on my departure?

■ How far am I pulling the client from their natural operating position and will it take them too far from the natural point of equilibrium and cause them to lose balance?

You must recognize that pushing people into a change strategy that is not appropriate will result in tears or reversion at a later date. Your role is to understand this and be able to diagnose what type of change is appropriate for the system.

Strength

The strength of any structure is measured in terms of the burden that will break the structure. This is known as the breaking load. (Gordon, 1978)

Some people can give up cigarettes easily while others fight a frustrating battle for years. This internal capability might be likened to their personal strength or power to combat problems. This level of strength can also be seen in organizations. Some companies have the potency to shrug off misfortune or overcome market downturn by reinventing themselves. Others seem to lose the will to live the moment they have a crisis.

Unless you are convinced that your client organization has the necessary stamina to see change through to its conclusion, then problems will occur at some stage. The change process might start with a flurry of flags and banging drums, but unless the organization has the willpower to see it through then both you and your client will be left with egg on your face.

❝ unless your client organization has the necessary stamina to see change through to its conclusion, then problems will occur at some stage ❞

It is important to recognize that strength is both a positive and negative factor. The positive side is an organization's ability to deal with and resolve problems that might cause other businesses to stumble and fall. The negative side is the organization's ability to shrug off change processes. Clearly, some major programmes might fail because the organization does not have the strength to maintain momentum. However, they might also fail because the inherent power within the organization's culture has the ability to resist external invaders. Simply diagnosing strength is not sufficient. You must be able to determine if the strength will be used to aid or oppose any change you are trying to deliver.

Ultimately, you must make a decision as to where the strength lies. You also need to determine if it will be an amplifying or attenuating force. If an amplifying one, then effort should be made to map the dominant areas and use this energy to enhance the change. If the strength is deemed to be lacking or an attenuating one, then urgent action must be taken to raise the profile of the problem and make the client aware of the possible consequences of the situation.

Surface tension

Surface tension: creating a force to resist external energy requires energy to be drained from inside the structure. (Gordon, 1978)

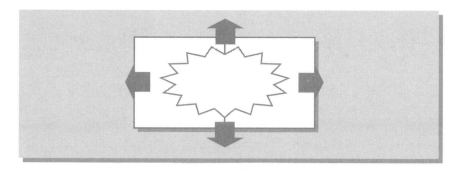

Surface tension, too, is both positive and negative. On the positive side, it is shown by an organization's ability to fight hostile takeovers or resist external agents. Just consider the flurry of activity that takes place once a company realizes that it is a target for possible acquisition and break-up. With the barbarians at the gates, it is amazing how quickly a management team becomes energized. Old missions and visions are dusted off, the five-year profit forecasts look increasingly rosy and the PR agent actively campaigns to sell the idea that a break-up would not be in anyone's best interest. All the energy and time that has previously been focused on internal issues is used to build a response to the alien invasion. The extent to which the organization can muster and co-ordinate such resources often determines the level of surface tension it can create. This in turn determines its ability to ward off the corporate raiders.

One example of this was the BTR bid for Pilkington Glass. When a bid for £1.2 billion was made, few gave the glassmaker much of a chance of escaping. Though Pilkington had gone public in the 1970s, it retained the dull air of a family concern. But Pilkington mounted one of the most extraordinary defences ever seen. In addition to wooing institutional shareholders with a blockbusting profit forecast, it gathered local support from staff, company pensioners and councillors. Raising fear about job losses, Pilkington even had trade union leaders demanding that BTR be stopped. The campaign worked brilliantly. BTR decided to withdraw its offer rather than overpay for the pleasure of taking on so much political pain (Randall, 1999).

The downside of surface tension is the ability to resist new ideas as they surface in the market. An organization is often able to build such a thick skin that it is unaware of significant changes. Companies have often disappeared because they were unable to adapt to a changing environment. In the same way that musicians, actors and authors need to be aware of changing trends and fashion, so company directors and product managers need to stay tuned to the changing business market. In the current climate where the product life cycle is shortening all the time, the development of a thick corporate skin can be disastrous.

Clearly, if you are about to start work with a client, surface tension will be key. If you are able to break through the outer membrane there is a chance that the change will be delivered. However, if the surface tension is such that you are unable to break through then there is less chance that the transformation will be accepted. As a consultant you can see this in your first presentation to the board – does it welcome you and value what you present, or is there a tacitly held view that consultants are parasites and offer little value?

Two issues will affect your ability to break the skin – the level of trust with the client and consumer and your ability to manage the marketing process. Trust is significant because it oils the hinges that open the door to the client. In cases where the surface tension is solid, there it little chance that you will penetrate the corporate skin unless people believe you are truthful, responsive, uniform, safe and trained. Second, unless you are able to position yourself and your services in an attractive way then the surface tension will doggedly resist any advances that you might attempt to make.

The first step is to determine the extent to which the surface tension will inhibit the change. Once understood, you need to create a strategy to help break through the membrane. To do this, it is useful to align the level of surface tension with the strength within the system. If you are faced with a high-strength system with impenetrable surface structure then change will face significant problems.

Stretch

Stretch is the extent to which something can stretch and contract in relation to its length and so store energy without causing permanent damage. This is seen in ropes, masts and trees: any structure that is capable of being flexed elastically. (Gordon, 1978)

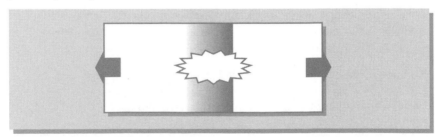

Stretch can be used to consider the extent to which you can encourage an individual or organization to move beyond their natural state of equilibrium. You might decide to offer ideas and suggestions that take the company into more exciting and emergent markets, thus adopting a potentially high-risk change strategy. Alternatively, you might feel that the organization is at heart conservative and hence would not be able to take on the associated problems that emerge with a radical strategic shift.

You must calibrate the extent to which the individual, team or organization is able and willing to stretch. The effective consultant will start this calibration from the very first contact with the client by talking about past change actions or problems that emerged in previous transformation projects. In doing this you are gathering both tacit and explicit knowledge about your client's ability and desire to change.

However, you must be wary of the gap between perceived and actual stretch. Imagine you have been engaged to introduce a statistical quality management process in a large manufacturing organization. The MD is bullish about the company's ability to adopt the changes. As such he encourages you to set demanding targets so that the change is implemented in record time. However, the MD is relatively new to the company and does not understand the cultural barriers that exist to this type of change. If the end consumer is unwilling to accept the quality project, it might turn out that you are pilloried for failing to deliver the change and in some cases forced to suffer financially.

In any case where stretch is being tested, you would be wise to undertake a simple triangulation exercise. Calibrate the capacity of both the client and the consumer to stretch and adapt to the proposed transformation process. You can do this by analyzing the system to be changed and mapping it against the structural factors. In the example shown in Table 4.4, the analysis indicates that the organization is in a highly stressed state owing to an impending cost-reduction and downsizing programme. As a result, the implementation of a new computer system might face problems. The combined problems of cost reduction, suspicion of a new reporting package and people's general unwillingness to help external agents pose real obstacles to change.

In this example, the solution is to add a restraining process that will remove some of the stress. Like the architect who uses steel beams to support a ceiling when a wall is being removed, you will need to import support forces to reduce the organizational stress. This could involve ensuring that senior managers are on hand to support and coach people through the process or offering to pay people overtime where longer hours need to be worked.

Table 4.4   **Structural analysis example**

Change proposition: Implement a new MIS financial reporting package to produce a set of monthly statistics on profitability by product line

Structure factor	Organization	Change impact
Stress	The atmosphere is one of relativity high stress as the business is operating in an increasingly competitive market and pressure is on to reduce costs across the business	Financial pressures within the business might cause the change to face problems: unless the system is eased in within existing budgetary constraints it might face problems
Strain	Internal politics form a major part of the company's operating system	It will be imperative to undertake a detailed stakeholder and power broker analysis – otherwise political blockages might occur
Strength	People are willing to make quite large personal sacrifices to ensure that the products and services get delivered on time.	If the change is positioned as a political and business imperative, then there is greater chance that people will support the change
Surface tension	The organization has proved adaptable at resisting the recent influx of management fads; it is content to ignore changing trends and work on its own ideas	The trick will be to sell the change as an internal transformation rather than an external imposition
Stretch	There is evidence that people are not able to stretch with any great ease; they can operate in their own confines, but, beyond of this, problems occur	The system should be eased in at such a pace that it does not overload the current processes

Structural analysis

A team or organization is like a house built with playing cards. It is often a fragile structure that can be toppled over with relative ease when the right leverage point is touched. The consultant's role is twofold:

- identify the areas that are able to accept and embrace the change;
- avoid those areas of the system that are structurally unsound.

There is always a risk that an inappropriate change could inadvertently topple the organization by pulling out the card holding up the rest of the deck. This approach to clarifying the change situation is a simple but effective way to understand where maximum leverage is placed while ensuring that inadvertent damage is not done.

A structural analysis is also a powerful tool to help the client and consumers to diagnose their readiness for change. Put the client in with a group of consumers and ask them to agree where they fit against the five structural factors. Although they might reach a general accord about the factors, any disagreement will offer valuable information on potential problems. For example, the client might believe that the organization offers little resistance to change programmes and there is little chance of surface tension causing a problem. However, the consumer might offer evidence of previous local initiatives that have failed because people were not willing to change. The simple fact that you offer the two groups a shared language and mental mindset will allow issues to surface that might have remained hidden until the critical point.

Stakeholders

Stakeholders have the power to influence, enhance or curtail an engagement. They can operate in both an overt and covert manner, often driven by their personal values and goals as opposed to those of the organization. Like beauty, stakeholders are viewed from a subjective rather than objective position. They are only viewed as stakeholders if perceived as having power by the perceiver.

To clarify the issues that surround any problem, it can help to develop a map that indicates who can influence the outcome of the change and to what extent they might wish to wield their power. Consider the consulting firm about to undertake a critical piece of work with a multinational client. Although the client might have set out the basic structure of the organization, indicating the key figures involved in the project, the consultant will need to take this a step further and understand who the real power brokers are and to what extent they can amplify or attenuate the flow of the project.

It is useful to map the organization's key stakeholders against the criteria used in the change ladder (*see* Chapter 3). It then becomes possible to use the five attributes of the change ladder to build a deeper understanding of each stakeholder group and how it might affect any proposed change. By constructing a simple matrix, you can quickly understand which of the key stakeholders need to be influenced.

For each of the four stakeholders listed in Table 4.5, it is possible to infer what effect they might have on your project. The benefit in producing the profiles is that it makes it easy to share the impact of the stakeholders with other members of the change team.

- **Stakeholder 1** (key person): A critical player. This person has both the power and ability to affect the change dramatically. The question is, which way will they choose to exert their influence? Will they act as the powerful benefactor, bestowing their grace and favour on the project and so help speed it to a successful conclusion? Alternatively, have they yet to be convinced about the need for change and so will they be a powerful opposing force? The golden rule in this situation is to get to the person as quickly as possible. Make time to meet the individual, understand their orientation and decide what action needs to be taken to ensure they will support the change.

- **Stakeholder 2** (loose cannon): Such people are a real problem. They hold all the aces in the deck but do not understand how to use them. They manage the assets used in the engagement, the procedures and have a real desire to be involved. The problem is that they do not have the appropriate knowledge and they do not have a real appreciation of the need for the transformation. You might therefore need to make a rapid and effective change to ensure they do not inadvertently derail the process by taking inappropriate action.

- **Stakeholder 3** (little interest): This person is on the fringe. Although they have the ability to affect the change, their interests lie elsewhere and they have no desire to get involved. While in some cases this is useful, the downside is that they can turn into a loose cannon if they choose to get involved later. Like a time bomb, this stakeholder might decide the day before implementation to disagree with the change and withdraw assets

Table 4.5 Stakeholder matrix example

	Stakeholder 1	Stakeholder 2	Stakeholder 3	Stakeholder 4
Asset	High	High	High	Low
Blueprint	High	High	High	Low
Capability	High	Low	Medium	Low
Desire	High	High	Low	High
Ethos	High	Low	Low	Low

from the transformation. Your approach with this person must be softly-softly. A low-key relationship must be formed and maintained over the life of the change, giving you the ability to know if the stakeholder is being energized and in what direction their energy will be directed.

∎ **Stakeholder 4** (Desperate Dan): This stakeholder has a high desire to get involved in the engagement but little capability, power or understanding of the need for change. Depending on how they are used, this person is a liability or an asset. Just as a willing person is worth ten pressed people, it might make sense to use them simply because of their energy and desire to help. However, if their association becomes too high-profile it is possible for the stakeholder to make inappropriate statements about the project. In this case, you need to make a decision whether their involvement in the project adds real value or could end up wasting time and causing trouble.

This methodology takes what is a very complicated and emotional process and turns it into a simple but practical diagnostic model. The value comes not from the map but the dialogue you go through with the client in developing the shared model. Such a dialogue helps to dispel many of the unspoken concerns about stakeholder groups and allows the client and consultancy team to operate on a common platform.

Life-cycle risk

The fact that consultants have been invited into a change process suggests that risk is an issue. The nature of any change is built on the premise that the future can be envisioned and delivered. The reality is that this is impossible to guarantee. Therefore you need always to be aware of the trade-off between the risks being taken and the associated reward.

Any risk–reward balance will fit into one the four quadrants shown in Figure 4.16. The first is the commodity quadrant, where the service being delivered is of little risk and any corresponding reward simply reflects the accepted market rate. There is no premium and little opportunity to maximize income. Examples are the delivery of a training programme or undertaking some desk research on a company's market position. Although this is seen as a low-value area, the benefit is that the effective consultant can use it as a launch pad to sell products and services that sit in the high-reward quadrants.

Next is the safe option, where the company is happy to pay a premium over the standard rate because of its confidence in your competencies. It might be that a relationship has built up over time or that you have a

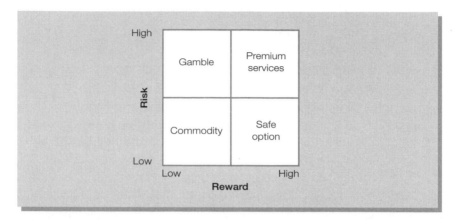

Figure 4.16 Trade-off between risk and reward

particular niche expertise or that you have a trusting relationship with the client.

The premium service quadrant indicates an area where the gains might be high but so are the corresponding risks. Often this will be seen in the Merger and Acquisition market where the payback and benefits can be substantial but the chances of the integration falling over part way through the programme are quite significant.

The last quadrant is headed as gamble simply because if you choose to take a high-risk contract for a low fee there is a chance that you will not achieve a payback. This scenario is often found with consultants who have just started. As new entrants, they need to gain income streams and market share fast and one way to achieve this is by taking the jobs that other companies reject – in some cases for less money. Although this is a good way to enter a new market, it is dangerous to operate in this quadrant for long as eventually the odds will stack up against you.

Wherever you sit in the matrix, there will be two key questions to ask:

- What chance is there that something will go wrong?
- How can I ensure that unseen problems are managed?

This breaks the risk element into two areas: risk assessment and risk management. The scientist who developed the Saturn 5 rocket that launched the first Apollo mission to the moon highlighted these succinctly: 'You want a valve that doesn't leak and you try everything possible to develop one. But the real world provides you with a leaky valve. You have to determine how much leaking you can tolerate'. (*The New York Times*, 1996).

Your job in an assignment is to determine the extent to which the project might fail and to do everything in your power to ensure that it doesn't.

Risk assessment

The issue of total risk is considered at the outset in the construction of the contract; in the Clarify stage risk is more about assessing the dynamics that will have to be managed. It is a continuous process of qualitative and quantitative analysis of what could happen and what should happen during the project. The key with risk management is not to try and stop problems from happening; rather it is to determine what problems can be tolerated without damaging the change process.

Consider a situation where the consultant has been asked to manage a large corporate project. Figure 4.17 shows that the consultant has thought through the key issues that might affect the change. The reality is that halfway through the process there is an unexpected change of CEO and this results in significant changes. Replacing the CEO is outside the consultant's control and all the consultant can do is ensure that any fall-out from the change is minimized. No matter how much you plan, it is impossible to anticipate all the risk factors. However, you can develop a state of mind that assumes that problems will happen and so be more prepared when they do.

❝ the key with risk management is to determine what problems can be tolerated without damaging the change process ❞

One of the factors that will indicate the degree of potential uncertainty is the extent to which the organization is viewed as risk-averse or risk-seeking. A risk-averse organization will avoid taking actions that have a potential for failure and will tend to take the safe option. The risk-seeking culture values both the rewards that come with risk and possibly the excitement associated with the gamble.

However, there is another factor in the equation that has as much impact on the success of the change – to what extent is the consultant risk-averse or risk-seeking? While the nature of the job might suggest that the consultant will have a risk-seeking nature, this clearly is not always the case. Many people turn to the consulting profession as a way to develop a set of latent skills, a way to survive following redundancy or as a hook into a new market sector. This stresses the importance of risk assessment within the consultancy cycle – to understand the risk drivers for both the client and consultant and what impact this might have on the relationship.

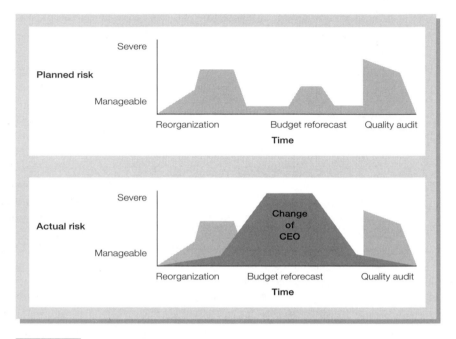

Figure 4.17 **Risk assessment example**

In clarifying the situation, you need to consider a number of key factors:

■ The nature of the organization: to what extent does it adopt a risk-averse style of management?

■ The nature of the consultant's engagement: to what extent do you feel that it is regarded as a high-risk venture?

■ The personal biases of the consultant: are you risk-averse or risk-seeking?

If these three factors are in alignment then the assumed risk is minimal. However, if there is a degree of misalignment, then issues might start to surface as the project moves forward. The classic problem is a risk-averse consultant implementing a high-risk project in a risk-averse company.

Risk management

Once the variables in a project are understood, steps can be taken to minimize the impact of uncertainty. This is risk management – or managing the uncertainty that can affect a successful outcome of the project. Since all projects will have unknown factors, at best all the consultant can do is reduce their impact. At worst, the high-risk factors might cause failure.

Good risk management can help to take the luck out of bad luck and build on the random opportunism of good luck.

Risk is managed by using a set of tools to control the issues that surface in the assessment phase. The tools you use will depend upon the context and content of the change. Three simple tools are:

■ **Pilot:** For any proposed analytical or change process, it is wise to test the deliverables and variables in a controlled environment, using the process with a small team before rolling it out.

■ **Risk list:** When considering the proposed change, you should attempt to agree with the client and consumer the potential risks over the life of the project. The risk list categorizes risks against a range of variables including probability, impact, owner, etc. Once the risk list is defined then a series of contingency plans is developed for each of the options.

■ **Contingency response:** When faced with a potential problem, the best option is to build a planned response to take away the element of surprise. There is a range of generic responses for each of the perceived risk factors:

– **Do nothing:** Simply ignore the risk in the hope that it will disappear because of other factors.

– **Deeper diagnosis:** Gather further information on the issue in the anticipation that greater clarity will lead to risk reduction.

– **Alternative strategy:** Is the risk sufficiently large that an alternative approach is warranted, one that bypasses the problem and does not attempt to tackle it?

– **Ignore and plough through:** Is the change momentum such that there is a belief that any obstacle will be beaten?

– **Hedging:** In some cases it is possible to build a basket of diverse responses so that at least one of them will minimize or eliminate the problem.

– **Specific response actions:** It might be that a response is built around all of the above, with the development of a highly complex response pattern to what is a highly complex problem.

At this stage in the change process you will have a real feel for the setting and symptoms to be addressed and the potential risks that will be faced in dealing with them. Managing risk is difficult and more of an art than a science. You will never be able to predict with any accuracy what will happen, but you can ensure that all of the pegs are in the ground so that when unplanned issues occur you will be able to reduce their impact.

5

Stage three: Create

Imagination is intelligence having fun.

At this stage of the project cycle your aim is to develop a unique and specific solution that will deliver the most appropriate remedy for your client's problem. This part of the process is among the most exciting but also the most frustrating.

The process offered in this stage of the model follows this pattern:

- **Managed creativity:** Use the CREATE model to originate and develop potential solutions for the core issue identified in the Clarify stage.

- **Divergent scanning:** Explore the possibility of finding ideas and solutions that might exist elsewhere, rather than trying to originate something new.

- **Convergent choice:** Assess the impact of the final decision to be presented to the client.

- **Solution storyboard:** Breathe life into the potential solutions and start to validate their potential to deal with the issue. Shrink to one single action plan.

- **Resourcing the solution:** Map the resources to the potential solutions to ensure that they are viable.

The whole process should come together to offer a diverse, imaginative but practical action plan. The history of science is full of inventions and ideas that emerged from creative thinking and were managed into working tools. It is also awash with ideas that failed to gain acceptance. The objective at this stage is to ensure that the solutions are not just created but also marketed to the client and consumer. Unless both sides of the equation are carefully managed, the change can easily fail at this stage.

Managed creativity

The development of a competitive advantage in the market place often hinges on creativity and invention – doing what others have not yet done. Virgin's approach to air travel, Sony's mass marketing of the Walkman, and Trevor Baylis's invention of the clockwork radio are all examples of people using creativity and innovation to break the existing market mould. In most cases, this type of groundbreaking innovation enters market areas that others thought unworkable or unprofitable.

How can you introduce this type of managed innovation into the Create stage of change? How can you help people to escape the attitudes and mindsets in which they take the simple, safe and stagnant approach to change?

In many cases, the only reason you will be working with the client is because of the creative value that you bring. If all you can offer is a slight variation on the previous offerings then your contribution will at best be marginal. However, by introducing more radical elements of wisdom and creativity, you might be able to help the client deliver a solution that breaks the current management paradigm. Your goal is to help the client move from a world that they know and shift them into the area of unpredictability and uncertainty (*see* Figure 5.1).

We all have our own mental models of the world and frameworks that we believe to be true. A teenage daughter wants to stay out late at night; her parents want to set a curfew. Each has a set of experiences, beliefs and views as to what is safe, practical and appropriate. But both parties are operating from the world they know and are not prepared to consider other options. Even more important, they are not prepared to sit down and think about solutions that neither of them has ever considered before. If you were asked to help resolve this issue, one of the ways that a collaborative solution might be found is by forcing them to move into the 'I don't know what I don't know' area and to generate new solutions to their impasse. This same approach can be taken when working with a client or consumer who has to find a solution to a seemingly intractable problem.

> **❝ help the client move from a world that they know and shift them into the area of unpredictability and uncertainty ❞**

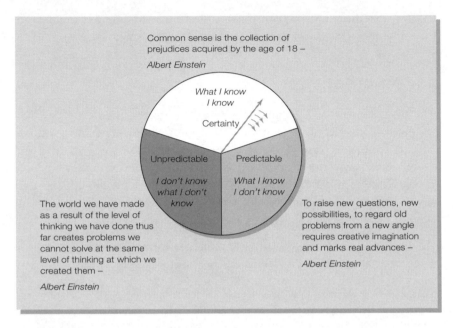

Common sense is the collection of prejudices acquired by the age of 18 –

Albert Einstein

What I know I know

Certainty

Unpredictable

Predictable

I don't know what I don't know

What I know I don't know

The world we have made as a result of the level of thinking we have done thus far creates problems we cannot solve at the same level of thinking at which we created them –

Albert Einstein

To raise new questions, new possibilities, to regard old problems from a new angle requires creative imagination and marks real advances –

Albert Einstein

Figure 5.1 Certainty and uncertainty

However, simply finding a radical solution to a problem is not enough. Anyone can create hundreds of ways to make their first million, but few manage to turn these pipe dreams into reality. You might be able to help your client to create new solutions to problems, but ultimately you must also help them to develop ideas that are practical. From this, you can help them to make the final decision on which ideas should go forward for implementation. Innovation is about managed creativity – taking the initial ideas and working through a process whereby the change is actually delivered and does not stay inside people's heads or on their lists of things 'to do'.

Thomas Edison, one of the most prolific inventors of the nineteenth century, demonstrated the ability to manage the creative process. He credited his success to the fact that he did not wait to be struck by an idea but found the solution through aggressive and careful investigation. He would often decide what he wanted to invent before knowing if it was possible. He would then work on ways to develop the product that he envisaged (Birch and Clegg, 1996). His process of invention was characterized by repeated trial and error, and experiment after experiment until these studies led to those flashes of insight known as inspiration. From this came his well-known comment that genius is 99 per cent perspiration and

1 per cent inspiration (Wren and Greenwood, 1998). The perspiration comes from the process of actively managing the process and not just sitting in a dream world waiting for good ideas to happen.

Many people might find the combination of the words 'managed' and 'creativity' alien or uncomfortable. They might think 'managed' implies a degree of control and planning while 'creativity' signals the need for an intuitive and unbounded framework. However, this is not an either/or situation. To achieve true commercial creativity, both arms must be used in partnership. This means delivering a style of working that can be described as 'loose-tight'. Clearly, employing wildly creative people might be fun, but unless they deliver ideas in a working format then it might prove to be fruitless. Conversely, a consultant may be highly skilled in managing change but does not take time to try to be creative in the way they work. The trick is to create something new and also ensure that it will add value to the client and consumer.

Two essential ingredients fuel the ability to create innovative solutions. The first is the ability to open your mind and remove inhibitions and blockages that prevent the generation of new solutions. By doing this you will be able to create a rich pool of innovative ideas that can be used as a well-spring for the next stage. The second stage is to consider the pool of ideas and filter out those that do not add real value.

Think about the last time your partner asked you to buy a bottle of wine. In the space of a few seconds you will go through a complex decision-making process to choose the wine. However, this is something we do intuitively and without realizing the strategies we use. So what steps do people actually follow?

The first stage is to have a clear understanding of the challenge: namely to find a wine that matches the meal. The second stage is to look for a store that holds the widest selection of wine. When the pool of potential wines is identified, you might start to read the labels to explore which wine will be most suitable. Once the options are understood, you move from an exploratory process to a decision-making approach. You might look at each of the labels in more detail and appraise them for suitability with the meal. As you go through this process, you will be testing each bottle against a set of criteria that probably includes cost, quality and reputation. Finally, you will prioritize and evaluate the options to make a choice. This process might take an hour or it might be over in the blink of an eye. However long, the goal is to follow a journey that takes you first down the divergent path of thinking, closely followed by a style of thinking that is convergent in nature (*see* Figure 5.2).

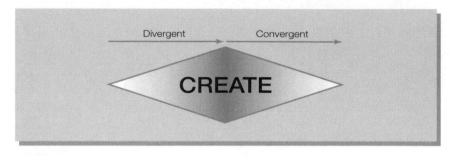

Figure 5.2 Decision-making process

The divergent part of the journey will have three stages:

- **Challenge** the status quo and break through the mentality that strives for the average level of mediocrity that often drives the creative process.

- **Randomize** potential solutions – a deliberate process to generate a rich tapestry of options.

- **Explore** each of the ideas and see which ones start to offer some real change options.

It is important at this stage to avoid any form of judgement or criticism. It can often be easier to adopt a critiquing role rather than take the position of someone who is being asked to bring forth new ideas. It is essential that you do not allow creative laziness to come into play in which a judgemental hat is worn as soon as the ideas start to roll. However, once the divergent or dream-like stage has helped to bring out a range of potential ideas, the next stage is to shift into a convergent style of thinking, where the creator can take a more critical role.

The convergent process is used to bring you from a dream state into that of critic or judge of the ideas generated. This process will typically draw upon three styles of thought:

- **Appraise** each idea and filter out those that intuitively do not help resolve the original issue.

- **Test** the remaining ideas, often by filtering them through an explicit criteria sieve to identify which of them can deliver a valued output.

- **Evaluate** each of the remaining options against the core requirement to ensure that the end solution deals with the problem.

Although the six stages of the create model are offered in a linear format, this can be difficult to manage, especially when working with a team. There might also be questions as to the extent to which such a linear process can destroy the opportunity to free-form or grab wild ideas that occur in the latter stage of the process. Certainly, you might argue that by using such a methodology there is a chance that people will be put off by its formality. Although all of these arguments are valid, it is still crucial that commercial and practical creativity is managed and not left to chance. As such it can help to use a process that is simple, logical and easily understood by all. The CREATE model, outlined in more detail below, is not the only way to manage the generative cycle, but it will help to ensure that ideas are originated and deployed in a practical way.

Challenge

The first stage of the divergent process is to ensure that you are mentally prepared to challenge the status quo. Norms exist in all forms of life: the conventions a family follows at dinner, the way pop songs are written, or the cultural norms that drive how an organization takes decisions. These norms are often so entrenched that people are unaware of their existence. So when any solution is being addressed it is important to understand the norms that underpin the context and in what way you are prepared to challenge this status quo. All change propositions will have a solution boundary – an implied or explicit limit that sets out how far the consultant, the consumer and the client wish to stretch or puncture this norm. It is important that this is understood from the outset so that time is not wasted and people do not feel let down when the final proposition is rejected.

Wherever possible, try to put a clear objective for the creative challenge in writing. Develop a clear and succinct statement that sets out what you hope to achieve at the end of the Create stage of the change project. This statement will indicate the problem (as defined in the Client or Clarify stage) and the type of solution. This can help all the people involved in the process to understand the amount of stretch required. It might be a category one solution, where the final resolution will not challenge any of the existing and accepted conventions; a category two solution, where the boundary is stretched but not to the extent that rules have to be rewritten; or a category three solution, where the final proposition must break all existing boundaries and set new standards for the industry.

Without this kind of initial focus, the Create process will start to address ideas that are off-centre and have little to do with the client's goal. Examples of this can be found in the US patent office – a diaper for parakeets, an alarm clock that squirts sleepers in the face, a machine that imprints dimples on the face (Michalko, 1991). Although there is a wild chance that a need will occur for these items at some time, there is a better chance that the inventor has patented an idea that will not generate a great deal of interest.

Randomize

If we are going to originate new ways of thinking, it is important to step outside the box – to take on board new and chaotic ways of viewing the world. The enforced randomization of potential solutions can help to push the boundaries back and also offer a new perspective. Leonardo da Vinci believed that to gain knowledge about the form of a problem you had to look at it from different perspectives. He felt that by simply sticking to the first view, you would be left with a limited impression of what the object is and what it might be. He would restructure his problem by looking at it from one perspective, then move to another and then another. With each move his understanding would deepen and he would begin to understand the essence of the problem (Michalko, 1998).

However, helping people to step outside their normal frame of reference is difficult, since they need to let go of their comfortable thinking styles and practices. One way to achieve this is to use different techniques that force the mind to operate in areas of uncertainty:

- **Randomize:** Take an encyclopedia or dictionary and pick random words. Use these to stimulate new ideas and actions associated with the engagement. Don't try to force anything, just let the back-of-the-mind thoughts trickle through to help originate new ways of working.
- **Connections:** Consider the change process and then link it with another idea. Ask yourself or your team to imagine how the change process might operate like a Chinese restaurant or how they might use the local library as a training location.
- **Opposites:** Exploit the fact that many new ideas are actually the opposite of what is traditionally being used: the shift from fixed telephones to mobile phones, private rather than public investment in the transport infrastructure, or disposable rather than long-lasting razors.
- **Explode:** Take one idea and then grow it, like an expanding balloon – see where it goes when self-imposed limits are taken away.
- **Reframe:** Take the issue being addressed in the engagement and reframe from a problem to a golden opportunity. Imagine that what is being offered is actually the solution required and then work through

how such an opportunity is used. Alternatively, take the issue and turn it into a negative. If the problem is how to improve morale in the office, reframe the statement into how to make morale worse. See what ideas this type of re-orientation produces.

■ **Why, why:** Take one of the issues or options and repeatedly ask why. Force people to dig deeper and deeper into the problem so that new and more divergent solutions are created. This can also be used in a revolutionary mode to encourage a business to break its own rules, especially if it cannot remember why those particular rules were instituted in the first place.

■ **Reminiscing:** Encourage people to use 'This reminds me of . . .' statements in relation to aspects of the change process. This uses the power of recall to stimulate people to make links with other experiences.

When in trying to originate new ideas, the danger is that both you and the client group will sit in a certainty box, offering ideas that do not step outside the comfort zone (*see* Figure 5.3). However, as you both start to learn from each other's experience, so it becomes easier to shift into the unpredictable area, offering up new and innovative ideas.

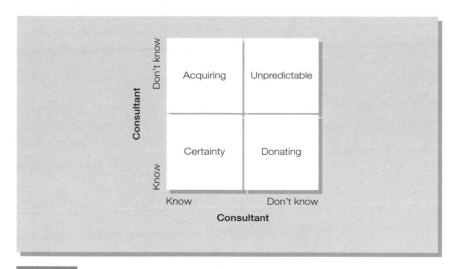

Figure 5.3 Shared learning

New ideas will emerge as people draw upon the ability to network and interact with others. There are times when something exciting happens between two people that would not have happened to an isolated individual. It is very rare that one could explicitly point to an idea that one person originated without help (known or unknown) from another human being. The development of new ideas will be a buoyant process where one person's thoughts will trigger an idea in another, which in turn leads to a prototype by someone else. So often in a creative process it is this social construction of ideas that adds the most value.

Explore

Once the wild and random ideas are generated, it is important to play with them and start to flesh out how they might be used. This means that each of the ideas is played with in the same way that a baby experiments with a new toy. Question the purpose of the object, see how it might be used and find out what practical value it holds. Try to put some flesh on all the ideas that emerge from the random stage and really understand how they might be applied in a practical way. While the randomization stage is 90 per cent idea and thought based, the exploring stage is 90 per cent hard effort – actually taking the wild ideas and really trying to understand how they might contribute to the problem at hand. You can achieve this by asking the following types of questions:

❝ ensure that all the ideas are really pushed to their limits to understand what value they might add ❞

- How would it work?
- Can it be used in any other way?
- What happens if it is used with another option?
- How would it be organized?
- What resources would it need?
- Where are the synergies?

The exploring stage is the final element in the divergent process. From this point onwards the goal is to close down the number of ideas. Hence it is important to ensure that all the ideas are really pushed to their limits to understand what value they might add.

Appraise

Building on the toy metaphor, when a child is faced with a floor full of toys it will naturally start to appraise which of them it will take out to the garden to use with its friends. In the CREATE model, the appraisal stage is used to make the transition from divergent to convergent thought patterns and so start the closure phase. Your aim at this point is to filter out those ideas that do not seem to add value or are less effective than others offered in the generative stage. Although this stage will often be instinctive rather than explicit, you must ensure that intuitive disposal is not used as an excuse to abandon those ideas that are too risky or step outside the normal mode of operation.

The basic process is to take all the ideas that have been generated as part of the randomization and exploring stages and subject them to a first pass of rejection. Using both intuitive and explicit knowledge and experience, take a first pass at all the ideas to weed out those that seem totally unpractical. One way to do this is to write all the ideas on paper and spread them over a wall or floor. Ask people to go through the list and mark those that they totally reject, are not sure about and really favour as having potential. Do this individually, without any discussion between the team. In a short space of time you will have broken the ideas into three separate groups. It is then possible to discard those that have been rejected by all the team, set aside those that offer a possibility and focus on the ones that all team members believe might add value. It is important to point out that those ideas in the possibility pile should not be pushed aside in favour of those that have full backing from the team. At some point these ideas can be tested. But where time is of the essence, this quick appraisal process can highlight the ideas on which to focus on initially.

Test

Once the intuitive appraisal process is complete, then you will need to be more explicit and rigorous in selecting the ideas that will be used. This is the final gate that the ideas must pass to ensure they offer effective solutions. Although this stage might be undertaken in many ways, one of the more effective approaches is to use a criteria-based selection model. At the very outset of the exercise, you can determine the criteria that any final solution must meet to ensure that an effective outcome is achieved. This criteria set might be a series of hard financial measures, a group or cultural factors or a stakeholder agreement list. Whatever the format, it is a clear indication of the factors that will ensure that any proposal will be accepted.

Evaluate

Finally, once the number of potential solution is down to a short list of two or three, they can be evaluated against the core challenge set out at the start of the process. De Bono (1992) suggests that the process of evaluation is logical and judgemental and is not directly part of the creativity stage. He suggests that evaluation can be based along four lines:

■ Is the idea feasible?

■ What benefits will it offer?

- What resources are required?
- Does it fit the need of the end client?

When any idea is being evaluated, it can fall into one of many categories:

- directly usable now;
- good idea but not for us or not for now;
- needs more work to bring it into a usable form;
- has value but cannot be used because of regulatory, environmental or other reasons;
- interesting but unusable – keep around for future investigation;
- weak value when really put to the test;
- unworkable because it has fundamental impossibilities that prevent it from being delivered.

At this stage it is important to ensure that emotion does not creep into the decision process. Although emotions are critical throughout the creation process, if people are allowed to push their personal fads or projects then the creative rigour of this model can be compromised.

One of the most important objectives in any consulting engagement is the drive to create a solution that is both innovative and practical. While the full creative processes need to be stimulated, any idea must be delivered within the given constraints. To achieve this delicate balance it is important to adopt managed rather than freewheeling creativity.

Divergent scanning

Sometimes it can be difficult or impractical to come up with totally new ideas. You might need to look outside your normal surroundings and scan the market. Although this can be done in a variety of ways, there are a number of common approaches. These are built around two key variables:

- **Breadth of the search:** Is the search based within the same industry or does it move into a totally different area?
- **Balance between a passive and active search:** For the passive search, systems are put in place and then left to react to ideas as they surface. Alternatively, you can search in a proactive way.

The relationship between these two variables produces the following activities (*see* Figure 5.4):

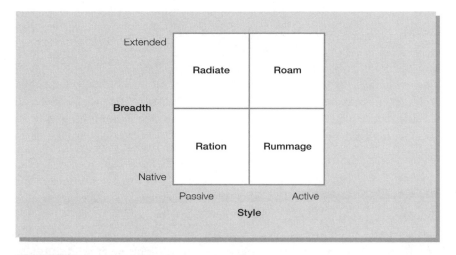

Figure 5.4   Scanning matrix

■ **Ration:** There is only limited interest in searching. Thus there is only a passing desire to subscribe to journals, join committees or scan the internet.

■ **Radiate:** Ideas from other areas are of interest but little positive action is taken to pick up on them. Benchmarking is one example of a positive process for identifying new ideas, although the extent to which other people's ideas are actually adopted will indicate whether a reactive or proactive stance is being taken.

■ **Rummage:** The creative team will take the time to interact closely with new people but the search is still limited to the local area. New ideas are forthcoming but they are likely to be in use already.

■ **Roam:** A positive decision has been taken to look aggressively for inspiration beyond the local area and to look actively for ideas from counterparts in other industries and across more diverse fields.

It is important to keep a balance. The danger is that people can be lazy and might try simply to transplant what other people have implemented. This is the approach when companies blandly climb on the total quality, re-engineering and downsizing bandwagons.

A crucial part of the scanning process is to develop the ability to recognize ideas that occur naturally. Stories abound of the various inventions that have emerged from the process of serendipity, such as Goodyear's accidental discovery of the vulcanization process for rubber or Fleming's accidental discovery of penicillin. All these inventions originated because someone (apparently) happened to be in the right place at the right time and was observant enough to notice something out of the ordinary. However, simply being around when an accident happens is not enough to bring about new ideas and discoveries. It is important that the development team is in a state of constant preparedness and able to recognize the difference between an accident and when fate offers the chance to create something new. A discovery based on serendipity is the fruit of a seed sown by chance in fertile ground.

The idea of 'fertile ground' is an engaging one. How can a consultant create the fertile ground to allow for surprises or serendipity? The list is probably endless, but a key role is to help individuals be in a state of readiness. An eagerness to challenge, desire to learn, a spread of relationships and the ability to reframe all contribute directly to creating fertile ground. It is also important to draw upon the unspoken ideas and thoughts that are held at a tacit level. Tacit knowledge is described as the thoughts, feelings, dreams and intuition that go on in the background while people are performing a task, or the natural acts that people perform without consciously thinking.

In one study, 82 of the 93 winners of the Nobel Peace Prize over a 16-year period agreed that intuition played an important part in creative and scientific discoveries (Cooper and Sawaf, 1997). It is this soft and intuitive aspect that can help to develop consultancy processes that break the mould. It is human emotion rather than any logical cause–effect analysis that drives intuition. It is the ability of the individual to have a hunch that something might work, even though everyone else says it will fail. Whilst it is not possible to systematize an inherently soft factor, people can choose to influence their ability to take intuitive decisions.

However, intuition does not preclude the notion of rationality. Although intuitive insights can appear not to make sense and might seem to be the opposite of a rational response, when brought together they form a more powerful tool. Einstein never discovered anything solely with his rational mind – the principle of relativity came about after he imagined himself travelling on a beam of light. This intuitive idea, coupled with his brilliance as a physicist, allowed him to develop a scientific theory that helped change the world's view of itself.

Once the power of unspoken knowledge is extracted, the tap is turned on from the pool of known explicit knowledge – the clear, known and unambiguous experiences that people bring to work. For example, product managers do not live that role for every hour of the day. They might also be parents who experience products on a personal as well as a professional level. This is just a simple example of the life experiences that an individual will bring to the workplace. The question is, to what extent can the consultancy team draw upon this fountain of knowledge and skills? If you are serious about creating new and innovative ways in which to assist your client, you need to offer freedom for the members of the consultancy team to present their whole self to the change process. You must value the rich diversity that resides within the workforce.

Convergent choice

There are many factors that help determine what makes the difference between a good or bad solution but often it depends on the rigour of the selection at the end of the Create stage. When you pick your final proposal from the list of evaluated options, how can you be sure that it is the optimum choice? It may look the best on paper, but when trying delivering a sustainable outcome in a live situation will the client really go through with the pain of change and will it hold up to scrutiny by the consumers?

There are six factors that can have a significant impact on the long-term success of a change process. These CHOICE factors are:

- **Control:** Does the client have all the necessary power to effect the suggested solution?
- **Hungry:** Does the client really want to do this to the exclusion of spending time and energy on other important activities?
- **Options:** Can we guarantee that all possible options have been considered?
- **Internalization:** Is this solution for which we/the client accept responsibility?
- **Consequences:** Have we fully considered what can happen as a consequence of the choice and still believe it is the best option?
- **End game:** Can we be sure that this choice aligns and supports the clients desired outcome?

Managing these six factors does not guarantee that the solution will be successful. What it does do is help you to become more conscious of the factors that affect the solution's chances of success.

Control over outcome

Are you making a choice about something where you have control or are you simply spending time and energy on something that is outside your area of influence? So many people spend time and energy bemoaning the problems in their life and whinging about things over which they hold no sway. Consider someone who sits on the outer ring of a children's round-about wheel and spends all their time moaning how sick they feel. They have a choice: stay there or move to the inner part of the wheel where the centrifugal force will stop acting on them (*see* Figure 5.5).

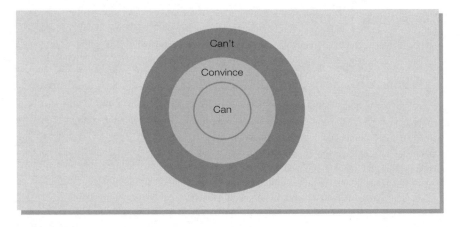

| Figure 5.5 | Choice circle |

Curiously, many change programmes are managed from the outer ring of the wheel. It is here where work is hectic, buzzy, political and fun. There are constant battles, fights raging every day and the testerone flies across the room as the change warriors battle out their private wars. At the end of the day people go home feeling like they have done a real day's work and earned their money. The trouble is that all this energy expenditure does not achieve anything useful – It is constantly focused on things that people cannot change.

It is far more productive to move into the centre of the roundabout and focus energy on things that are under immediate control and can be resolved within the change team. The intriguing thing is that the more choices that are made in the inner circle, the more chance there is to make a choice that is successful. As you become recognized as someone who chooses choices that work, so other people will both follow your lead and ask you to help with their problems. Your 'can' circle becomes wider and the 'can't' circle shrinks. The result is that your personal leadership power grows proportionally.

The third area in the choice circle is the 'convince' area. This sits between the 'can' and 'can't' wheels. It offers a solution when you want to make a choice but do not have direct control over the situation. In this case it makes sense to focus on either convincing others to help you achieve the outcome or tackle those people directly to convince them to change.

There are three types of choice

■ you can deliver the intended outcome

■ you would like to but can't actually deliver the intended outcome

■ you need to convince others to support your desired goal.

The great consultant spends time in the area that will realize the most payback. The question; does your proposed solution sit in the 'can' wheel? If not, then the effort expended might offer limited return.

Hungry for success

This stage attempts to understand the emotional content of the choice and gauge the desire or motivation of the client for the decision. An intelligent choice made without the emotional quotient may be brilliant, but is unlikely to be either sustainable or successful.

Diets don't work. This is an often-quoted maxim but generally with good cause. The reasons why they don't work are many, but one of the factors that can cause them to fail (in the long term, if not in the short term) is the fact that people don't really want to lose weight. They say they do, the television says they should, the magazines suggest that it is great to be a size eight, but the fact of the matter is that it isn't really something they deep down want to achieve. Maybe they say they do – but not enough to give up the late night chocolate bar or get up for the early morning jog. The reality is that some people are really hungrier for the chocolate cake than to lose weight.

The heart is the emotional epicentre that provides the inner strength and compass of leaders, regulating the desire and ability to make choices about important things. When we are energized and engaged we can make tough choices with clear purpose. When less hungry, the choices can be lacklustre and short-lived.

Knowing what you want to do and how to get there are not enough. You need passion and perseverance. It is this emotional self-management that is needed to manage and overcome the problems and obstacles that arise after the choice is made. Take any consultant who creates a new company strategy in partnership with the client. It is rarely the choice of what strategy to deliver that makes the final difference. In most cases it is the passion the consultant wraps around the choice – creating a dream for themselves and others that is supported by charisma and confidence. For someone who is about to diet, selecting the dietary process is simple; the difficulty comes two or three weeks into the process when it is your best friend's birthday party. Can you really say no to the cake or the glass of champagne? It is at this point that the direction and energy provided by the emotions need to kick in and provide the strength to say no. Without this support then any choice will be short-lived.

> knowing what you want to do and how to get there are not enough. You need passion and perseverance

As consultants we often have to get emotionally engaged with the choices we make and not feel shy about saying so. We must be prepared to stand on a soapbox with the client and shout out loud what we are going to do and why. We must find a way to communicate the choice that comes from our heart and build an instant connection so that it touches the hearts of the consumers of the change. Hunger leads to desire, desire leads to dreams and dreams lead to passion and committed action.

Options for action

This stage of the CHOICE model is the head or logical part of the equation. It provides the wisdom and clarity of purpose that can regulate the excesses of an emotional heart. The head function remains above our emotional needs and helps us formulate plans and make decisions relating to how we lead others and ourselves. The heart says, 'I know where I'm going and I'm going to get there by hook or by crook'. The head says, 'Fine, but let's make sure we actually make it in one piece so it's a really effective journey'. To do this the head needs to have breadth of choice. It needs to be able to call on a range of views and ideas to ensure the direction set by the heart is achieved – even if it is not necessarily by the route the heart had envisaged.

We often restrict our options for choice unconsciously. This occurs for a number of reasons, including:

■ **Dead choices:** Sometimes people act as though the commitment they made with a previous choice means that they have to keep going down the same route. When this happens we can fall into the trap of religiously following 'dead' choices. People want to believe they are good at making choices and so persist in believing that the original decision was a good one, even when it appears not to be. This might be where we have spent so much on a car to keep it running that it seems silly to trade it in to get a new one. We have an emotional investment in the current car in the form of investment decisions; getting rid of the car would be like saying that the earlier choices were bad. Sometimes we have to accept that choices made are lost and cannot be recovered. Once made, they are dead and gone and we have to focus on the rationality of the choices still to be made rather than those made previously. An example of this can be seen in wartime when it becomes impossible to back out of a situation – even if more lives will be lost on a wasted cause.

■ **Decision rules:** We all create frames of reference that contain decision rules. These are the unspoken internal policies that we use to get through the day. It might be only one cup of coffee a day, fish on Fridays, or a bird in the hand is worth two in the bush. At the time of setting the personal rule it may have been correct, but does it still make sense in the current situation? If not, then make sure you are prepared to discard the rule.

■ **Discounting:** People set their own discounting rules. Research suggests that young children faced with a choice between getting an attractive toy in five minutes or a less attractive toy immediately will choose the latter. We can all become temporarily myopic (nearsighted) and just focus on those options that give the earliest payback. This is known as impulsiveness and can be seen in problem-solving situations where the tendency is to respond quickly with a solution rather than waiting for one that offers a better outcome. By doing this we are discounting the value of the future option. This is because we believe that by taking the sooner option we start to accumulate interest (in the form of benefit) through use of the choice now rather than later. This can restrict variety because we ignore possible choices that do not deliver an immediate benefit. Examples of this are the depletion of fish stocks, eradication of the forests or depletion of the world's natural energy sources.

The objective is for the consultant to ensure that they have helped the client to develop sufficient options to deliver the required solution. This is known as Ashby's law of requisite variety. Ashby suggested that any regulator must have as much or more variety than the system it regulates. The same can be seen in a game of football or chess. Winning either of these is not just about the level of skill or intelligence. It is also about the ability to generate a variety of responses to moves taken by the other side. The more options you have in your kit bag, the better placed you will be to respond with a winning move.

Internalization of responsibility

It is important to understand whether the choice is intentional or imposed. Is it one that I choose to make or is it a choice that I feel is forced on me by someone else? This is often referred to as the locus of control. Locus is the location: the place where you believe the controlling elements of the choice are coming from. Do you believe the choice is being controlled by an external circumstance, or do you believe that it comes from within and that you determine the course of your life? This is a reflection how far people see themselves as being in control of, and responsible for, the course of occurrences (desirable and undesirable) that they experience.

People who internalize operate from a self-concept that says 'I take responsibility for both good and bad things that happened in my life'. People who externalize take the view that 'I can't take responsibility for the good or bad outcomes because they stem from the action taken by other people'. Most of us fall somewhere in the middle, believing that the life we have is a combination of our own effort and the outside circumstances that affect the outcomes of events in our lives. So at times we are under the pressure of others and sometimes life is under our control. For example, school students who have a very external locus of control often believe that it is solely the teacher's responsibility to teach them and not their responsibility to learn. Because they put the responsibility for learning on the teacher, they always fall under pressure to do rather than taking the choice to do things themselves.

Many people will not try to achieve something if they do not believe it is attainable. People who have an internal locus of control ('internalizers') think that they are responsible for their successes and failures. They believe that if they succeed it is because they try hard and have the ability to succeed. Other people may feel they do not have control over what happens to them. If good things happen it is due to luck, circumstances or other people. These people have an external locus of control (externalizers). Many people will fall between these two extremes and possess characteristics of each type.

Listen carefully to your thoughts and speech patterns. Also listen carefully to language used by people around you. Compare your language with the examples in Table 5.1.

Table 5.1	Internalization and externalization
Internal locus	*External locus*
I can control my feelings	She made me so mad
I was sick and chose to rest	I couldn't do my homework
I decided not to call you because . . .	I couldn't go to class
I prefer or I chose . . .	I must . . .
I chose not to . . . because. . .	I can't. . .
I will get my degree	If only I had my degree

If people believe they have control over future events, then they will attempt to exert that control in order to achieve a positive outcome. It does not matter whether an outcome is or is not attainable; the perception of control determines if one will try to attain it. For example, if Sue believes that it is in her control to meet an extremely difficult goal such as getting straight As in school, she will try to get them even though the odds may be against her. On the contrary, Steve may drop out of school because he does not believe that he can choose to determine if he passes his classes, even though passing grades may clearly be within his ability. Locus of control has a significant impact on how individuals' expectations shape the goals they set for themselves and the choices they make to achieve those goals.

If the client is externalizing the choice and simply doing it because someone else says it must be done, then they are likely to opt for any outcome without any particular focus. The choice may lack any emotional support and certainly will suffer from any test of intellectual rigour; hence alternative options will not be explored. A successful solution is one where the client views it as theirs to solve and they feel that the solution is under their control.

Consequences understood

Choices are crossing points in time. Each choice is a branch on the tree, terminating in a list of consequences that follow if that branch is selected. Often these consequences lead to a new set of choices and consequences (*see* Figure 5.6).

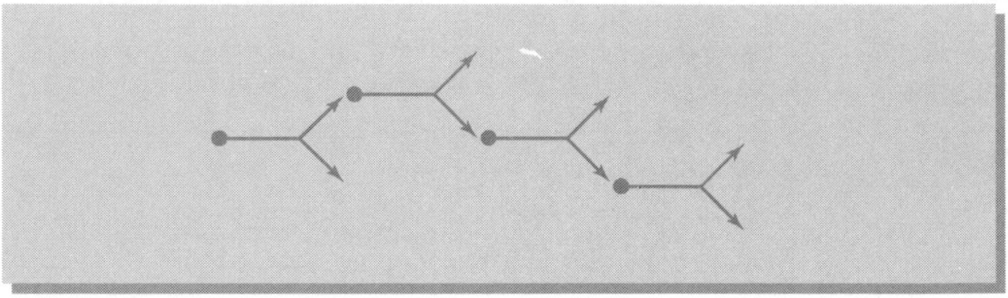

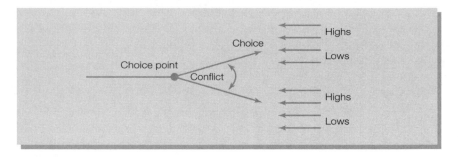

Figure 5.6 Choice points

Each choice point signifies that an ongoing state or process is about to change into a new state or process. For example, you are at the movies with an old friend; you've never done it before, but you now decide to hold your friend's hand. At the choice point you interrupt the automatic flow of past into future – you take control. Every choice creates a new future and with this a set of (virtually infinite) consequences. But more importantly, choices represent or anticipate the future they are trying to create.

For each choice that you might make there will be a set of consequences. These will have a range of possible benefits and problems, but in simple terms we can assume that no matter what choice is taken, the consequences will fall into highs and lows (*see* Figure 5.7).

Figure 5.7 Choices and consequences

The highs are those consequences that will give a positive return on the choice investment. These repay the time and energy invested in the choice process and validate that the choice was the right one. The lows are the outcomes that offer less benefit and can actually act against the value of the choice, thus negating its primary value. It might be that there are so many lows or one of the lows has such intensity that it negates the choice made and a further choice might need to be taken to resolve the situation.

Every choice has at least two options, each of which has positive and negative consequences. When choosing one option, you receive its positive consequences and avoid the rejected option's negative consequences; but at the same time you must accept the chosen option's negative consequences and miss out on the rejected option's positive consequences.

Although we try and anticipate the future consequence when taking the choice, we can never know all possible future consequences of our choices – and even if we could, we would not know how many of the possible consequences may come true. It is this uncertainty of the impact of each choice that leads to conflict in the decision-making process. These implications upset your natural goal to select good things and avoid bad things. A feeling of confusion can accompany your choice and can be felt even after you choose.

One way that we can manage this confusion is by working with the client to evaluate each option and map all its possible consequences. Once the possible highs and lows for each choice are understood then it becomes easier to take a stab at a choice that will deliver the best sustainable success.

End game fit

Sometimes we look around at our lives and wonder how we arrived where we are. What happened was that we made choices along the road and those choices had consequences – which we live with every day. And each day that we live we continue to make more choices. So, if our lives are not exactly where we want them to be, maybe we should consider whether the choices we made have actually taken us towards where we want to go or if they led us into a place that is not quite right, or in many cases feels distinctly uncomfortable.

It is important always to try to step into the future – to understand the end game so that decisions are taken with the end in mind rather than what feels right today. For so many people, pivotal choices have been made based on the situation of the moment, and not on the basis of their personal life goals. Choices made without consciously knowing where you are going can leave you wondering how you got there. These are often the choices that we 'blame' others for making, even though we made the choice.

> **❝ choices made without consciously knowing where you are going can leave you wondering how you got there ❞**

Part of the role of the consultant is to help the client consciously make their choices and ensure that wherever possible the choices take them towards rather than away from their end goal. The key question you have to ask when helping the client take a choice is whether they have an end game to measure it against. If they do not have a clear outcome developed in the Client stage of the Seven Cs, how can they know if the choice they are about to take is moving them towards or away from the end point?

One day Alice came to a fork in the road and saw a Cheshire cat in a tree. 'Which road do I take?' she asked. 'Where do you want to go?' was his response. 'I don't know', Alice answered. 'Then', said the cat, 'it doesn't matter'.
(Lewis Carroll)

Solution test

Once you understand the CHOICE model then it is relatively easy to apply these criteria to the solution that has been selected as the best option. For example, consider the last project you managed and pass the final choice to implement a solution through the following CHOICE map in Table 5.2.

Table 5.2 Solution test

Control	The client does not have all the necessary control and power to deliver the solution	1	2	3	4	5	The client has all the powers required to deliver the desired solution
Hunger	The client is not passionate about taking the action	1	2	3	4	5	The client wants to do more than anything else at the time
Options	This is the only option the client considered	1	2	3	4	5	The client has selected the action from a wide range of options
Internalization	Someone or something else required the client to take this action	1	2	3	4	5	The client will take this action because they want to and not because of anyone else.
Consequences	The client does not have a clear picture of what may happen once the choice is taken	1	2	3	4	5	The client is clear about all the possible consequences that might follow the choice
End game	The outcome will not take the client towards where they want to be in the future	1	2	3	4	5	The client can describe how it will take them to their end game.

It is very easy with this type of test to begin to allocate scores that miraculously predict if solutions will be successful. Clearly this tool cannot do that; however, what it can do is help surface the issues that might cause a problem and more importantly help communicate these issues to the client. By explaining the model and highlighting the differing profiles that can emerge from the model it will be easier to have a high-value conversation with the client and consumers about the chance of success with the proposed solution.

As an example, take the three CHOICE profiles shown in Figure 5.8. With profile (a) the problem might have been hunger and the solution is chocolate. While the first five parameters offer a high solution rating, the fact is that the whole end game (losing weight) has been discarded. This can happen in life where people panic after losing sight of their objective and take the first thing that comes along. It also happens in organizational change where companies say they are in for the long-haul transformation and then make silly short-term decisions just to satisfy the political or financial master.

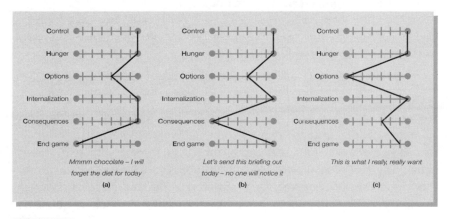

Figure 5.8   Choice profiles

With profile (b), all the parameters apart from consequences have been considered. This is the 'knee-jerk' solution. It can be seen where organizations jump for a solution because it fits all the criteria but they fail to think through the consequences of their action. It is this type of solution that often leads to industrial action following the introduction of ill-thought-through policies; downstream costs increasing as inappropriate process changes are introduced; or the departure of staff after pay plans are changed that drive up sales of a product but result in bonus reductions for key managers.

Profile (c) is a pattern that has been found time and time again across a range of industries and countries. This is the 'fad' solution. After yet another new book comes along espousing that businesses need to upsize, bright-size or downsize if they want to survive, we see a sheep-like mentality as managers and consultants say 'That is the answer for me' and do not take the time to consider other options. Over the past 30 years we can see wave after wave of fads that have entered mainstream business thought, hung around for a while and then drifted away as people begin to realize that maybe they don't offer the magic answer. The challenge for the consultant is always to ask the question 'And what else could you do?'. Never accept an either–or range of options. As a minimum there will always be a third option and in most cases more. Unless these are thoroughly tested in the Create stage, how can you and the client be sure that you have the optimum rather than the only solution?

The CHOICE profile cannot determine if a solution will work. What it can do is to help you to understand the deeper dynamics of a potential solution that emerges from the CREATE model and acts as a checklist before you take the final step to implement the solution.

Solution storyboarding

Once the final solution is selected, the team will need to understand how it will actually be deployed in the field. This can be achieved through the use of storyboards. The storyboard is a sequential model of both text and pictures that describes the journey a change might take. The team will take the ideas generated and use them to construct a number of potential story-lines. The idea is to allow people to piggyback and bounce off each other and from this instigate a range of optional stories and patterns. Typically, each storyline will follow the pattern used by most good books or films, with a compelling start, engaging middle and a strong ending. Each of the stories offers a potential solution to an issue.

Imagine a team trying to resolve a poor morale problem in a large insurance company. As part of their group session they might identify three different storylines. Each storyboard offers a different approach that might resolve the situation:

■ **Storyline 1:** Undertake a cultural audit to determine the key drivers for the problem; map issues and share them with selected focus groups to confirm target areas; create action teams from the focus group members to own and manage the problem; provide expert support to the teams; central project management team to oversee and report back to board on resolution of issues.

■ **Story line 2:** Run a series of large team meetings and allow people to voice concerns; allocate project leaders to each issue; project leaders to report back on progress at regular group meetings, possibly monthly; publish progress in house magazines.

■ **Story line 3:** Invite unions to a meeting to consider problems; identify what they believe the issues are; set up union/management teams to resolve issues; if this proves to be successful, consider setting up a joint team to deal with all future staff issues.

Within each of these three storylines, the basic start and end are similar but the content is quite different. However, by building the storylines using words and pictures, the team can quickly understand the total picture and options. In the same way that it only takes a few seconds to draw the essence of a story from the front page of a newspaper, your team can rapidly assimilate and communicate a large amount of data.

This ability to communicate ideas and patterns quickly will allow the team to modify and rebuild the storyline in a matter of minutes. As a result, the team can quickly test which of the three storylines will be most effective. It also means that the team can readily test the risks associated with each option by pushing each of the storylines through a range of different scenarios. Finally, if the team wishes to involve others in the decision-making process, it becomes quite easy to share the stories.

This approach can also be useful when you start to design the transformation process. Whereas many change programmes use a hard approach (substantial objectives, plans and structures) to build the change plan, storyboarding allows a softer style (holistic, loose relationships and metaphors). One of the primary problems with the hard approach is the tendency to mentally lock into the first design that emerges, thus restricting any real opportunity to search for innovative and interesting solutions. With the storyboard approach, the options are framed in such a way that the first plan is not necessarily the final one. The use of pictures framed in a loose structure means that once a story has been placed on the wall, it can be cut and pasted in seconds to create a totally different change model.

“ a narrative style can help people to make emotional as well as logical sense of the change ”

Although this approach feels simplistic, it can help develop a complex and detailed framework. Behind each panel in the storyboard there are a series of sub-panels that underpin the ideas and these can in turn hold a greater level of detail. Using this system, quite complex and detailed propositions are framed in such a way that all players can readily understand them.

The use of a narrative style can also help people to make emotional as well as logical sense of the change. Like a cartoon film, powerful messages are delivered in a short time with little embellishment. A good story can bring together diverse elements and help people to make sense of a complicated message. Whereas many project plans can be quite adversarial and impersonal, the storyboard aims to be engaging and inclusive. The idea is to use it as a way to help a group of people design, develop and disseminate a simple story.

Some might view this approach as fuzzy, lacking in rigour and overly driven by intuitive frameworks. However, storyboard modelling is as rigorous as any harder approach because it still includes logical and linear relationships found in formal development systems. It just presents them in a more palatable way. Rather than developing the change plan using dates and numbers on a Gantt chart, the creation process uses pictures, shapes and colours on a storyboard.

At this stage, the team should be able to work through the various options and agree on one single storyline that will form the backbone of the consultancy process. With the final proposition in place, you can start to understand the implications of the decision and test its viability. In particular, you can begin to understand what resources will be required, who will own the work activities and what specific actions need to be undertaken.

Resourcing the solution

There is clearly a big difference between the design and the delivery of a solution. In general, the initial design element is theoretical and idealized, where people work on the basis of what they would like to happen. Managers are still in the euphoria stage and will possibly offer total commitment and promise to deliver the necessary people, plant and finances. You are the saviour who has arrived on the white charger to rescue the organization from a dastardly problem. However, partway through the transformation, the promised resources either start to disappear or, worse still, never actually materialize. Like the pull of gravity from a black hole, the energy and resources start to be sucked off to deal with other pressing issues – 'resource shrinkage'. As a result you are left to deliver the contracted change without the necessary resources.

Although resources are often agreed at a senior level, they will generally be deployed at a lower level. You might have a formal sanction to use a resource but trying to gather and hold it can be difficult. The final delivery of a project is based more upon your ability to bargain for and leverage resources than making a sales pitch to the client. In a perfect world your engagement would be the primary initiative for the whole company and support would be ensured. The reality is that organizations are a boiling pot of ambitions, politics and changing priorities. Your initiative will therefore only have a limited honeymoon period, after which you will have to get inside the system to fight for resources.

Successful resource management depends on your ability to negotiate in an internal market. To ensure that the resources stay allocated to the engagement you will have to develop a range of tactical and strategic actions. These include (A–F):

■ **Amass:** Like the farmer who stores supplies for the winter or the mechanic who keeps a secret stock of parts for when the local suppliers have run out, a consultant often needs to amass a pool of local talent and resources to be drawn upon when sparse times surface. These people will generally be friends who have offered to help or people with a real interest in your proposition.

■ **Borrow:** When resources become difficult to hold, you might need to resort to a process of surreptitiously borrowing. The difficulty comes in defining the boundary between borrowing and stealing. It is important that you operate within the spirit and letter of the contract but always seek to deliver the agreed outcome. If active borrowing outside the agreement of the contract is necessary, then you must ensure that the dominant stakeholder is aware of the situation and is willing to underwrite the action.

■ **Complement:** It is often difficult to obtain the exact skills to deliver a specific outcome. Trying to find an IT specialist who has experience within the travel industry might prove difficult. However, by adopting a fusion mentality it is possible to generate the necessary resources. Is it possible to identify an IT expert who can work with a travel specialist to create a collaborative partnership?

■ **Demarcate:** When you agree the initial contract, it is important to delineate the general broad resources required to deliver the outcome from the core resources that are mission-critical. If this is a core group of people, they must be ring-fenced to prevent anyone from trying to pull them from the project. Where possible, this ring-fenced group must be included as part of the contractual arrangement with the client.

- **Economic:** The appropriation of human capability within an organization is based upon an economic model – people are traded in the same way as equipment, office space and IT software. You must therefore understand the barter value of the individuals within the project and where necessary trade to ensure that they remain locked into the process. For example, one trade-off might be that you could hold on to a programmer if you are prepared to be responsible for their travel and training costs.

- **Favours:** In Tom Wolfe's novel *The Bonfire of the Vanities* (1987) there is a suggestion that 'everything in the criminal justice system in New York operates on favors. Everybody does a favor for everybody else. Every chance they get, they make deposits in the Favor Bank.' This same principle can be applied to the appropriation and management of resources. People are loaned across functions, teams and geographic areas. Therefore, it can pay the consultant to maintain a log of individuals who are in debit and credit with regard to resource sharing. Although this is an option that might only be used as a last resort, it can help to resolve issues that seem insurmountable.

Resource management will always be complex, because the nature of your relationship with your client is grounded in a collaborative, but competitive framework. Although you have been invited in to help resolve a problem, to the consumer you are probably just a temporary member of the team so they will be loath to offer you access to their scare resources. Instead, you must master the ability to acquire, manage, retain and deploy people with all the expertise and guile of a general in battle. However, the moment you actually view the acquisition of resources as a war rather than a collaborative effort, then the battle is lost. You will always be playing against local managers on their home turf and so they will have the dominant position. It is far better to work at a desire level within the change ladder (*see* Chapter 3). Convince them of the need for change and the benefits they will gain from helping you. Then you will be able to resource a team that has the capability and desire to help.

6

Stage four: Change

Consider how hard it is to change yourself
and you'll understand what little chance you
have of trying to change others.

Jacob M. Braude

Change is the fun part of the whole process. This is where the action
takes place, careers are made and reputations destroyed. At this stage, as a
consultant you might put on your project management hat, pull out the
25-page work-structure breakdown and launch into a highly technical
discussion about milestones, critical paths and percentage-completion
factors. Clearly, these issues need to be included, but this aspect of the
process has been sufficiently well documented elsewhere so need not be
covered in this book.

The focus here is on the softer factors – the issues that have a subtle but
significant impact on the change process. It is these intangible factors that
are often pushed to one side. However, only by taking care of the soft issues
will the hard deliverables be achieved. As Senge *et al.* (1999) suggest, most
change initiatives fail. In many cases the supposed failure rate for total
quality and re-engineering initiatives is around 70 per cent. Kotter's study
of 100 top management-driven corporate transformations concluded that
more than half did not survive the initial phase (Kotter, 1999).

The failure to recognize or resolve this problem is often shielded by the
cloak of political intrigue or the simple fact that organizations change so
fast that the failures are lost in the mists of time. But effective change is not
about increased technical or project management capability, it is more
about the need to understand the meta-processes that drive and support

change. These are the actions that need to be understood, irrespective of the nature of the change or the industry. However, these factors are often viewed as the soft processes, the intangible elements that are swept aside once the ball is in the air.

Yet within an engagement, the soft issues are often the hardest. Although the development and management of the project plan are difficult and often labour-intensive, it is important to ensure that the more intangible issues are not overlooked as the heat is turned up.

The Change stage of the Seven Cs model includes the following themes that seek to help to understand and address the human elements of change:

- **System dynamics** – What are the deep systemic issues that will cause the change stage to hit problems?

- **Organisation and disorganisation:** What factors related to the organisation of the system will impact on the success of the change.

- **Understand the resistance:** How can people be encouraged to be involved in the transformation?

- **Change spectrum** – What type of change interventions can be effected to help people through the change?

- **Consumer segmentation** – How can the consumer be segmented into groups based on their desire for change.

- **Methodology:** Determine from the outset what methodology will be used to drive the engagement.

- **Energy mapping** – Understand where the forces are who can impact on the change.

System dynamics

Look at the list of words in Table 6.1. Why is it that so many consultants sell their services using words from the left-hand column while so many clients believe that the words on the right are more indicative of the outcome? Wherever you go, whatever industry, the role of the consultant is generally under attack. People are dissatisfied with their doctors, householders complain about builders and directors moan that yet another consultant has left them with a mundane solution. Clearly the consultancy industry might have a few rogues and the odd bad apple but the huge growth in consultancy spend over recent years seems to run counter to the view that consultants do not add value to the client and consumer.

| Table 6.1 | Intent and outcome |

Consultant's intent	Perceived outcome
Action	Aberration
Better	Bluff
Cure	Chaos
Deliver	Delay
Easy	Embarrassment
Faster	Fails

One of the reasons is because so many consultants do not pay sufficient attention to the nature of the system in which they are working. They act on the evidence of a single event and give little consideration to the deeper issues that underpin the system. Consultancy projects are often designed on the premise that the issues revolve around a simple, predictable component. In reality, this is the tip of a problem that involves a complex, dynamic and integrated system. As Senge (1990) suggests:

Business and human endeavours are systems . . . they are bound by invisible fabrics or interrelated actions, which often take years to fully play out their effects on each other. Since we are part of that lacework ourselves it is doubly hard to see the whole pattern of change. Instead we tend to focus on snapshots of isolated parts of the system and wonder why problems never seem to get solved.

For example, the incident the police most dread is a family dispute. In this situation they are being asked to dive into a situation that is volatile, emotional and unpredictable. There is often no 'solution' since the issue is possibly about a perceived rather than actual problem. No matter what action they might take they are likely to end up in the firing line, often being abused by both parties. They are effectively being asked to intervene in a system where they have little or no control over the process or outcome.

As a consultant asked to help resolve a problem within an organization, you are often in a similar position. You will be asked to unravel problems to which people are emotionally attached and will defend against outside interference. Moreover, you will rarely have to resolve an issue that involves just one person.

In all cases the effective consultant will focus less on the issues (tasks, content or facts) than on trying to understand the relationship between them. For example, the only way a marriage guidance counsellor will be able to help resolve a problem is by understanding the nature of the relationship between the husband and wife. Just understanding each partner in isolation will only produce a rubber-band solution, where the old problems bounce back after a few days. In the same way that 2 + 2 is vastly different from 2 × 2, the relationship is as much a part of the system as the component parts. In other words, the whole of the system is more than the sum of its parts. Unless you are able to see this then any project will be flawed from the outset.

> **❝ you must see (and help others see) the big picture ❞**

You must see (and help others see) the big picture. The view that an individual, team or organization can be improved by focusing just on one part in isolation is seriously flawed. Senge (1990) makes this point when he suggests that:

From a very early age we are taught to break apart problems, to fragment the world. This apparently makes complex tasks and subject more manageable, but we pay a hidden, enormous price. We can no longer see the consequences of our actions; we lose our intrinsic sense of connection to a larger whole. When we then try to 'see the big picture', we try to reassemble the fragments in our minds to list and organize the pieces.

Once this dissection has taken place it can be difficult to resolve the problem. Actions are taken on the separatist's principle with the result that a short-term fix might be delivered but a bigger long-term problem is planted. The consultant's failure to take account of the total system will often lead to one of the following scenarios (A–F):

- ▪ **Action/abort:** Systems that are made up of people do not react passively to an outsider. They will fight back with all the energy they can muster. Change makes things worse – it is difficult for a stranger to fix a problem because they do not have sensitivity to the context and situation. Thus it is impossible to make a change in one area without some impact being felt elsewhere. The end result is that the consultant has to close down the project or call in other people to help untangle the mess. Interestingly, in many cases consultants will make a good living on the back of projects that previous people have failed to resolve.

- ▪ **Better/bluff:** Things often get better before they get worse. Like the car mechanic who changes the spark plugs when your car is running rough, you might get a short-term improvement in performance, but the mechanic realizes that the clogged-up spark plugs are caused by excessive oil being burnt, then the issue has not been resolved. The real problem is that the piston rings are worn and no amount of short-term fixes will produce a long-term improvement.

■ **Cure/chaos:** In this case the cure is worse than the original problem. A doctor may happily prescribe Valium for a depressed patient. But unless the doctor tries to understand the root cause of the depression, the individual is led down a rocky road to possible long-term addiction. An insidious cycle of shared dependency can be generated with this approach. As the system falls into chaos because of an inappropriate cure, so managers look to the consultant to help them resolve yet another problem. Dependency is created between the consultant, client and consumer, with each believing that the real cure is just around the corner, if only they can have just one more fix of the latest consultancy fad.

■ **Deliver/delay:** When a change causes a problem for the system you can take immediate action to resolve the issue; however, the difficulty comes when a time delay creeps into the reaction and problems are caused downstream. You might make a change on the assumption that it has been effective, but you might not be around to see the impact of your actions. In 99 per cent of projects the consultant is not around after six months to understand the impact of the change.

■ **Easy/embarrassment:** If you are asked to help resolve a problem, the temptation can be to use the tried and tested techniques on the basis that what worked before will work again. You are like someone with a hammer who believes that all problems can be fixed with a nail. The danger is that after trying for the fifth time to push 'a square peg into a round hole', you might have to accept (with some embarrassment) that the easy, quick-fix solution might not be the most appropriate. Just because one system looks like another, it does not mean that solutions can be easily replicated.

■ **Faster/fails:** The pressure valve on a cooking pot or the governor on a steam engine are examples of how things are set to operate at their optimum level. In the same way, any system will have an optimum level at which they will operate and any effort to push this over the limit will be frustrating for you and damaging for the system. This can be seen in the way that people try to resolve difficult issues. Rather than stepping back from a situation to consider what deep structural issues are causing the problem, the tendency is to work harder, do more research or involve more people. In many cases, it might be that the slower or smaller action would actually deliver the desired outcome. Rather than trying to overcome resistance and force a change through, it might be easier to understand what limiting factors are causing the resistance and try to eliminate them by more subtle means. You can spend an hour arguing with your daughter about the need to keep her bedroom tidy, but it might be simpler to suggest that the tidiness of her bedroom will be directly linked to her pocket money.

Although each template tells a different story, they have a common theme that has a serious implication for any consultant. They suggest that when embarking on an engagement, you need to ensure that the situation is understood from the whole perspective and not in isolation (*see* Figure 6.1).

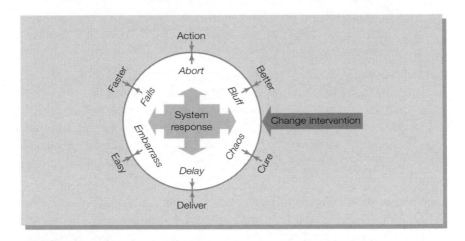

Figure 6.1   System responses

When undertaking any change engagement, you must pay careful attention to the systemic nature of the organization being changed. The systematic nature of the engagement can either fuel the drive towards a successful engagement or leave a problem legacy for the future – a problem that you, a colleague or client might be forced to resolve.

Organization and disorganization

Another issue that is beginning to have a significant impact on the way that change is deployed is the organization of the business unit. Historically, consultants may have been able to assume that the client group would have an organization build that was broadly based on a hierarchical business model. Today this assumption cannot be made. With a constant shift in organization shape, location and reporting structure there is often a move away from the formal hierarchical model to a more networked-based formation.

For those organizations based on mechanistic or machine-based operating principles they will have typical assumptions that drive the formation of an organization's management system (Cope, 1998):

▓ equilibrium, stability and control are the desired states;

▓ organizations can be separated into discrete components (function, department, product groups, etc.) and these elements can operate independently of any other unit within the business;

▓ organizations should always allocate resources in trying to determine what the market will look like in one, three and five years time;

▓ cause and effect relationships can be traced through the business;

▓ when something goes wrong in one part of the business, it can be isolated and repaired without affecting other areas.

These assumptions are driven by a set of deep underlying ideas:

▓ **We can know the future:** Organizations are often awash with market forecasters, business planners, strategy builders and economists who advise the organization of what is likely to happen in the future. The whole premise on which these positions exist is that the future can be predicted and managed.

▓ **Divide and conquer:** There is often a desire to divide the organization into management chunks on the assumption that things can be taken apart, dissected and split asunder (as with business functions and academic disciplines). The conjecture is that by comprehending the workings of each piece, the whole can be managed (Wheatley, 1994). The chunking that might typically be seen in organizations is by function (marketing, engineering, finance, etc.), geography, hierarchy, product groups or project teams.

▓ **Let me tell you what is wrong:** Most systems operate on negative feedback. Control systems such as objective setting, budgetary structures and resource allocations, are driven by a common approach. People are asked to forecast what is required, report any variance against the forecast, and then take action to rectify and limit the variance.

▓ **The boss knows best:** The common structural map is that the people at the top – the managers – know best and only need to draw upon the views of the lower teams to pick up a few tit-bits and give them a pat on the head.

■ **Don't feel – think:** Organizations are typically (overtly) driven by tasks, business goals, corporate objectives and the assumptions that people come to work for the love of the business. Often there is a view that people's feelings are left at home. Many organizations work on a repressed model, where any mention of emotion or sentiment in a business meeting can be enough to cause an apoplexy for the traditional manager. The base (espoused) assumption is that business decisions are based on logic and sensible decision-making processes. The reality is that decisions are often driven by personal ambition, greed and fear as much as for the good of the business

The network organization is founded upon an entirely different set of operating principles. It is built around the idea of a community that can spontaneously self-organize itself and adapt to changing market conditions. It can be seen as the ability of group of people to manage itself without any intervention or control from an external agent. Self-organization demands that a system draws upon its own resources, not that of the hierarchy, in order to meet the challenges that it faces (Goldstein, 1994, p. 3). Like birds flocking in the sky, children in the playground, people leaving a football stadium, or massed peace rallies, once the boundaries are set, and simple rules are offered, then harmony can emerge from a situation that is apparently chaotic – this is essentially 'order for free' (Kauffman, 1995, p. 71).

One of the significant factors with the mechanistic organization is the emphasis that is placed upon the cogs in the system. This means that people have defined roles, objectives and their place in a robust hierarchy. With the self-organization model, the emphasis is placed more upon the nature of connectivity within the system – on the interconnections, the configuration and the map of the relationship between the components, as well as the role of the people. This can be seen as the network organization – one that is likely to increase with the proliferation of web-based connections, remote working and global expansion.

Organizations that operate according to network model have the following characteristics:

■ **Self-stability:** There is a high degree of stability – not in the traditional sense of being fixed or unvarying, but in the capability to maintain the same overall structure in spite of any changes or replacement of component parts. The nature of the system means that it is able to remain steady, even when small disturbances occur. Since the inherent design of the system is based upon adaptability and self-regulation, it is able to contain any surprises that might occur that could have been disruptive. If the people in the network want to be in the network, then it will survive. It will change and adapt every day, week and month, but it will survive.

■ **Self-reproduction:** The network can continually reproduce itself in order to meet its goals. While the overall structure of the community remains the same, the components or people in the network will continually change. Thus the network modifies its internal elements but retains its overall identity. An example of this can be seen in the way that people rebuild their pancreas every 24 hours, their stomach lining every three days, and blood every month. The body is able to do this because it continually regenerates and changes the cell structure within the body (Capra, 1997, p. 213).

■ **Self-regulation:** Underpinning this idea of the self-sustaining organization is the notion of intrinsic self-regulation. Intrinsic regulation is where the network has its own capacity to regulate its operation and hence its output. Extrinsic regulation is where the control comes from outside the natural system. Networks will typically be intrinsically managed because no one person has the right to say what is and is not right or wrong.

■ **Self-organization:** Natural organisms can have a tendency to be attracted to an instinctive style or pattern of working. This natural or stable state is often known as the attractor state – it is a way of operating where order naturally arises out of disorder. For example, look at a group of school children playing at lunchtime. There is apparent disorder and chaos, but if the picture is considered in terms of patterns and relationships, different shapes and behavioural patterns will emerge. It will be possible to see patterns in the guise of repeated games that instigate a set of behaviours. Football will set up one pattern whilst the game of tag will drive another pattern. Networks will intuitively set up self-regulated patterns that form around a common point of interest. If you can understand the nature of the attractor then you will start to understand the nature of the network and how it self-organizes.

As people migrate from a mechanistic or organized system to operate in an open network they might need to lose some of the beliefs in the gods of direction, stability and consistency. If this is the case then consultants must develop the ability to effect change across organizations that do not have a network mentality. It is easy to 'install' a new vision, mission or strategy into a business where everyone meets in team meetings, logs in to the company web every morning and is paid through the same payroll system. The challenge will be for consultants to effect change across organizations where none of these things can be taken for granted – where people work with and not for the business, or where people log on at different times, depending on where they are in the world.

In many cases the change style adopted as norms by many change agents (command and control) may need to shift toward as much more negotiated and softer style to ensure that sustainable change is realized. As the formal organization structures begin to change, so too will the resistance that people offer to change imposed by external agents.

Understand the resistance

People don't resist change – they resist being changed.

Resistance to change is one of the most significant but least considered issues. This is because many people view opposition as a negative issue – something to go into battle with and defeat. However, unless people are already moving in the direction of a proposed transformation then it is natural to expect some form of resistance. This might be minimal, such as the odd joke or sarcastic comment about the new corporate uniform; or major, such as company-wide industrial action triggered by proposed downsizing. Although these two examples are different in scale, they follow the same underlying process that is a natural response in reaction to something people regard as unfair or inappropriate.

Although it is impossible to identify every type of behaviour where resistance is encountered, there are a number of common reactions that can be observed as people experience the adaption process (Kubr, 1976):

- **Lack of conviction that change is needed:** If people are not properly informed and the purpose of change is not explained, they are likely to view the present situation as satisfactory and any effort to change as useless and upsetting.

- **Dislike of imposed change:** In general, people do not like to be treated as passive objects. They resent changes that are imposed on them and about which they cannot express any views.

- **Dislike of surprises:** People do not want to be kept in the dark about any change being prepared; changes tend to be resented if they come as a surprise.

- **Fear of the unknown:** People do not like to live in uncertainty and may prefer an imperfect present to an unknown and uncertain future.

- **Reluctance to deal with unpopular issues:** Managers and other people often try to avoid unpleasant reality and unpopular actions even if they realize that they will not be able to avoid these for ever.

- **Fear of inadequacy and failure:** Many people worry about their ability to adjust to change and to maintain and improve their performance in a new work situation. Some of them may feel insecure and doubt their ability to make a special effort to learn new skills and attain new performance levels.

- **Disturbed practices, habits and relations:** Following change, well-established and mastered practices may become obsolete and familiar relationships may be altered or destroyed. This can lead to frustration and unhappiness.

- **Lack of respect in the person promoting change:** People are suspicious about change proposed by a manager whom they do not trust and respect or by an external person whose competence and motives are not known and understood.

The common theme with all these issues is that resistance often occurs when people do not feel engaged by the change process. In general, people can live with what they know but find it difficult to live with the unknown.

The first reaction to such resistance is often to try to minimize any response to the proposed change. But all this means is that valuable time is spent on avoidance routines – trying to work out ways to hide the elements that people might not like. For example, think about the hours people spend trying to find a politically correct way to present an idea that is obviously not politically correct. Hence the rebadging of 'downsizing' to 'rightsizing', or 'decruiting' as a way to manage people out of a business in a controlled way. All these actions indicate a change process that is being squeezed through the back door rather than being presented honestly.

❝ resistance often occurs when people do not feel engaged by the change

Natural resistance

It is normal for individuals, teams, organization or even nations to react adversely when faced with something different or unexpected. This reaction can be mapped in the form of a Y-curve, mapping time against the stages the individual(s) will pass through. The Y-curve is a powerful and effective change model that clearly illustrates many of the feelings associated with change and learning. People will especially feel these emotions where the change process affects their self-esteem or position in an organization.

Letting go

The Y-curve consists of two distinct stages (which may overlap). The first stage is the letting-go or disposal stage. This is where people learn they will have to modify how they currently think, feel or behave and be expected to adopt a new set of behaviours (*see* Figure 6.2). Such a change in a person's lifestyle can push them over the edge of the cliff into a downward spiral. External events, or stressors such as the death of a significant other, personal injury, illness or change of residence, will tend to force a person out of secure patterns. While the loss of a loved one through death or divorce is unquestionably shattering, humans mourn other losses as well: the end of a secure relationship, loss of a homeland, loss of favourite job or even access to the local playing field to play soccer can be quite devastating for some people. Humans experience grief at any time their life role is seriously changed and can be seen to move down the slope.

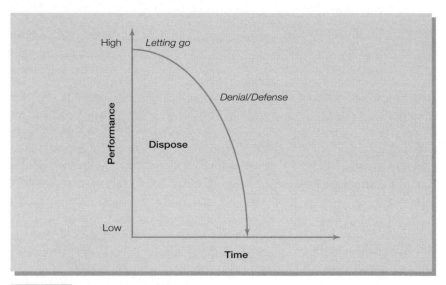

Figure 6.2 Letting-go phase

An important process in this stage of the cycle is to allow the person to express their feelings. Don't try to 'sunshine' them out of their grief or distract them from what they need to express. Recognize outbursts of anger as a natural part of the grieving process and expect people to become selfish, childish and angry. They may well experience concern, denial, shock, worry, anger, grief, excitement, depression and frustration This is the normal process and one that needs to be supported not shut down. Most importantly, watch out in case you or the client tend to avoid these grieving people just because they might be difficult to deal with.

Before people can adapt and adopt the news ways of thinking, feeling and behaving, they must unlearn – they have to let go of the maps that are of no further use. This is not the same as throwing away ideas. The brain does not erase memories, it changes the connections – renewing some, letting others fade away – under a form of selection. When we remember, we recreate memories, which are based on those strengthened or weakened connections. To rebuild our cognitive maps and emotional memories, we have to throw away the old pattern (Battram, 1999).

However, simply letting go of knowledge is not always as easy as it sounds. Because knowledge is associated with power, prestige and political clout, we are often loath to release it for others to use. In addition, unlearning is emotionally difficult because the old way of doing things has worked for a while and become embedded in our beliefs and behaviours (Schein, 1993, p. 87). We have to shift from the comfortable domain in the existing organizational environment and be prepared to migrate to the new form – we have to discard and forgo any existing mental models that might have held the status quo. This can be difficult because we often remain prisoners of our conceptual framework, where there is a general reluctance to leave the old way of thinking (Meznar, 1995).

The disposal process is critical to the change process, yet it is one that is rarely considered. Few change programmes really examine the process of unlearning and how to help people let go of redundant ideas and feelings. Unless we learn how to let go of past and redundant beliefs, then we will find it difficult to accept and embrace new forms of knowledge.

Looking forward

Once people have been able to let go and dispose of the old way of thinking and feeling, then they can start the journey to discover the new ways of being that is expected of them. The discovery phase is the point when people will look forward in anticipation of what is to come (see Figure 6.3).

Discovery is the process by which we enhance the quantity and quality of our ability to think, feel and behave. This might be through a range of processes, including reading, writing, conference presentations, working alongside someone, daydreaming or working in a management team. The one thing the processes all have in common is the acquisition of knowledge.

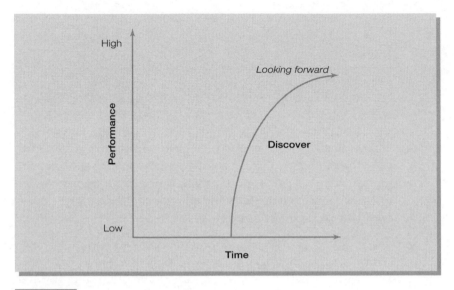

Figure 6.3 Looking-forward phase

At this stage in the change cycle the new thoughts and feelings do not have to be newly created – they only need to be new to the individual or organization. BP gives a 'Thief of the Year Award' to the person who has 'stolen' the best ideas in application development. The company recognizes that, when it comes to organizational knowledge, originality is less important than usefulness. Texas Instruments has created a 'Not Invented Here, But I Did It Anyway' award for borrowing a practice from either inside or outside the company. The knowledge-focused firm needs to have appropriate knowledge available when and where it can be applied, not just generate new ideas for their own sake.

The important point about the discovery phase is that people have to make a decision to let go of the past and move forward. Critically, this is a choice that must be made by the individual and not imposed by an outside agent. This might be an explicit decision in the form of a conscious choice to accept that they have to think, feel or behave in a new way. This might be someone who looks in the mirror and realizes that they really do need to get fitter or the company that finally accepts that the current processes are not up to scratch and they need to look for new operating models. Or it might be a tacit decision – an emerging acceptance that things must change. This might be the realization that a couple come to when they accept that problems in their relationship need to be addressed or the organization that slowly begin to focus on the real issues as more and more people surface the shadows and talk about the problems they face. Critically it is the fact that the decision must own and internalized. Without this then the change will be short-lived. For example lots of people go on a training course – but few learn. So often they have been sent by the boss and did not make the personal choice to change. Without this conscious choice to change then little knowledge acquisition or change will occur.

The looking-forward phase is important because it is a building block to the value to be created from the change. Unless people are helped to look forward and climb out of the dip that they may have hit with the letting-go phase then their personal performance will diminish over time. If the personal performance of people in the organization dips, then so will the business performance – no matter how robust the management systems and processes might be.

The Y-curve

As we bring the two stages of disposal and discovery together we see the emergence of the Y-curve – the pattern that people follow as they go through change (*see* Figure 6.4).

The Y-curve has a shaded area on where the letting-go and looking-forward phases cross. This is the point of the doldrums where nothing is moving. The person has disposed of the old way of thinking and feeling but has not yet climbed up the discover side to find a new way of being.

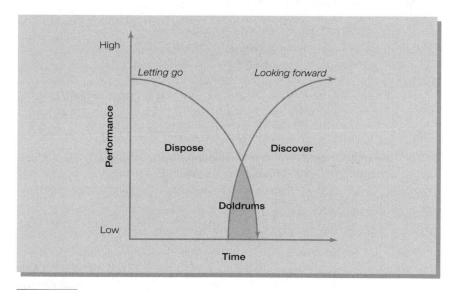

Figure 6.4   Y-curve

In *The Phantom Tollbooth* (Juster, 1971): this fantasy novel the Doldrums is where the Lethargians live. These are minute creatures who live in perpetual boredom. They change colours to match their surroundings and sometimes enforce laws against thinking and laughing. The Lethargians spend their life busily doing nothing:

Well, if you can't laugh or think, what can you do?' asked Milo.

'Anything as long as it's nothing, and everything as long as it isn't anything,' explained another. 'There's lots to do; we have a very busy schedule:

'At 8 o'clock we get up, and then we spend

'From 8:0 to 9:0 daydreaming.

'From 9:0 to 9:30 we take our early midmorning nap.

'From 9:30 to 10:30 we dawdle and delay.

'From 10:30 to 11:30 we take our late early morning nap.

'From 11:00 to 12:00 we bide our time and then eat lunch.

'From 1:00 to 2:00 we linger and loiter.

'From 2:00 to 2:30 we take our early afternoon nap.

'From 2:30 to 3:30 we put off for tomorrow what we could have done today.

'From 3:30 to 4:00 we take our early late afternoon nap.

'From 4:00 to 5:00 we loaf and lounge until dinner.

'From 6:00 to 7:00 we dillydally.

'From 7:00 to 8:00 we take our early evening nap, and then for an hour before we go to bed at 9:00 we waste time.

'As you can see, that leaves almost no time for brooding, lagging, plodding, or procrastinating, and if we stopped to think or laugh, we'd never get nothing done.'

Walk through any organization that has embarked on a change process that is not working well. Find business teams where people feel that they are not being supported, told what to do or where they are going and you will get a sense of the doldrums. These are people who are angry, moaning to each other, busily searching the web for the latest free software and doing anything they can to fill the day.

The theme of *The Phantom Tollbooth* story is that that a mind is a terrible thing to waste. In the same way it is a terrible waste to push people into the crutch of the Y-curve and not offer a ladder they can use to help themselves to climb out. This is the role of the consultant in the Seven Cs. It is to act as an expert – not to pull people out, but to offer strategies to the client by which people can be helped to find a way up the discovery curve and back to peak performance.

The D-spot

The one consistent activity that will help anyone who enters the Y-curve is to help them understand *why*. Why has the change happened, why does it affect them, why should they give up what they are doing and why do they have to do something new in the future? Without the why factor then people will often fail to step through the Y-curve and simply revert back to their old ways of thinking, feeling and behaving.

The critical point on the Y-curve is the point where the dispose phase meets the discover phase. This is the D-spot: the point where a conscious or unconscious choice needs to be made (*see* Figure 6.5). This is where to make the choice to move forward into the next stage or to reject the potential change and regress back to the previous way of thinking and feeling.

As people go down the disposal curve they will naturally get upset, angry and despondent. They will fall down the curve until they reach a point where they say enough is enough (either consciously or subconsciously): this is the point where one of three decisions can be taken (*see* Figure 6.6). The first choice that people might make is to go back to point 1. In this case

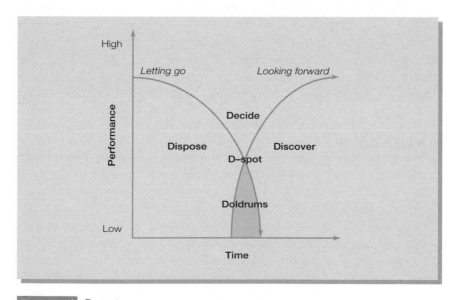

Figure 6.5 **D-spot**

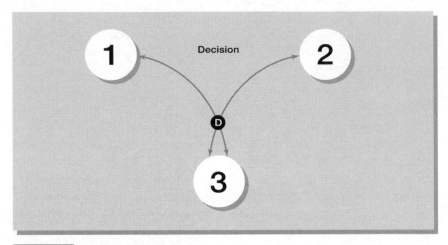

Figure 6.6 Choices at the D-spot

they will say this future position is not for me and refuse to go forward. This often happens in organizations that are embedded in rigid bureaucratic models, for example government organizations or family firms where change seems quite untenable for people who want to hold on to the current status quo. Point 2 is where people hit the low point and do not come out. They just sit feeling angry, upset and as a consequence can be quite disruptive. Point 3 is where people choose to internalize the future and move out of the dip and into a new way of thinking, feeling and behaving.

This is a choice, but not always a conscious one. The role of the consultant and client is to manage the D-spot and to help all the participants in the change process make the choice that will support the overall transformation the client wishes to achieve. It is a failure to consciously address what choices people are likely to make at the D-Spot that often leads to successful short-term change but unsuccessful long-term change.

Change spectrum

Before setting out on any change, you have to consider the strategy that will be used to underpin the transition (Hersey and Blanchard, 1972) and help make this decision to change. When push comes to shove, what rules will govern the decisions to be taken? To decide this, you need to agree what ethos will underpin the assignment. Will it be one where the client and consumers are given the freedom to decide their personal rate of adaptation or will the consultant own the process and be responsible for controlling the change? Although there are degrees between the two extremes, any change will often have a bias in one direction (*see* Figure 6.7).

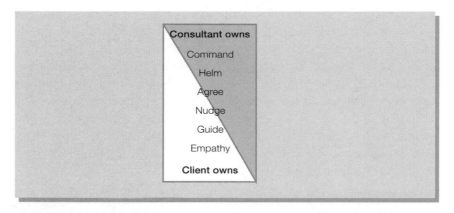

Figure 6.7 Change spectrum

At the 'client owns' end of the spectrum the assumption is that giving people a new knowledge base modifies their behaviour. This is like the government campaign that tries to stop people smoking or avoid drinking and driving. The objective is to offer people information about the destructive impact of cigarettes or drink. In the same way, an organization might try to modify behaviour by offering people knowledge about a new quality system, ideas scheme or advanced competitor product. The problem with this approach is that it can take time and often requires a high level of back-up. The benefit is that the change will last over a period of time and is not dependent on a directive transformation process.

At the other end of the spectrum, the consultant decides that urgent change is necessary and stimulates rapid behavioural change across the organization in the expectation that everyone will quickly adopt a new range of behaviours. This is seen in the way that the UK government introduced car seatbelt and motorbike helmet laws to curb the high death rate on the roads. For an organization, this type of action is seen in the introduction of new process measures, quality audits or enhanced personal objectives. Each action will be reinforced by the idea that failure to reach the prescribed target will result in some form of disciplinary action. However, although behaviours will have been modified, people are doing it under duress. In many cases, deep-set attitudes and beliefs will not have been modified. Only over time might people start to embrace the new ways of working and accept that the new knowledge is valid as part of their normal working style.

Where the consultant owns the process it is dependent on the people or system that originated the change. If the support mechanism is taken away, there is every chance that the transformation will collapse and there will be a shift back to the original behaviours. Imagine a school that has been beset with problems of ill discipline, drugs and violence. A new headteacher might be able to ride in to save the day by enforcing a code of discipline. However, until the change has worked its way deep into the culture, there will be a high level of dependency on the new head. If for any reason he or she leaves there is a chance that the old problems will return. This approach may be acceptable in a school environment, where the staff turnover rate is relatively low, but in fast-moving industries such as electronics, communications or marketing, such a strategy is risky. As people move on to new positions, so the initiatives they introduced fade away, with their replacement introducing a new set of changes.

Therefore, when a client asks about the difficulty and length of time associated with a consultancy project, they might need to be educated about the trade-offs that must be made. You might be able to deliver speed and ease of implementation but add the caveat that it might not include true and deep gain in the short term. For example, a company that wants to improve its level of quality has a decision to make. Does it look for a quick implementation, on the premise that it will be owned and driven by one of the senior managers? Or does it take a longer view and allow people to absorb and adapt to the new ideas at their own rate of change? Although you can help facilitate the decision, the ultimate responsibility for the judgement must be down to the client.

> **❝ as people move on to new positions, so the initiatives they introduced fade away ❞**

Change levels

One way to help the client make sense of the change process is to offer a simple tool that can describe the levels of change that sit across the change spectrum. At one end of the spectrum the consultant takes charge and at the other the consultant simply supports the client while they make all the choices. Working from one end to the other down the spectrum it is possible to identify six types of change:

- **Command:** The consultant owns the process and does not delegate any of the power to the client or consumers.

- **Helm:** The consultant gives away some level of control and does not have absolute power over the direction of the project, but still retains significant authority over the direction of the project.

- **Agree and negotiate:** The consultant gives away significant areas of the power, but does this through agreement (because of the desire to protect the change process).

- **Nudge:** The consultant has conceded over 50 per cent of the power to effect change to the client group. However, the consultant keeps a presence and encourages people to take small steps to try the change out – perhaps key people are encouraged to get involved so that others feel like joining in.

- **Guide:** The consultant's role is to help people to understand what is coming and how it might impact upon them. This is primarily an education intervention where the role is to help the client and consumers understand what is happening.

- **Empathy:** The consultant shows an understanding of potential problem – giving people time and space to acclimatize to the proposed change.

At any time in the change process the consultant has to make a choice as to the most appropriate level of control they need to retain and how much is managed by the client. This raises an issue that must be clearly dealt with in the Client stage of the change process: just how much control will the consultant have to effect the change process and how much do they want or need? It is the failure to agree such a simple factor that can lead to confusion and chaos in the Change stage. When this happens there is one guarantee: the client will suffer in the short term as the change falls apart and the consultant will suffer in the long term as the value of their brand is eroded.

However, assuming that the consultant does have the necessary level of control, they will have to make choices about how to deploy the control and where on the change spectrum will be most effective. They do this by taking into account the change, the client's level of experience and the client's desire to accept control of the project. Implications of managing some of the levels include:

- **Command:**

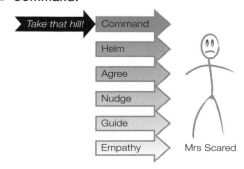

Clearly this is a powerful change process. It offers speed, simplicity, and a power of autonomy that can ensure that things get done. However, the risk is that in getting things done, people can get scared. They can be worried by the loss of jurisdiction and power and this can have a dramatic impact on the performance of the business. The moment people are scared then it might be beneficial to consider other options in the change spectrum – to help them understand why you are taking absolute control over the change.

■ **Helm:**

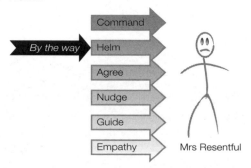

Mrs Resentful

Where the helm style is being used the consultant has handed over a degree of control to the client. This offers the benefit of signalling a desire to include others in the change process and so helps the movement towards independence. However, the risk with this approach is that by giving people a taste of the action they want more. Like the father who lets the young child play in the front garden, the child then wants to play in the street and feels resentment when the parent says no.

■ **Nudge:**

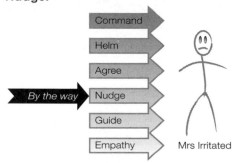

Mrs Irritated

The nudge is often used where companies need to downsize. For example, there might be a combination of factors – including legislation, union power and political implications – that prevents a company from moving to a full-blown redundancy programme. However it needs to lower the staff costs over time and so instigates a number of semi-soft actions to help nudge the people out of the door. These might include briefings in the company paper about poor market conditions, briefs to union representative about poor trade conditions, and grapevine or lobby stories about the fact that sacking will start if people do not leave. All this action leaves a large degree of control with the individual but the management offers a gentle nudge – like a tap dripping overnight. Although this strategy can (and does) work, it can become a major irritation and provoke a backlash once people become really irritated.

■ **Empathy:**

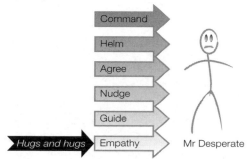

Many people would argue that it is important to give people time and responsibility to make their own choices to effect a sustainable change. However, often people do not want this. There have been many instances where teams have been left to find their own conclusion about a problem and have ended up shouting at the leader to just tell them what to do. So although empathy has its benefits, it is not always the answer.

Change spectrum options

There is no right option with the change spectrum. You need to be aware of the following:

■ What latitude do you have to regulate your control over the change activities?

■ What type of intervention does the client group prefer or expect?

■ What preference do you have? (Often consultants will favour one particular type of intervention based upon their psychological preference and personal beliefs.)

■ What budget is available to support the intervention? (The cost of effecting each of the levels will vary quite considerably – both for short and long-run costs.)

■ What internal support processes are available? (This will vary, depending on the type of change effected.)

In most cases there are no single miracle cures or single-shot solutions to deliver successful change. Single shots rarely hit a challenging target. The delivery of sustainable value through change involves introducing and sustaining multiple policies, practices and procedures across multiple units and levels. So one engagement might start with a command action by the consultant; be followed by a round of guiding or education sessions to help train the consumers and a series of nudge processes to stimulate action; and finally there will be agreement with the staff associations to open the door for movement. The key is to be able to develop a cohesive and coherent change strategy that will help realize sustainable value and not introduce the knee-jerk change that delivers short-term fixes but long- term decay.

Consumer segmentation

There will be occasions when resistance starts to stall change. All consul- tants will have war stories of the time they spent battling with a group or individual that refused to change. If this happens, it can help to segment the target audience to ensure that energy is applied in the right places. The worst thing that a client or consultant can do is to spend time and resources trying to change someone if that person does not really contribute to the end transformation process.

The change process can be considered along two specific lines of interest. First, the extent to which people are actively involved in the change. For a retail organization about to implement a new stock control system, it might be that certain groups of people are critical and need to be introduced to new ways of working at the outset. However, there will be people that might need to know about the system but whose training can take place at a later date. Second, consider the level of resistance to change. This ranges from high (where there is a real blockage to the change) down to low (where the people are quite happy to take on board the new ways of working). The different groups of people are shown in Figure 6.8.

■ **Leaders:** This quadrant includes those people who are viewed as the early adopters – people who will respond to the change initiative in a proactive and visible way. They have a critical role in the final change outcome and have a low resistance to change. Hooking in these people early gives a clear signal that the project is serious – people are buying into the new ways of working and the new model is socially acceptable. As an example, consider the cable TV company that has merged with another similar group and needs to relocate to a site over

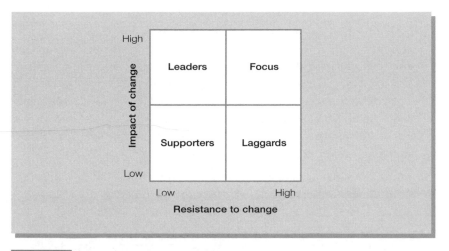

Figure 6.8   Change segmentation matrix

100 miles away. Resistance to this shift is likely to be fierce and could lead to protracted negotiations and conflict. However, it will be useful to identify one or two people who are happy with the change and are willing to support the strategic need for relocation. Their visible support sends a positive signal so that other people will become more amenable to the change.

■ **Supporters:** These are the people who have limited involvement in the change but are committed to its success. They are people who enthuse about the change but in reality it makes little difference if they decide to change or not. In the case of an IT upgrade, the small customer services team may be enthusiastic about the proposed shift to a new platform. However, the shift has actually been proposed to reduce the product delivery time. So their support is only a limited by-product of a shift elsewhere. However, if this team is committed then it makes sense to use their enthusiasm. You could use them as internal communicators, trainers or facilitators. Although their involvement might add little to the formal engagement, it might have a substantial impact on helping others to see the need for a system upgrade.

■ **Focus:** The people who fall into the focus quadrant will resist the change but must be converted to ensure success. They are the key players. If you do not identify these people early on then there is a chance that valuable resources will be deployed elsewhere. As a result, you will not be able to spend time and energy working with them to help them make the necessary change. This can be seen in the case of a project to implement a new financial package within a local government office. It might be that the government has mandated a system change to deliver the necessary data to the Treasury. However, if the chief executive does not accept that the system will add value in her domain then she will have the capability to put every possible obstacle in the way. You must put every available effort into working with the individual and her team to convince them of the benefits. Failure to shift their viewpoint will turn the project into a nightmare and might result in a loss of your future income.

■ **laggards:** These people will fiercely resist the change but have little involvement in the outcome. In many cases it is better to say, 'Fine, we will make the change in your absence and when the time is right you can make the shift in your own way'. An example is a technical department that refuses to accept the need to attend customer skills training. While the chief executive has decreed that everyone should attend a two-day event, this group has little contact with other people. The consultant could force the situation, but the end result will be a great deal of game playing by the unit manager and a disruptive crowd of people at the change workshop. By giving them the option to adopt the new techniques at their own rate, these people are able to do so in a way that suits their needs. As a result, they might become leading exponents of the need to adopt a more customer-focused approach within their work and actively start to promote this ethos to their suppliers.

Methodology

In this context, methodology refers to the underlying ethos and approach that will be used to underpin all the decisions and actions taken by the consulting team and client group.

In recent years, change has become a discipline in its own right. It is now recognized that it is important to pay attention to the underlying dynamics that drive successful business transformation. In particular, you must understand what choices you have when faced with change issues. Although these choices are many, two factors should be taken into consideration.

■ Will the programme be planned in advance of the change? Should every detail be strapped down well in advance or can things be left to chance?

■ Will receivers of the transition be aware of what is happening? Is the change to be conducted in the public domain or will it be hidden from view, so any shift is seen as happening naturally as opposed to an external change?

When considering these two drivers, it is possible to identify four schools of change management that are commonly seen in industry: accidental, backstage, controlled and debate. By looking in more detail at each of these four styles, it becomes possible to develop a simple change management matrix (*see* Figure 6.9). Each of the four quadrants has a particular management style that may be applied in different circumstances.

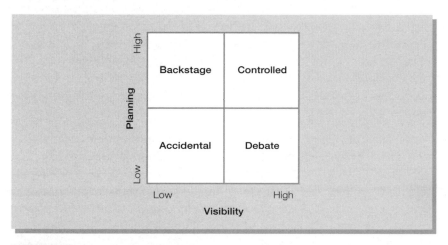

Figure 6.9   Change management matrix

Accidental style

When a group of young children play together, the overall behaviour of the group has a chaotic feel. An observer sees the chance of anything productive coming out of the antics as accidental in nature. It is often left to the capability of a single teacher to manage the demands, tantrums and excesses of over 200 apparently wild animals. However, within this zoo-like scenario, there are a number of powerful rules that control how the group operates.

The children are effectively operating as a self-organizing system. Although the teacher has set out ground rules, within these the children operate as free agents. Examples of these rules are: keep on the hard surface, no swearing or fighting, and everyone must line up for dinner at a certain time.

Since the teachers are also aware of these rules, they can initiate a change and within reason guarantee that a desired outcome is achieved.

For example, if a football is left in the playground at the start of break then within minutes a football match will start and will keep the children amused for the duration of the break. Alternatively, just drawing some white lines will trigger specific games associated with the patterns. The children also understand that if the teacher suddenly walks out into the middle of the area and blows a whistle, they are expected to stop what they are doing and listen for instructions.

Let's assume that organizations can operate in a similar fashion by conforming to a shared set of common rules and norms. As a result, rather than trying to dominate and deliver an outcome, some consultants might choose to spend their time trying to understand the rules that drive an organization. Once understood, they can make engagements that might seem chaotic or random but which will deliver the desired outcome. The engagements are not highly planned and have little visibility – but they still have a clear purpose.

For example, a regional manager within a retail organization might have a level of stock wastage higher than the industry norm. It must be reduced to an acceptable level. Clearly one option is to issue dictates, discipline people or change the formal stock control procedures. Now this might 'apparently' work but the ingrained behaviours are likely to surface once the manager's attention is focused elsewhere. However, by using the accidental methodology, the manager might attempt to understand what rules or norms drive the wastage to happen and why it is seen to be acceptable by local managers. It might be that, at the store level, wastage costs are attributed to a hidden budget line, visible only to the regional manager and the finance department. This rule means that the operational managers are not actually affected by the wastage, so it is not part of their frame of reference. By simply changing the bonus indicators, for example, the regional manager might be able to deliver a radical reduction in wastage. The change will have been managed without any real control or planning and its visibility would have been limited, but the end result is a successful change.

This is clearly a high-risk strategy and is reliant upon the trust of the organization to adopt any changes that are promoted by the management team. The consultant's role in this management style is more about helping to develop a suitable environment for the change to occur rather than formalizing any direct approach.

Backstage style

Millions of people watched the movie *Titanic*. The boat scenes are amazing, to the point where the audience believes they are actually part of the production. Although star actors play a critical frontstage role, it is often the backstage people that can make or break such a film. Compare the technical prowess of *Titanic* with the out-takes shown on television: doors won't open, walls fall over and props fail to perform. Taking these two scenarios together, the power of the backstage processes is apparent.

The key to managing any backstage process is preparation, preparation and more preparation. Just to generate a simple scene in a film will take hours of pre-production effort. This process is invisible to the audience since they just see a two-second jump off a cliff. In the same way, some transformation programmes are stage-managed by consultants. The installation of a new IT system, the shift to a new quality directive or the adoption of a new legal ruling, will all be highly managed and planned but will in the main be invisible to the end user until the point of handover.

❝ the key to managing any backstage process is preparation, preparation and more preparation ❞

The change process is often concerned with the exercise of power, persuasion and political skills. It involves intervening in political and cultural systems, influencing, negotiating and selling ideas and meaning to the owners and recipients of the change and mobilizing the necessary power to effect the backstage activity (Buchanan and Body, 1992).

Imagine that you are to install a new quality system into a medium-sized manufacturing company. You might choose to operate across a number of backstage areas. The first step is to agree the content of the system with the directors of the company, since the structure of any quality system will potentially lock in a set of standards and processes. Next, you might need to undertake a degree of negotiation with all the key stakeholders to ensure that the content of the system fits with their map of the world. Firstly, much of the backstage work will be focused on managing people's feelings. The quality system is right for the business, but if people 'feel' upset or concerned about its adoption then the whole change process will be fraught with problems. So although there will be effort applied in developing the new system, a large chunk of the work will be focused on the backstage issues – the unseen aspects that will never be apparent to the end user.

The backstage model is one that people use intuitively every day. Persuading the child to eat their cabbage, hiding a pill in the dog's food, or flirting with the boss's PA so as to get some time in the diary. The question to consider is the extent to which such stage-management is undertaken as a manipulative tool for personal gain. When it is overtly used, you must be careful that you are not seen as using the process in a duplicitous way just to further your personal goals. Working with a client group always involves a degree of suspicion about your actions. When this model is used it is therefore imperative that it is used openly and without any hidden agendas. This does not mean that you tell everyone what is happening, but that if people ask about the process being used then you take time to explain it.

Controlled style

This type of change is like the processes used to manage a large construction project such as the Channel Tunnel. The scale and risk of such projects mean that everything down to the last nut and bolt must be forecast and controlled to ensure that the change is managed to time, cost and quality.

The control model is based upon a deterministic framework. The consultant makes the assumption that it is possible to predict and control the future according to a set of rules. Plans are made, resources booked and people hired, all on the premise that the change will follow a known path. The change is then managed using the exception method, where the goal is to minimize any variance or disturbance in the system. Accidents will be frowned upon, deviation is not allowed and failure to hit a milestone will cause apoplexy.

Where the surrounding issues are managed by the consultant or client then this approach is clearly effective. However, where you or the client do not control all the levers then it is quite dangerous. Building a rigid plan and locking people into a controlled system puts all of the eggs definitely in one basket and sudden changes in the environment can result in costly and time-consuming last-minute actions.

This methodology is perfect for the delivery of fixed outcomes, particularly where the plan is built using logical cause and effect reasoning. This is why it is used so frequently in the construction of missiles, houses and a host of other projects. However, its success is dependent on your ability to control all the environmental factors.

Debate style

Think about the case of a merger between two large organizations. Project managers, probably using the control methodology outlined above, will wrap up all the mechanistic issues. However, there will be elements of the merger that cannot be managed using a highly planned style. In particular, how will the two cultures come together?

When you try to merge cultures, the desired outcome is reasonably clear but it is very difficult to plan down to the last detail what will happen and when. People are people and have their biases, preferences and particular styles of thinking and behaving. Any action plan will have some critical milestones or tasks, but there is still likely to be much debate as people struggle to come to terms with new ways of working. Only through a process of sharing and working together will people start to understand what value their new partners will be able to contribute.

The debate style of change is seen in many areas. Think about the traditional way that a senior team will develop vision and values. It often falls to a consultant to organize a workshop. This will be preceded by a meeting with each of the directors to develop an understanding of their beliefs about company values. This initiates the debate process, in which each person is encouraged to talk about their views on what the company values should be and offers people the necessary time and space to share their schematic view of the world. As they talk to the consultant, people start to firm up their beliefs so that once they get to the workshop they will have a clearer view of their desired outcome. At the workshop, these personal schemas are displayed, shared and (if all goes well) will merge to become a shared schema – one that is communicated to a wider audience.

Another example is the way that strategy can slowly develop within an organization. One view is that the control approach should be used, where logical processes are used to build a corporate strategy. Another view is that strategy emerges from dialogue and debate that goes on between the key players in the business. This might happen in formal meetings, but in many cases it is the odd comment as people meet in corridors or coffee rooms.

The debate model happens all the time but is often not recognized. As a process it is difficult to recognize because it is so natural and embedded in the content of the change. Trying to understand how a decision was made, or a mission or strategy developed can be quite painful – people struggle to understand how the change took place. However, the benefit is that when this style of change is used, it is locked in at the desire level in the change ladder. Therefore, the change will have a greater degree of passion and permanence.

Four-quadrant model

Bringing these change styles together results in the four-quadrant model seen in Figure 6.9. In this simple matrix each quadrant represents one style: accidental, backstage, control and debate. This suggests that in many cases you might have to take a decision to use one particular style. Should the change be controlled or is it best to take the accidental route? Should the development of the outcome be through open debate or is it more appropriate to push the discussion into the backstage and develop answers that people are mandated to follow?

However, it is possible to offer a holistic framework – a hybrid model that builds on the strengths of each of the four quadrants and yet tries to avoid their weaknesses. By drawing upon each of the four quadrants, it becomes possible to develop another option, that of the emergent style – a fifth way that sits in the middle of the matrix (*see* Figure 6.10).

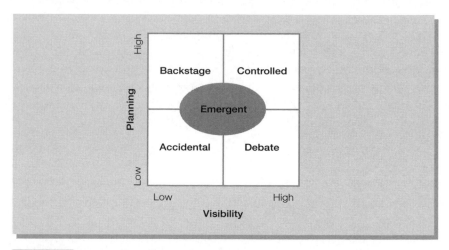

Figure 6.10   Emergent change

Emergent style

If a group of people decides to travel around the world on a backpacking holiday, which of the four styles would be appropriate? The accidental approach is exciting but could leave the group sitting as hostages in a war zone. The backstage model would be ineffective because only the travel agent would know the itinerary. The control model seems to be the most practical, but using a deterministic approach in a chaotic world will only lead to frustration and cost increases as the group struggles to get back in line with 'the plan'. Finally, the debate model is inappropriate since the group might have fun discussing where to go next but the trip will probably take three years longer than expected. The option is to adopt a change process that allows for clearly defined outcomes but with the flexibility to be adaptive.

The emergent model allows an agreed outcome to be delivered through people interacting according to their own sets of behaviour. It creates a framework for action without specifying the action to be taken. As consultant, you will set the goals, boundaries and basic operating rules but leave the action and detail up to those directly involved in the engagement. The benefit is the development of a flexible plan that allows people to respond to changes.

This type of approach is often seen in culture development programmes where the end goal may be understood but the deployment process needs to be flexible enough to cope with the needs of different managers. Imagine that you have been asked to deal with a problem of poor morale in a large corporation. You might have agreed a measurable outcome with your client but the actual processes and tools can only be determined once you are inside the system. This is because the needs of the group rather than your client's needs drive the choice of a change tool. For example, if the morale issues are in the open and being discussed at a team meeting then it is useful to rely on peer review and open events between people and their managers. If, however, the issues are buried deep in the culture then focus groups and one-on-one coaching sessions are more appropriate.

Five-segment model

In the five-segment model, each of the four primary models (accidental, backstage, control and debate) has a clear role to play in managing change. However, when change is being managed according to one of the four primary styles, any deviation from the preferred approach is viewed as a failure. Hence, the person running a project using the control model might view deviation and variability as a problem. Similarly, someone using the accidental style might forcibly resist any attempt by the organization to impose formal controls or milestones on to the engagement.

The emergent school of change is something that people use all the time but not always knowingly. For example, it is used in a manager's diary system. A manager's life is often in tension between planned and unplanned events. It is a battle between order and disorder, seen in the deletions and changes to most people's diaries. However, it is the practised ability to manage unplanned and emergent interactions that allows a manager to respond to changes in the marketplace. Once the boundaries are set and simple rules are understood then it is possible to create a balance between accidental and controlled change.

Although this model segments your approach into five different methodologies, clearly it is never so simplistic. Any change methodology must be focused entirely on the needs of the client and the context, so each change process is unique. However, what this model does highlight is that there are alternatives to the more typical command and control approach to managing change.

Usually the change process will use all the options at different times. Imagine you have been asked to lead a project team to develop a new Christmas toy. You only have nine months left to design, develop and deliver the toy to the shops. With such a tight deadline, and with the fact that the environment is under your control, you may well opt to take a control approach – clearly setting out the goals, milestones and delivery dates for each of the project teams. However, you should also recognize that this is a creative as well as a delivery process and as such it would be unwise to constrain people's freedom to innovate and make mistakes. Therefore, you may also try to ensure that the lower-level change processes have a degree of freedom and space so that people can experiment within the teams. A map of the change style used for different elements within the project might look like the list set out in Table 6.2.

> **" the decision to adopt a particular change style is not black and white "**

The decision to adopt a particular change style is not black and white and in many cases might not actually be a decision that has to be taken. In some cases, it is best to let things happen naturally and simply be aware of the choice that is made in case things start to go wrong.

| Table 6.2 | Change styles within a project |

Project activity	Change style
Project plan	**Control:** This is necessary because of the fixed delivery date and the ability to manage the close environment
Review meetings	**Debate:** This allows the necessary flexibility to find out how the project is progressing, but with space for some shadow issues to surface
Design meetings	**Accidental:** The need to offer the designers space to innovate is paramount at this stage
Customer focus groups	**Accidental:** The primary goal is understand the customers' expectations and to give them the space to talk and describe their feelings
Pilot trials	**Control:** Since feedback from this stage will affect the launch decision, the marketing data must be very accurate and controlled
Measurement process	**Backstage:** Since the primary focus should be on delivery of the product, the goal is to keep any project measurement procedures to a minimum: they will only operate in the background, using exception reports where issues surface

Energy mapping

By definition, change is about modifying the status quo – managing a shift from one state to another. This transfer requires energy. It might be the energy required to climb on the exercise bike; that burst of energy to read the latest management book; or the physical and emotional energy required to run yet another quality workshop. Alternatively, it is the energy required to stop something or someone from taking action when they want to be a change inhibitor. Just think how often you work with an organization where people spend more time stopping action from happening rather than making a change work. In a change process you need to have a clear appreciation of where energy will come from and how it might affect the change. Carter (1999) makes this point when he suggests that:

The energy that people put into organizations is absorbed in a number of ways. Some of it is used for actually doing things for the customer, such as adding value to a product or service, but little of it is directly productive in this way. Much of it is spent communicating with other people within the organization, co-ordinating activities, planning, motivating, managing, being managed.

To understand how this energy can affect a change, you might map three aspects:

- the source
- the mass
- the direction.

You can then set out a strategy to harness the energy and use it to support the change. Or you might develop counteracting energies that will help to overcome any resisting forces.

Energy source

This is how and where energy is dissipated across an organization. Simplistically, power is bestowed as part of the formal governance system (in reality power germinates and accumulates in a range of areas within any system as a result of energy used). When you are dealing with an organization, you must determine where the power lies. Then you must use this knowledge to determine what strategy will be appropriate to influence how the energy is directed and applied.

Consider a touring group performing Shakespeare. If you look closely it would be possible to deconstruct the energy within the group – to identify who owns and dispenses different type of energy and so power. One of the group might manage the finances; another the interactions with the various theatre managers; yet another might act as the group's soul, with the energy to ensure that effective relationships are maintained within the group. It is possible to map the various energy levels and, more importantly, how the energy is deployed within the group.

The same idea can be applied to organizational change. Looking around any organization, it is possible to see where the various streams of energy sit. Some of the possible groups are:

- **Financial:** In many organizations you only have to walk through the door to realize that the financial controllers have their hands on the tiller. Evidence is in the construction of the tender documents, the people that have to sign off your contract or the extent to which financial prudence dictates the building decoration.

- **Operational:** In some types of business the operations managers are seen as the gods. In organizations where production lines are key to the business, they will dictate what changes are acceptable and how programmes should be implemented.

■ **Professional:** In some companies the professional groups hold control over the key decision-making processes. For example, lawyers, IT specialists or marketing groups often feel that they are above transformation programmes and do not need to be involved.

■ **Interest groups:** Sometimes the power actually exists outside the organization. In the UK, for example, government regulatory bodies hold sway over the regulated industries. In other countries lobby groups have amassed power over the petroleum industry.

■ **Customer facing groups:** In professional service firms there is often an absolute focus on the customer experience. For example, in large consulting or accounting firms, the core driver for all resource allocation and decision making takes place on the yield figure, so the billable time booked to the customer is key. Since any transformation programme will take people away from this billing activity, you will have to justify the true business value of any change.

These groups may not be the absolute sources of energy within an organization, but they do highlight how energy can surface in different shapes and forms. Your role is to build an ability to smell out where the sources of power originate when developing the change implementation programme. However, simply understanding where the power resides is not enough. You also need to determine the extent of the power under each group's control.

Energy mass

The mass of a body in terms of the physical world is its weight, which is measured in terms of its inertia or resistance to acceleration. This mass is actually nothing more than a bundle of energy – even when an object is at rest it has energy stored in its mass. Within an organization, it is possible to consider the energy sources in terms of their ability to release energy.

In any organization, different functions will have differing energy levels. So for one company it might be that the finance department has a significant mass of energy and is able to exert a great deal of influence over the business. In another business it might be that the IT group has a significant energy level but its true ability to exert a force over the company is limited because the real energy is held by the customer-facing teams. To understand the energy mass within a system, it can help to calibrate it against a set of levels:

■ **Dense:** Absolute power and energy to drive or resist change within a business.

- ▓ **Medium:** Some energy to effect a control over the change process but is subservient to the dense groups.

- ▓ **Light:** Limited energy to effect change and will always lose to the medium and dense groups.

Thus the IT department with a light mass level will not be able to force through an idea in opposition to a finance department that has a medium or heavy mass. Although many groups with a light mass level do attempt to take on the stronger opponent, the reality is that unless they are adept political animals they will waste their time and energy in a fruitless battle.

Trying to find a way to map these energy levels accurately can be difficult. One way is to look at the profiles that the groups promote within the organization. Who is featured in the internal house magazines? Which people sit on the financial approval committees? Who has the ear of the managing director? Finally, and most important, whose budgets are cut first every time there is a reduction in expenditure? Across most industries, training is the first budget to be reduced when a downturn comes – this is indicative of the limited mass that the personnel function is seen to have.

This approach to mapping energy mass does not offer the definitive answer but it might help to point you in the right direction. The other approach is to follow the money. In the majority of cases the dominant group will have a significant amount of influence over the way that cash is received and distributed.

Energy direction

The final issue to consider when mapping the energy sources within an organization is their direction. Imagine a company facing a crisis. Sales are falling, costs are rising and the market does not look rosy. In the midst of this the marketing director suggests that part of the problem is the fact that the espoused brand values are not being lived by the customer-facing teams. So while the company sells its products on the basis of 'a quality product with a quality service', the service end is not being delivered. There are reports from customers of rudeness and inefficiencies, and the marketing director believes this is causing sales to fall. The marketing director therefore proposes that the company embark on an organization-wide 'living what we value' programme, where everyone goes through an intensive series of workshop and coaching session. Clearly, in such a difficult time, this individual might find it difficult to introduce a change programme that will temporarily raise costs. The key point will be what energy other directors have in resisting his proposal and in particular where the energy is directed. If the finance director has sufficient mass, and chooses to focus it in the marketing director's direction, then the change programme might well be blocked. However, it might be that the finance director has the mass to stop the proposition but chooses to focus energy on the engineering functions in the belief that their costs are the cause of the problems. If this is the case, then the marketing director can use this space to push the change programme through.

So when trying to understand how any one person or group is targeting their energy, it is possible to allocate it to one of three categories:

▓ **Driver:** A positive force that is supportive of the change.

▓ **Doubtful:** An in-between force – not quite a supporter but not quite willing to resist any change process.

▓ **Driven:** An energy source opposed to the ideas put forward by the consultant – so has to be pushed to take every action.

Allocating such a category to any person or group is bound to be at worst a guess and at best open to contradiction, but it does have some useful benefits. The first is that it offers a benchmark against which other stake-holders can be calibrated. Although as an absolute measure it is inaccurate, at a relational level it is possible to build an accurate picture of your supporters and opponents. Second, it offers a dialogue tool that helps to clarify the views of different individuals. Often when people come together to effect a change, each will have different experiences of the various power brokers and independent views of their orientation towards the project. Bringing these views together into a single picture helps to create consistency within the project team.

Energy map

By now you should have calibrated where the energy is contained within the organization. This will indicate both the energy level and where this force is directed. Now you can construct a map, to bring this knowledge into a single view.

Imagine a company is being pressured into adopting an environmental quality programme. Figure 6.11 shows how an outside pressure group is threatening to take the company to court if it does not implement a new environmental directive. The legal department realizes that the company must take urgent action, but the work will incur significant cost and disruption. The net result is that the legal department is applying pressure to three key organizational groups: the finance department, the operations managers and the customer service groups. The legal department has sufficient mass within the business to drive the latter two groups to change without much resistance. However, when dealing with the finance team, it is tackling a group that has more mass and so will have a problem in trying to effect a change. The map indicates that in trying to take on the finance team, the professional unit is unlikely to succeed. However, if it uses the additional energy contained within the operations and customer facing groups, the combined force might well offer sufficient power to effect a change.

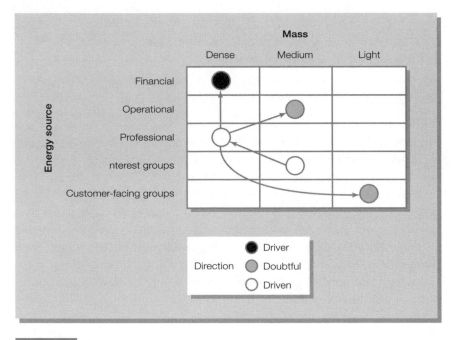

Figure 6.11 Energy map

This approach is not about accurately calculating the energy within any group in relation to another group. But it should be possible to calibrate such detail intuitively and use the knowledge to ensure that blockage does not occur.

7

Stage five: Confirm

Not everything that can be counted counts,
and not everything that counts can be counted.

Albert Einstein

With any new engagement, passion flames when you first met the client, curiosity emerges as you clarify the situation, adrenaline begins to flow when creating new ideas and the real buzz emerges when making a change. However, when the excitement is over, someone has to confirm that what was wanted has actually been delivered. At this point, everyone looks around to find a willing victim, someone who is prepared to put his or her neck on the line to measure the outcome.

Your motto must be 'Start to measure before you start'. You would not start a diet and then wait three weeks to see if you had lost any weight. Unless you take an initial measurement, there is no way to confirm that the change has been effective. So although the Confirm stage is shown at a relatively late point in the cycle, this does not mean that you should wait until the change has been completed before thinking about the issue.

Even when you first agree the contract, it will have insufficient bite to make it worth signing unless you have thought about the measurement process. As an ideal, the contract should include both the process of measurement and the targets that are to be achieved. However, if the situation is one where a degree of uncertainty exists about the outcome at the start, then the measures will be implied in the goal and objective statement used in the contract.

The following seven steps are offered in the Confirm stage:

- **Responsibility:** Agree who will own and manage the measurement process.
- **Climb the ladder:** Decide where on the change ladder should the measurement take place.
- **Cockpit confirmation:** Set the end point in terms of cognitive, affective and behavioural criteria.
- **Quantitative–qualitative mix:** Ensure that a rich mix of soft and hard measures are employed.
- **Measure thrice, cut once:** Understand the impact of the timing of the change on the perception of the outcome and your final remuneration.
- **Confirm the costs:** Analyze the impact of cost on the different measurement processes and the types of costs found in the Confirm stage.

All too often, the charge levelled at the consulting profession is that its people do not stop around to see how any transformation process turns out. Although the outcomes of the change may not be expected until a later date, you need to ensure that the measurement phase is clearly designed and locked in as part of the cycle. By applying the seven Confirm steps, you will ensure that real clarity is gained and that your client understands the process by which the outcomes will be measured.

Responsibility

The first step is to agree who will own and manage the measurement process. The client, consumer, external verifier, stakeholders and yourself all have a valid reason for owning the measurement process, but all might have a hidden agenda as well. Perhaps you need to prove that the change has been a success and the client needs to identify areas that have not worked so as to question the amount being billed. There is no one answer to this conundrum as it will always depend on the context in which the confirmation process is taking place. However, it is possible to offer a model by which the debate can take place in a structured and controlled manner.

It is important to appreciate the importance of schematic variation and the need to bring together people's separate mental models. An individual's schematic map acts like a filter – letting some things through and screening out others. It helps to bring certain elements of the world into focus while making others blurred and fuzzy so that they are ignored or overlooked. It is this screening process that causes a problem with the measurement stage, since two people staring at the same object or issue can view it from totally different perspectives. While one person might think that the quality project has resulted in a reduction in faults, the other might feel that training costs were so high that it will take years to recover the investment.

ff your goal is to bring together the players' perspectives to give a sense of balance to the measurement process JJ

Your goal is to being together all the players' perspectives to give a sense of balance to the measurement process. As any boating enthusiast will appreciate, it is impossible to get an accurate bearing by taking a single point of reference, since a true position can only be determined by taking two independent references. It is through this process of triangulation that a true position is derived and it is by the same process that you can confirm that the correct output has been achieved. When confirmation of the change process is required, as least two of the players shown in Figure 7.1 should be involved.

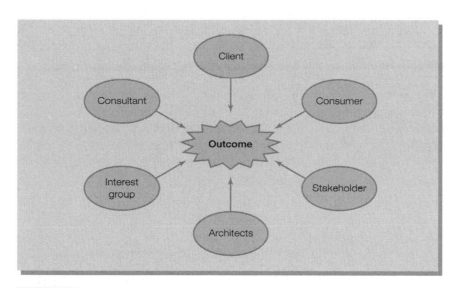

Figure 7.1 Different perspectives

This triangulation process can include any mix of players. The most common triangulation will be one that uses you and the client. The problem here is that the real issues that are being faced by the consumer are poten-tially left out of the equation. For example, when reviewing the outcomes associated with re-engineering, your view might be that you have delivered the agreed reduction in time to market and the client's view is that the overall costs of the business will be reduced. The problem is that no one is around to voice the issues that have surfaced as a result of the change. The increase in sick leave, reduced quality and general cultural dissent are all potential issues that would not be picked up in this triangulation.

The natural response is to include the consumers in the confirmation process. However, who then raises the concerns of the interest groups and the fact that the change might result in a serious gender or racial bias within the company? You must understand this problem and be able to take on a multiple personality role – to be able to represent objectively the views of the various actors and ignore the subjective personal interests within the engagement. Although this is difficult in the short term, by presenting an approach grounded in integrity, the long-term payback more than covers any losses. If you are able to demonstrate the capability to deliver a reasoned and impartial view on the success of the change then this increases the chance of gaining further contracts.

So at the end of the engagement your aim must be to stand in the shoes of each of the various groups and experience how the change might look and feel to them. For the re-engineering project there might be real evidence that the social structure of the organization has been damaged; for the consumers perhaps a fear culture has surfaced; and for the financial stake-holders there may be an indication that the financial investors are not happy about the change strategy. If you decide to ignore these feelings and thoughts, they may well create problems in the future. If there are confirmation issues for any of the players, then it is better to deal with them immediately rather than waiting for them to fester.

Climb the ladder

In the Client stage of the Seven Cs life cycle (*see* Chapter 3) we tried to understand what the problem really is: what type of change the client believes would be needed, what the 'real' problem is and the likelihood of being able to effect a sustainable change within the given confines. The tool used to map and measure this is the change ladder. This deconstructs the system that is to be acted upon into component parts, each of which contribute to the success of the change intervention. It also makes sense to use this tool in the Confirm stage, as it will demonstrate if the change has been successful across all five levels on the ladder (*see* Figure 7.2).

It is a failure to measure the change delivered on all five levels that so often leads to the accusation of poor service by the consultants. For example, it is very easy to put a new computer system in (asset) along with a few processes (blueprint), but unless people have been trained and want to use this system then it may look bright and shiny but will not be used. Conversely, you may have spent a week in the rain and fog dragging people back and forth across rivers as part of a team motivation programme (desire) and in support of a new vision (ethos), but unless the engineers have got the right tools and equipment to do their job (asset) then it will all have been a waste of money.

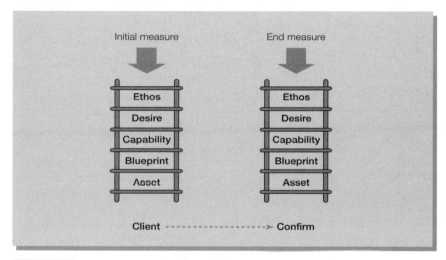

Figure 7.2   Using the change ladder at the Client and Confirm stages

The difficulty comes in trying to define the types of measures that can be used on the five levels. Although some of the measures can be relatively simple (count the boxes, measure the process, ask people to sit a test) others can be difficult because they are intrinsic to the people going through the change process. Table 7.1 offers examples of diferent measurement processes for the five levels on the change ladder.

Table 7.1   Measurement processes

Level	Factor	Measurement process
Ethos	Espoused: What they 'say' is important	▧ Language used
		▧ Company promotions
		▧ Senior manager's conference speech
		▧ Budget allocation (sometimes)
		▧ Published priorities
	Actual: What their behaviour demonstrates as important	▧ What people actually do when not in the spotlight
		▧ What people do under pressure
		▧ What people say in private
		▧ Actual business priorities
		▧ Listing beliefs in priority order
		▧ What money is actually spent on
		▧ How time is actually spent – reading past not projected diary
		▧ Choosing what to give up – what would be given up first?
Desire	Primary: What they say they want to achieve	▧ Company vision statement
		▧ Published strategic plans
		▧ The need for extrinsic support and pressure
		▧ Lists of things to do and well-prepared plans
		▧ The use of logical or head language to describe
	Secondary: What they really want to do	▧ Unpublished strategic plans
		▧ Genuine advocacy in conversation
		▧ Projects undertaken with intrinsic energy
		▧ Speed – what people rush to achieve may be an indicator of strength of motivation
		▧ Willingness to defend when faced with criticism of the goal
		▧ How time and money is spent
		▧ The use of emotional language
Capability	Explicit: Codified and captured capabilities	▧ Demonstrable skills, ideas and emotions
		▧ Practical tests that determine level of capability

Level	Factor	Measurement process
		■ Written tests, e-tests and remote observation
		■ Job descriptions, process descriptions and people specifications
	Tacit: Intangible and intuitive capabilities	■ Longitudinal studies – to understand application of skill over time
		■ Personal association – to feel the skill
		■ Response in pressured situations
		■ Stories, anecdotes and metaphor
		■ Personal construct theory
		■ Critical incident analysis
Blueprint	Structured: Planned approach to organizing	■ Observation of process in action
		■ Sample technology
		■ Survey processes
		■ Statistical process analyis
	Flexible: Adaptable way of organizing	■ Input/output comparison
		■ Deviation tests to ensure boundary limits are not exceeded
		■ Longitudinal observation – degree of variance over time
		■ Parallel running – A/B testing to compare systems
Asset	Functional: Practical use of asset	■ Is it physically there?
		■ Can it be counted – how many are there?
		■ What space does it take?
		■ Depreciation rate
		■ Rate of decay
		■ Can it be easily replaced?
	Symbolic: Emotional meaning attached to asset	■ What would people do if you tried to take it away
		■ How they respond when you install it
		■ Possibility of industrial action
		■ Potential resignations
		■ What could be done to replace it?
		■ Will it help attract new people?

The change ladder offers a powerful tool that will confirm if the change has been successful. This is not just at the relatively easy levels – where a good result is obvious by an object's presence – but also in areas that both client and consultant may shy away from. What often happens is that the consultant and client both agree to measure the new system, process, policy, structure (delete as necessary) using tried common techniques. Is the system working, has performance gone up, are people using it, does it do what it says on the packet? All these measures tend to be at the asset (function), blueprint (structure) and capability (explicit) levels. When only these measures are used it becomes very easy for people to fake a positive outcome.

Just think about the number of people who buy a new treadmill or exercise bike after the excess of Christmas. Come the next dinner party they proudly shows their friends the new machine (asset: functional), enthusiastically points to the exercise schedule they have put on the wall (blueprint: structure) and even jumps on for a few minutes to demonstrate how to use the machine. The reality is that six months later (at best) it is just another exercise bike that sits waiting to be used. At worst it is sent to the car boot sale as the owner desperately tries to recoup some of the investment. The problem here is that the measurement took place at the easy levels. What the dinner party guests did not do was challenge why the host had a huge plate of chips when he needed to lose weight (ethos), why he talks about the need to do something every time they meet but it always seems to be jam tomorrow (desire) and why when he got on the machine did it take him a while to remember how to set the special features up (capability: tacit). However, the guests would not challenge the host on these things because it can seem rude and confrontational. So they smile happily, nod and agree how great the machine is and how it will help him to lose weight.

What we can see when confirming change using the change ladder is a sense of cognitive and affective dissonance. Like the smoker who knows that smoking has the potential to kill them they still find reasons to make a choice to have another cigarette. The same can be seen with the managing director who believes that they are best able to deliver high performance when the stockholders do not constrain them with rules but then turn round and argue the case for imposing even more process controls on the operational teams.

It is cowardice not to ask the right question, at the right time and of the right people: avoiding these questions leads to short-term fix but long-term failure. It is easy to measure at A and B (asset and blueprint) on the change ladder, but it is the brave client and consultant who opt to measure at D and

E (desire and ethos). It is an even braver set of people who are then prepared to share openly the measures they get at this level!

Cockpit confirmation

When commercial pilots fly a plane, they navigate by following a series of radio navigation beacons (VORs), which take them from their departure point through to the destination. While on the ground at the departure airport the pilot will enter all the en-route navigation aids and the flight level they want to fly at and the onboard computers calculate the track, identify the routings required and also calculate arrival time, fuel usage etc. During the flight, they have onboard equipment, which picks up the signals from these VORs and tells them the track to fly and the distance from the beacon. Meanwhile air traffic control (ATC) may call up and ask the aircraft to make deviations from its planned route to avoid conflicting traffic; the aircraft makes these deviations and at some point is given permission to resume track until finally it arrives at its destination. So there is an initial plan with precise measurements of time, distance, fuel, etc., which is then modified as the journey progresses to take into account ATC, weather avoidance etc. until finally the plane arrives at its destination.

The flight stage can be compared to the Change stage in the Seven Cs process because of the need to balance two conflicting goals – to maintain a steady direction but be flexible in the face of unexpected surprises. However, the closer to the final destination the plane is the less scope there will be for variation in the flight. The need to increase directional accuracy will increase because quite simply the pilot does not want to overshoot the runway. In the same way, the consultant will need to be flexible in how the change is managed but will need to become more focused in the Confirm stage. Neither the client not the consultant want to overshoot or undershoot the goals and objectives agreed in the Client stage of the engagement.

Aeroplanes now land at airports that do not have vast expanses of vacant ground around them. They have to land in highly congested areas, where any deviation from the landing plan would result in death and destruction. To do this, airlines use the instrument landing system (ILS), which is especially useful in conditions of poor visibility. A plane fitted with appropriate equipment can approach an airport and receive high-precision signals from an instrument landing system: it is automatically guided down on to the runway, has its engines throttled back and its brakes applied, all without the aid of the pilot. Now fitted to many airliners, the system was first tried experimentally in 1964 and first used commercially in 1965.

In the cockpit, the pilot has a flight display as seen in Figure 7.3, which has a lateral scale (called localizer) and a vertical scale (called glide slope) next to the altitude display. This display indicates where the plane is in relation to the ILS beam. The pilot can use these displays to define where the plane is in the descent, if it is off track and then make a corresponding adjustment to the landing. It is the ability to fly against a reference beam that enables the pilot to land in conditions that would otherwise make the flight impractical and dangerous.

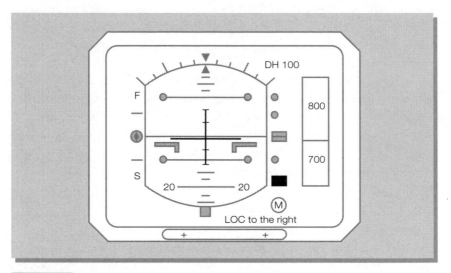

Figure 7.3　Flight display

In the same way, an effective consultant will be able to plot a directional heading and set a course to deliver the change programme, even when hampered by poor visibility and bad conditions. To do this, the consultant has to find reference measures that provide an indication of success and use these as the landing reference points.

the one common reference point for all change programmes will be people

The one common reference point for all change programmes will be people. No matter what change is being delivered, the success of the project will be impacted by the people's desire, understanding and capability to use the resulting product.

All human beings have three core dimensions that impact how they manage and respond to change. The key dimensions are affective (how people feel about the change), cognitive (what they know or understand) and behavioural (what they actually do). These three dimensions can be described as the heart, head and hand drivers (*see also* Chapter 3):

- **Heart:** Evaluates the affective domain – the way in which we deal with things emotionally, such as feelings, values, appreciation, enthusiasms, motivations and attitudes. For example, consider a corporate change programme where a new system has been installed. The heart factors to be measured might include how people feel about the system, whether they are angry about the way it has been implemented, what language is used to describe the system, or they feel the system impacts upon the business performance. Techniques to do this might include focus groups, peer observation, diaries or open-door sessions.

- **Head:** Evaluates the cognitive domain, which includes the recall or recognition of specific facts, procedural patterns, and concepts that serve in the development of intellectual abilities and skills. This is often a tested written test or a performance test. A criterion-referenced evaluation focuses on how well someone knows something against a known standard or criterion. You can also use norm-referenced evaluation, which focuses on how well a learner performs in comparison with peers. In the example of the new system installation, a head test will ensure that people understand how to use the system, know how to deal with specification upgrades, how to follow the processes, or how to describe problems to the service engineers.

- **Hand:** Evaluates the ability to do something physical. This is measured in terms of speed, precision or techniques in execution. A performance test is also a criterion-referenced test if it measures against a set standard or criterion. A performance test that evaluates who can perform a task the quickest would be a norm-referenced performance test. In the newly installed system example, you might measure the capability of people to translate their feelings and knowledge into tangible behaviours. The test might be to observe people using the system while dealing with a client call, or peer training at a team meeting to cross-test performance standards.

Although the specific engagement will have a set of specific measures that relate to the function specification of the process or system being implemented, it is important to understand and manage these three dimensions. It is all very well implementing the biggest and brightest new system in town, but unless the users care for it, know how to use it and can use it under pressure then the investment will have a limited return.

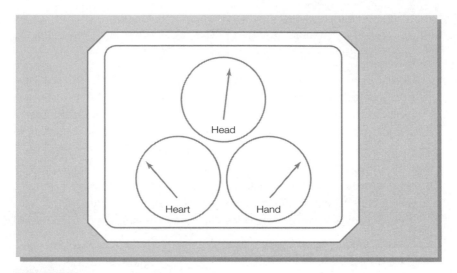

Figure 7.4   Confirm cockpit display

This is where you can use the idea of the confirm cockpit (*see* Figure 7.4). In partnership with the system and process measures, you need to define what measures will be necessary around the heart, head and hand factors. These measures are then tracked for the duration of the engagement – and ideally beyond, to a point where you and the client are satisfied that the value will be maintained. Hence, the three dimensions are tracked on a longitudinal basis as seen in Figure 7.5.

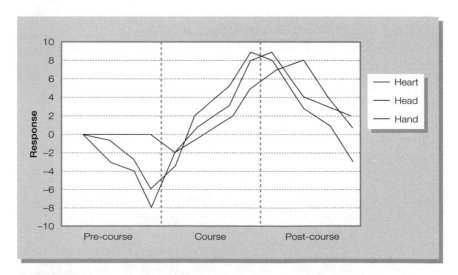

Figure 7.5   Three-dimensional tracking

This chart takes a common example of a change process – the quality training course that your boss says you needs to attend. You don't want to go, your in-tray is full and, even worse, one of your colleagues went on it last month and said it wasn't great.

- ■ **Pre-course:**
  - **Heart:** Even before the course the emotions take a dip. The reaction to colleagues comments, concern about the in-tray and a sense that the course is unnecessary turn you against the course even before you find out about it.
  - **Head:** Because the heart is dipping, the head starts to follow. The heart convinces the head that this is a waste of time. The head then forms sensible reasons why it is not worth attending.
  - **Hand:** The behaviour then follows through. You argue against the event, find other appointments, and even the day before make a big stand against the boss to say you cannot go. However, the boss says you must.

- ■ **Course:**
  - **Heart:** First morning on the course and you have the sulks. You don't want to be there and feel really upset and fed up with going to events that have no value. However, by lunchtime you start to enjoy the event, realize that it is not as bad as you thought, meet some interesting people and start to enjoy it.
  - **Head:** The opening head position is for the internal voice to argue constantly against the tutor. This internal argument sometimes leaks out into disagreement with the course content and other people on the event. However, as the heart position improves, so the inner voice begins to understand why the event is important and moreover sees the logic and sense in tackling the quality issue within the company.
  - **Hand:** The behaviour at the event begins with arms crossed, staring at the floor, late back from tea break and all the body language that signal dissent. However, once the head signals an interest in the context then the physical behaviour changes. Both the body shape and language become more open, inviting and welcoming.

- ■ **Post-course:**
  - **Heart:** Finally you leave the course all buzzed up and ready to go back and change the world – until you hit the in-tray. Then the passion disappears, leaving confusion, then frustration and anger. You question why the company talks about making sweeping changes when it does not resolve the basic problems of a PC that will not work.

- **Head:** Because of the frustration, the ideas and maps that were learnt on the event are ignored or forgotten and you revert back to the comfort zone of the old way of thinking.
- **Hand:** The net result is that you do not use behaviours that support the course goals. Because the feelings, thoughts and behaviours have taken a pounding then the overall impression can be a negative one, so you tell other people that the event is not worth attending.

When the airline pilot comes in to land, they will use a number of reference variables to understand actual against planned trajectory. Where the deviation indicates they are off course then corrective action can be taken to get back into alignment. By a simple process of cross-checking against planned data, it is possible for the pilot to land safely. Consultants and clients can also use this process to ensure that the change project lands to the planned cost, quality and time budget. However, although most change projects will focus on management of the task and process deployment, it is also important to pay careful attention to the human dimensions.

At the very outset of the change project, the client and consultant should agree on the three dimensions that should be measured both during the change and once complete. Try to agree what factors will be apparent if negative emotions are surfacing, if people are not buying in to the programme or if there are shadow factors causing dissent. Also consider what signs will be apparent if things are going well, how to measure when people are enthused and what techniques can be used to measure the corridor conversations. On a head level, try to define what thoughts people will have if things are not working and what mental maps they will need to have for the programme to be effective. Finally, from a hand perspective, if problems are surfacing, analyze what people will be saying and doing and conversely what their behaviours and conversations will be when things are going well. By defining dimensional criteria, it becomes easier to fly a precision approach and land the change project on the spot every time.

Qualitative–quantitative mix

The measures outlined in the previous section offer an extremely robust process to map and measure the change. However, no matter what the measurement framework is used to assist the process, all data will tend to sit between two camps – quantitative or qualitative.

Qualitative measures

Qualitative measures are based on a 'world view', which is holistic and built around the idea that there is no single reality or view of the world because reality is based on personal perceptions rather than an objective fact. This approach involves perceptually putting different people's viewpoints together to make a whole picture. From this process, meaning is produced. However, because perception varies with the individual, many different meanings are possible. As a result, the data gathered only has meaning and purpose within a given context.

Qualitative research methods are sometimes criticized for lack of rigour, but this is often because the critics have attempted to judge the rigour of qualitative studies using rules developed to judge quantitative studies. Rigour needs to be defined differently for qualitative research since the desired outcome is different. In quantitative research, rigour is reflected in narrowness, conciseness and objectivity and leads to rigid adherence to research designs and precise statistical analyses. Rigour in qualitative research is associated with openness, scrupulous adherence to a philosophical perspective, thoroughness in collecting data, and consideration of all the data in the development of a theory.

Typically, quantitative data is collected by in-depth conversations in which the researcher and the subject (informant) are fully interactive. Analysis begins as soon as the first data is collected. This analysis will guide decisions related to further data collection. Data collection usually results in large amounts of handwritten notes, typed interview transcripts, or video/audiotaped conversations that contain multiple pieces of data to be sorted and analyzed. Thus the analysis process is initiated by coding and categorizing the data.

Quantitative measures

Quantitative measurement is an objective and structured process in which numerical data is utilized to obtain information about the success of the engagement. It has a tendency towards numeric analysis, which is used to generalize and make decisions about the area under investigation. Broadly speaking, quantitative research is seen as objective whereas qualitative research often involves a subjective element. By interpreting quantitative data, the researcher can remain detached and objective. This is less the case with qualitative research where the consultant may be more involved with the content under investigation. For example, consider a study being under-taken into customer response waiting times in a high street store. A quanti-tative study, measuring how long people wait, can be purely objective. However, if the consultant wanted to discover how customers felt about their waiting time, they would have to come into contact with the customers and make judgements about the way they answered their questions.

Quantitative analysis is also inclined to be deductive in that it measures against a prior theory, idea or thought. Where data is not structured using numbers, it is considered to be qualitative. Therefore, objectivity, deduc-tiveness, generalizability and numbers are features often associated with quantitative research.

Primary stage: data collection

When a consultant selects the approach to manage a Confirm stage the choice should be what is most suitable for the project. However, it may also reflect the bias of the researcher. Much of the work undertaken by the harder consultancy schools (systems, sortware, processes, etc.) tends toward the harder or numeric approach. In contrast, the softer schools (organizational development, training, coaching, etc.) will tend towards the qualitative approach.

However, the question is often not what data has been collected as part of the Confirm stage, but rather what will people do with the data. Very often the primary data collection process is the simplest. It is in the secondary stage – when the data interpreted, manipulated and presented – that the problems can start to occur. It is here that the consultant and client need to be rigorous in the way they manage and analyze the data.

Secondary stage: data analysis

A common activity that can be seen in any major engagement programme will be a staff survey once the project is complete. The purpose will be to understand the emotive forces that reside in the company once the painful stages are over. The typical approach will be to send out a questionnaire, maybe meet a few people over coffee and possibly run a focus group. In some cases where the consultant is really keen to understand the thoughts and feelings of the teams they will invest in large group diagnostic sessions, web-based discussion or use 'moan' boards to pull out all the shadow issues. At the end of this diagnostic stage, the consultant will be left with masses of data to analyze. The question is how best to do this.

The first and perhaps most radical approach is to present the data in the form in which it was gathered:

■ **Qualitative data:** This can be held in its primary form and presented as qualitative output. For this to happen the board might be offered verbatim scripts of what people think about them and their change programme.

■ **Quantitative data:** This can be presented in numeric form. This might be a chart showing numeric representation of the samples, or tables that offer a periodic analysis of the shift in perception over time in percentage terms.

However, there is another option. It is also possible to reverse the process. Sometimes it is easier to take the date collected in one format and represent it in another, as seen in Figure 7.6.

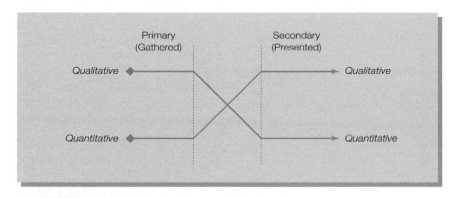

Figure 7.6   Data crossover

This approach offers the following variations:

■ **Qualitative data can produce quantitative data:** For example, the researcher exploring feelings of patients can analyze the responses in clusters that are negative or positive, to produce a figure/percentage of negative patient and positive patient feelings.

■ **Quantitative data can be presented in qualitative terms:** For example, it might be useful to take a cold percentage score of a team perception survey that shows a 10 per cent fall month on month and communicate it using a parable or anecdote. In this way, the presenter seeks to touch the emotive centre and encourages the audience to feel what it is that the teams are experiencing.

None of these options is the 'right way' to manage the Confirm stage. What is important is content and context. The content of the change programme will dictate how data is best gathered and presented, and the context will affect the impact of the acquisition and presentation of the data. In a corporate environment where numbers rule, any attempt to gather data on how people 'feel' and to present this using soft techniques to the management board may at best result in complaints and at worse a complete cancellation of the contract. Conversely, walking into a counselling company and explaining a change project in numbers while excluding the feelings of the group members will potentially generate an uproar and complete negation of any data.

When embarking on any Confirm stage the client and consultant will be faced with a choice of how to collect the data and how to format the presentation. Their choice will sit in one of the four boxes seen in Figure 7.7.

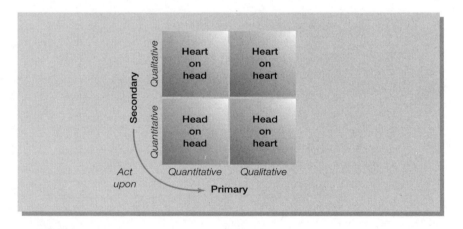

Figure 7.7   Data collection and presentation

- **Head on head:** In this case quantitative data is being presented using quantitative techniques. This is by far the simplest process to follow. Count how many you need, count how many you have and any gap indicates if you have under or over-performed. The risk with this approach is that it is often used to corrupt and manipulate data. The debacle of tampered hospital waiting times, yearly profit-and-loss scandals or altered car mileage figures are all sorry testaments to the ease with which head-on-head data can be manipulated when presented to the general public.
- **Heart on heart:** This seems to be quite simple: the consultant runs a focus group to ascertain people's thoughts and emotion following a

large redundancy programme. The text of the narrative is then condensed into a series of verbatim comments that are presented to the board. However, all is not so simple. First, to present the verbatim comments from a focus group could result in a very large report. With such a large report goes the time necessary to read and interpret the data. In most cases, senior managers do not have the time to wade through page after page of highly emotive comments. They often need a summary version of the themes and undercurrents that emerged so that they can mandate action. The problem is who should reduce the data. In the quantitative process, 2 + 2 will (nearly) always equal 4. But with qualitative data five people will interpret a single statement in five different ways. So again, this confirmation process can be open to corrupt practices.

■ **Head on heart:** This is a common process that makes life easy but is very open to abuse by people who wish to present a rosier picture of their work. For example, a company decides to enhance its leadership capability and runs a 360-degree feedback process. In this, leaders are expected to receive constructive feedback from six peers and subordinates on their performance as a leader. Now although the data being gathered is qualitative, because people describe what it feels like to be led by the individual, the resulting summarised data is translated into percentage terms that indicate the extent to which the leadership team is getting good or bad figures and showing improvement over time. Although the data set offers a rich seam of indicative information that highlights real leadership issues, all the board receives is safe numbers, pie charts and normal distribution curves. This makes their decision making easier but does not really expose them to the deeper issues that might need to be addressed if they truly wish to understand leadership in the company.

■ **Heart on head:** In this case people will try to take numeric data and present it in a way that conveys a deeper sense of emotions and richer understanding. This can often be seen in the way that general election races are presented in the media. At the end of the day, an election is about numbers. How many people vote directly equates to the person or party who gain power. However, the media tend to enrich the data as it flows in during election night. They might do this by using panoramic displays that subtly suggest 'landslides' and 'sweeping' gain for the left or right. They will add colourful language to the reporting, show party members being humiliated as their count is announced and finally use vox pop interviews with ingoing and outgoing party members to enhance the emotional issues around the data. The benefit of this approach is that it can help to convey meaning to the data; the risk is whose meaning is being added. This is a case of the 'half full– half empty' syndrome. Since most media groups will exhibit a party bias, this bias will often manifest itself in the qualitative spin added to the quantitative data.

The overriding message with this model is to use it with caution. Be especially careful in the Confirm stage because it is so often the point at which data corruption will emerge. This may be direct corruption because the client or consultant may wish to bend and bias the result in their favour; or indirect corruption because time and cost problems are surfacing so pressure emerges to reduce the effort and spend and just 'Get some numbers to the bosses to keep them happy'. It is all too easy to succumb to any pressure to corrupt the data because of short-term political or budgetary pressure. However, the risk with this is that your brand and the client's business will suffer in the long run. In the same way that you can only reverse the mileometer on a car for so long before the engine blows, you can only fake organizational or human change for so long before the system explodes. It will do this in the form of dissent, strikes, resignations, or the introduction of corrupt accounting practices. You can't buck nature and you can't hide a problem for ever. It is better to deal with a problem while it is still resolvable rather than covering it over with sophisticated accounting processes, glossy words or corrupt measures.

> **❝ you can only fake organizational or human change for so long before the system explodes ❞**

Measure thrice, cut once

Although the Confirm stage appears late on the Seven Cs process, this is not the case in practice. Confirm is something that the client and consultant will be doing all the time from the very first moment they meet, right through the Close stage when they look at each other and ask 'How have we done?'. So Confirm is both a state of mind and a specific stage in the life cycle.

However, there is one other stage with which Confirm has strong links and this is the Clarify stage. The point of Clarify is to ask 'What is going on?': by doing this you will be measuring the opening state of the system that is about to be changed. With any change process, there is this pre and post-test. So the essence of the Seven Cs stage process is to measure the 'current' state – both while 'doing' the change and once it is 'done'.

The measured success of a project is often linked more to the timing of the assessment than to the delivered benefit. Some change processes will kick in overnight, others might take weeks or months and some large-scale processes might take years to realize a payback for the company. As Senge *et al.* (1999) stress, you must not judge the ultimate success or failure of your efforts solely on early results. Managers often want to pull up the radishes to see how they are growing; pushing the measuring process can disrupt the delivery of the desired outcome. Too often we disregard the importance of time delays in the engagement and assume that we live in a mechanistic society where an input leads to an immediate output. The possibility that we actually live in a complex and dynamic world – where change is unpredictable – is forgotten in the rush to deliver hard outputs.

Consider a consultant who has been employed to introduce a culture change programme to a medium-sized organization with the goal of improving performance in the customer service department. The consultant decides to run a series of workshops that introduces some new human resource processes, specifically team meetings, appraisal system, upward feedback meetings, etc. The programme is launched in a blaze of publicity, with the active support of the MD and the board. All goes well until news comes in that the company will be purchasing a smaller competitor in order to rapidly grow its market share. Although the MD and the board believe in the need for a cultural shift in the business, their time begins to be taken up with the acquisition. The result is that many of the people start to doubt the senior team's belief in the changes and stories start to circulate about how the new appraisal system is being abused in some departments.

Clearly the consultant has delivered the changes specified by the client. The problem is: when does the measurement take place to confirm that the outcomes have been achieved? Through no fault of the consultant, factors have conspired to affect the assignment to the point where major remedial work will be required to bring the transformation back on-line. The timing of the change will affect the perception of the outcome and might well even affect the final remuneration that the consultant receives. There are four different time slots where confirmation of change might take place (*see* Figure 7.8):

■ **(T1) Shooting star:** Any consultant who wants to impress the client will measure the change when the momentum is at its peak. At this stage both desirability and capability to become involved in the change is quite high, hence the confirmation process is likely to show the change to be a raving success.

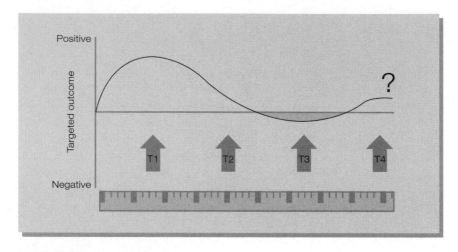

Figure 7.8 Confirmation time slots

- **(T2) It wasn't me:** As new toys and interests come along, the organization will eventually tire of the change. Undertaking the confirmation process at this stage will be the kiss of death. The negative bias that people put on failed projects will potentially put the chance of any further work in jeopardy.

- **(T3) It's over:** In many cases, the negative spin applied to the change can actually result in the view that the company should never have embarked on the change and that it caused more problems that it cured. Measuring the transformation at this stage would be like committing professional suicide.

- **(T4) Never give up on a good thing:** Once the dust has settled and a sense of reality returns, most change projects are seen to have added something. It is then possible to measure a residual outcome – one that is deeply embedded in the culture of the business.

This model might seem unduly pessimistic. However, although this cycle will not be typical of all change processes, it will happen in a number of them. Your goal must be to ensure that the dips at T2 and T3 are never actually reached and that sufficient energy and momentum is maintained to hold the gains. You need to develop a process that truly measures the value of the change as opposed to the impact of the uncontrolled extrinsic factors. Unless you have the ability to see into the future, you will never be able to predict where your change is on the curve. Therefore you must build in as many measures as possible to ensure that you obtain a true picture.

Four types of measurement can be used to confirm progress (*see* Figure 7.9):

■ **Quantitative outcomes:** Against this, it would be practical to set many of the factors that may have contributed to the approval for investment in the strategic engagement. These could include the number of people undertaking external training programmes, the cost of internal workshops, the increase in intellectual capital, etc. However, this measure is often abused: people can try to achieve the measures rather than try to change the culture. It can also create a false sense of end goals – 'We meet the 75 per cent criteria so we can back off now'. Finally, remember that any manager with a degree of common sense can meet targets by simply juggling resources and spreadsheet data.

■ **Quantitative in-process:** This includes many of the standard project management measures: achievement of milestones, number of completed tasks, cost overrun, etc. As a tangible measure, it is very effective for keeping minds focused on the process of change and ensuring that resources are carefully managed. This is appropriate if the organization is installing a new computer system or building a new extension, but people are not plant or equipment. People are unpredictable and social change is uncertain. While hard measures for the process are helpful, but there has to be a degree of care to ensure that the measures do not become more important than the desired

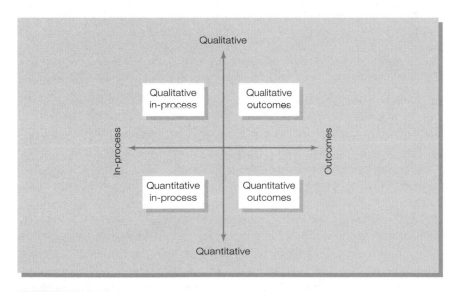

Figure 7.9   Balanced confirmation

outcome. If this were to happen, the measures tend to take the focus away from the end goal and act as an attenuator that restricts the change and learning process. The old adage that 'What gets measured gets done', often becomes 'What gets measured gets bluffed'.

▪ **Qualitative in-process:** This approach is concerned with understanding how people feel about the engagement. It is driven by how people perceive the change at an intuitive and emotional level. The difficulty is that it offers nothing that an accountant can really use to produce a cost-benefit chart and little for the whole business to hold on to so that they have a feel for the change. The only way that people can really get a feel for progress is by becoming a part of the change itself. By doing this they will also derive an intuitive appreciation of the progress made and where the change is heading. Businesses are not run for pleasure – they are run to maximize the profitability of shareholder investment. If shareholders cannot be satisfied that the investment is worthwhile, there is always a chance that any resources allocated to the engagement will be withdrawn.

▪ **Qualitative outcomes:** This approach is virtually the same as the qualitative process, except that it is concerned with the change in daily life as perceived by people in the business. These measures might be drawn from interviews with people after they have been through some experiential parts of the change initiative. The interviews will help people to understand how the deeper issues around the culture are transformed. One approach is to map people's perception of the changes in the cultural artefacts within the business against the stated outcomes.

No matter what the change process being managed, there is no reason not to use all four quadrants in this model. You need to measure both the soft and hard factors while doing the change and once it is complete. A failure to measure any of the four sections will lead to a huge gap in the data – and this can only result in change that may fail to deliver sustainable value.

Confirm the costs

Safety is a difficult issue for an airline. Although the ultimate goal is to spend as much money as necessary to ensure the safety of the passengers, there is a point on the expenditure curve where it becomes uneconomical to invest any more money. The same applies to the investment in the measurement process. Clearly you, the client and the consumer all need to have an appreciation of the impact and value of the change. But there is a cost associated with any measurement process. At some point you will need to agree with the client when it becomes uneconomical to measure.

Consider the implementation of a customer service training programme within a large organization. While the client might wish to undertake a full measurement and evaluation process to confirm that the engagement has worked, there is a downside: the cost of developing the confir- mation system; the cost of taking people away from dealing with customers; and the potential cultural corruption that is incurred as people play games with their responses. The alternative view might be that if the programme has worked, then any change will be apparent in the way customers are dealt with – so why bother with a grand confirmation process? Neither argument is right, but the consultant must understand the two extremes in order to develop an appropriate and cost-effective confirmation process.

> 66 at some point you will need to agree with the client when it becomes uneconomical to measure 99

When making this decision you need to have a clear view of the various costs:

- ▓ **Design:** These arise from the initial front-end work that takes place in the confirmation process. This might be sizing the market to be measured, designing the survey criteria, developing the questionnaires and arranging for people to attend a focus group. Depending on the process being used, this is biased heavily towards the use of a professional to design or administer the process.

- ▓ **Deploy:** These are the direct operational costs incurred from running the measurement process. They include printing and mailing questionnaires, paying for meeting rooms, paying professional interviewers and telephone charges. Usually these will all be quite predictable.

- ▓ **Deliver:** These costs are associated with taking the primary data from the measurement process and turning it into something that has value for the consultant and client. They can include data modelling with a software package, aligning the data with industry benchmark information or preparing a slide presentation for the client. These costs might have a tendency to overrun, since they are difficult to pin down. Just one stray comment from the director who wants a 'bit more information on the slides' can result in cost overrun.

| Table 7.2 | Costs of measurement processes |

	Design	Deployment	Development
Postal survey	Standard costs, most of which will be in the design of the questionnaire	Mail and administration time; money is saved if an e-mail system is used (which can also indicate if people have received and read the survey form)	If the questionnaire has been designed properly and is quantitative in nature, then analysis is relatively easy and cheap
Open interviews	Limited up-front costs, but is high in preparing people for the interview process	High costs in taking people away from their day job, plus the costs of the interviewer	High potential costs in coding and analyzing the final data; time is saved if interviewee does partial coding
Structured telephone survey	Costs of questionnaire design	Telephone costs and interviewer's time; also costs of taking people away from their jobs	Analysis should involve relatively low costs, especially if response is fed online to a computer system
Observation	Little up-front costs – but assumes that observer will have necessary skills and knowledge to do the job	No direct costs from people being observed – just observer's time	Potential high costs associated with coding and analyzing what is apparently wild and diverse data
Diary	Low up-front costs apart from diaries	Time costs of the person who is filling out the diary	Potential huge costs as data is so random and diverse
Focus groups	Some up-front costs in design and administration costs for getting people together	High time costs of facilitator and participants	Potentially high costs of analysis and presentation

When you discuss the costs associated with the Confirm phase, you should have a few facts and figures ready to answer questions from the client. Typically the 'What happens if' type questions can end up either costing you a great deal of money or put you in the embarrassing position of having to tell the client the confirmation costs are much higher than anticipated. As a result, you must consider the measurement processes that are available and start to understand what cost drivers will affect the final figure. A few examples are shown in Table 7.2.

Although there will always be pressure to reduce confirmation costs, there is a risk that too much downward pressure will increase the level of errors within the process. A decision to reduce expenditure in any of the confirmation areas will increase the error cost. These errors arise because the returns are not truly representative of the final situation or the data is incorrect and has to be gathered again. You must always be aware that at the run-down stage of a project people's minds will be elsewhere, the budget will be drained and careers are always made on the next project. Hence there is a tendency to cut corners. This is a false economy and every effort should be made to ensure the robustness of the confirmation process.

8

Stage six: Continue

Many receive advice, few profit by it. Publilius Syrus

The most common criticism of consultantcy work is that once a consultant's report has been completed it is put on the shelf to gather dust along with all the other consultants' reports. As a result, the change is only short-lived and the problem returns. Imagine if you went to the dentist only to find that your toothache returned the following morning or employed a builder to construct an extension and found cracks appearing two weeks later. The goal is real long-term results, not short-term fixes. Czerniawska (1999) aptly makes this point: 'Although as a consultant, you recognize that the prime responsibility for implementation lies with the client, you also know that your job is not done – or not done properly – until you have helped the client achieve real results'.

The key question that the dentist, builder or consultant must ask is: 'How can I ensure that any changes or recommendations that have been offered will continue following my departure?' Failure to consider the issue of continuance can result in a warm rosy glow at the celebration party but an eroded brand six months later when people revert back to the old way of working or the system fails to deliver the anticipated benefits.

You therefore need to ensure that the following actions are considered from the outset of the change process:

■ **Sticky steps:** Ensure that slippage does not occur once the project has been closed.

■ **D–E dissonance:** Look for the gap between what people say they want and what they really want.

■ **Listen to the language:** Often the only tangible legacy left by the consultant's intervention is changed language – hence it is important to understand what language needs to be changed to underpin the process.

■ **Gravitational pull:** You must always make sure that any supporting administrative system does not become a bureaucracy that will strangle it.

■ **Knowledge transfer:** If the benefits are to be maximized, both the client and the consultant must ensure that a learning transfer takes place so that key elements of the consultants' competencies remain in the business following their departure.

■ **Learning levels:** Be clear about the level of expertise that the client must develop to be self-sufficcint.

■ **Sell the story:** You must undertake a practical analysis of the client's capability to diffuse new ideas across the organization.

The continuance of any change depends on the extent to which it becomes embedded in the client's system. However, you cannot do this in isolation. In the same way that a doctor cannot resolve patients' problems without their support, you must work with the client to ensure that they take ownership of the outcome. Working with the client through the ideas in the Continue stage will help to ensure that the change will survive once you have moved on.

Sticky steps

For the majority of change programmes, you must help the client to hold on to the gains. Slippage is one of the most difficult issues to resolve. People may have the necessary energy to deliver the transformation but they do not all have the power and desire to continue through until the end of the engagement. Even when change is complete, many organizations tend to drift back to their initial state after a short period.

Change is often not sustainable because it has been enacted at the asset, blueprint or capability level of the change ladder, but not locked in at the desire or ethos level (*see* Chapter 3). Imagine a racing car driver who is unable to attain peak performance on the track. His car has been re-tuned, he has been on a development programme to enhance his driving skills and has been coached by the best guru possible to develop a positive mental attitude. The unspoken problem is that he has reached a breakpoint – the thought of speeding around a track at 200 mph no longer appeals. His real personal goal is to become a teacher, specifically to help young teenagers to learn how to drive. The end result is that any action to improve his performance might work in the short term, but will eventually fade away because there is little deep desire to change. In the same way, any organization that tries to install a quality culture, create a customer-focused ethos or develop a cost-focused culture must ensure that the change aligns with the basic purpose of the business.

Another factor to consider is the extent to which the change is driven by extrinsic or intrinsic forces. Imagine you are trying to encourage your children to brush their teeth every day. One option is to stand over them every morning and force a change in behaviour. However, until the behaviour is locked in, the moment that the parent is away the children will forget or choose not to brush their teeth. For the organization, if the managing director drives the change then the moment his or her attention is diverted, people will ignore the change and revert to type.

You must also understand how change fits in with the political system. When individuals operate in teams or organizations, they will be attuned to the political shifts within the business. The political actors, who either use the energy behind the change to further their political agenda or to resist the change because it potentially erodes their power base, will eagerly seize upon any new initiative or project. For the change to be sustainable, you must present it in a non-threatening way to people who may be damaged by it.

> **for the change to be sustainable, you must present it in a non-threatening way to people who may be damaged by it**

If you are designing a new computer system that will reduce the headcount in the IT department, then you must market the change in such a way that the systems people recognize the opportunities that will emerge. Otherwise there is every chance that the teams most affected by the change will do everything in their power to sabotage the process once you have left.

You must also develop a deep appreciation of the governance system. How are decisions made? How is the management board constructed? What is the process for logging actions? Who has control over the deployment of resources? All these factors can either drive or kill a change process. You need to understand both the overt and covert governance system and ensure that the change being proposed is able to operate in such a system.

Suppose you have been hired to install a new stock control system that allows requisitions to be managed at a local level. The governance system might react badly to this model if financial control is normally held with a financial director who likes to get involved in all the purchase decisions. There is every chance that once the system is installed then the first action that the financial director will take is to bring the process back in line with the existing control systems. The consultant has two choices: either to work closely with the financial director to change his or her values about the level of financial accountability with the organization or, second, build in sufficient low-level system controls to ensure that management of the system will be held at the devolved level.

Sustainability is not something to be considered at the end of the cycle. Although it is positioned in stage six of the framework, you must be tuned into the potential for sustainability from the very outset. When addressing any of the other six stages sustainability must be at the forefront of your mind:

■ **Client:** If there is a risk that the project is a stopgap and cannot be sustained, then it is better to say no to the project. Although rejecting potential income will always be difficult, the danger is that if you accept a non-starter, the client will eventually regard your input as worthless and may even say this to other people.

■ **Clarify:** The cultural and political issues need to be brought out in order to find the basis for longevity. This might include aligning the change with the organization's strategic goals, embedding the transformation into the company HR systems, or modifying the reward system.

■ **Create:** You need to develop ideas and process that align with the organization values and do not work in opposition to the natural forces. If a revolutionary rather than evolutionary change is required, make sure that the engagement has plenty of supporting hooks to lock in the transformation once you have left.

■ **Change:** When you map the energy being used to drive change, ensure that it will continue after your departure – if not, then try to lock in alternative energy sources to maintain pressure on the organization. If, for example, the change is the installation of a new accounting system and you think the IT group will lose interest, prepare the accounting team to take over once the system is installed.

■ **Confirm:** When you design the confirmation process, the tendency is to measure how things work now – especially if your client is looking for proof of output to guarantee payment. However, it is also important to look for proof of sustainability – have people really accepted the change and is it embedded into the behaviours or management systems?

■ **Close:** The client must be aware of the sustaining hooks that have been used in the engagement and understand what action needs to be taken to ensure they hold in place.

Sustainability will always be affected by the structural surround that supports change. There is little point in pushing one department to re-engineer its systems and processes if the rest of the organization continues to use out-of-date processes; and there is little chance that a new accounting system will be used if people are not trained. If change is to be sustainable then is must be in alignment with the structure in which it sits and the appropriate hooks and links must be tied in with the transformation process.

D–E dissonance

It is always interesting to consider change programmes that have obviously failed to produce their intended benefits, yet there is no (overt) acceptance of this failure. When we look closer at the situation, we can see a number of games being played. There is the 'life has moved on' game, whereby people suggest that because the environment has changed then the intended outcomes are no longer viable or of any importance. Another game is 'changing the guard', where the originator of the programme has moved on so everyone blames that person for its failure and the general antipathy towards the objectives. This game is interesting because of the extremity of shift in the stated desire to make a change. One week a certain objective is the only way to solve the company's problems, the next week it is the worst idea in the world. This failure to achieve change and the games that are played out to justify why the change failed to materialize can be seen in the personal change areas. For example, there are the constant failures of diets and the rush to find a new regime or blueprint because the last one was no good.

Much of this game playing can be traced back to confusion between four areas on the change ladder, as seen in Figure 8.1. It is the confusion and dishonesty that occurs at these levels (intentional and unintentional) that is so often the reason why change is non-sustainable. People say they are about to achieve great things, don't quite achieve them, cover up, retro-spectively make justifications for the failure and then move on to the next great change programme – just like the constant rush to find a new diet, the machine that will help us get fitter or the miracle cream to look younger. Because these change interventions fail to deliver success (though few admit it), they create a demand for more newly packaged instant-success solutions.

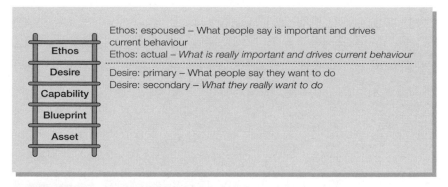

Figure 8.1   Change ladder confusion

The root of these ideas come from the work of Leon Festinger who originated the concept of cognitive dissonance. He argued that pairs of cognitions (elements of knowledge or belief about something that is true) could be relevant or irrelevant to one another. If two cognitions are relevant to one another, they are either consonant (in alignment) or dissonant (in opposition). Two cognitions are aligned if one follows from the other, and they are dissonant if they disagree. The existence of thoughts that do not agree creates a sense of discomfort and unease that the person will naturally wish to resolve. The greater the level of the dissonance, the greater is the pressure to reduce discomfort.

An example might be someone who has a deeply held belief in the need to protect the environment and argues against the use and abuse of fossil fuels. However, they work for a company based a long way out of town where access by public transport is difficult and would add an hour to the journey. As a result they use their car to get to work. On the one hand they hold a belief that it is wrong for people to drive unnecessarily, but on the other they have taken a conscious decision to drive because the use of public transport would mean that they would have to get up an hour earlier every day.

If we consider this in relation to the change ladder, there are two forces in action. The first is an espoused ethos (E) that it is wrong to damage the world and that people should not act in a way that is detrimental to society. The reality is that their actual desire (D) is to stay in bed to get more sleep (see Figure 8.2).

Another example can be found in someone who smokes. A regular smoker who begins to understand that smoking is bad for health will experience conflict, because the knowledge that smoking is bad for health is dissonant with the desire to smoke. They can reduce the pain by changing their behaviour and

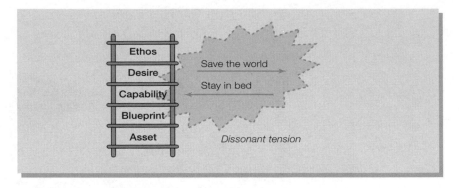

Figure 8.2　D–E dissonance

give up the cigarettes, which would be in alignment with the belief that smoking is bad for them. Alternatively, they could reduce the internal tension by changing their ethos-level beliefs about the effect of smoking and convince themselves that smoking does not have a harmful effect on health in their particular circumstances. Or they might look for the upsides and focus on the fact that it helps to reduce tension and keeps them from putting on weight. Or they could argue that the risk to health from smoking is negligible compared with the danger of being knocked over by a car on the way to work.

The main point of this desire–ethos (D–E) dissonance is that humans will not wish to maintain this level of internal tension and will seek to minimize it. They will do this either by modifying their ethos and belief in what is right, or by changing their desire to achieve something. This is indicated in a story told by Aesop about a fox that tried without success to reach a cluster of grapes that dangled from a vine just out of his reach. Although the fox leapt higher and higher to grab the grapes, he could not quite reach the fruit. After a few attempts the fox gave up and said to himself, 'These grapes are sour, and if I had some I would not eat them'. The fox's failure to achieve action on the desire level meant that he could not live with the dissonance created by the failure and so took internal action to minimize the conflict. He did this by changing his beliefs about the grapes; he provided an acceptable explanation for his behaviour.

D–E dissonance games

This apparent ability to adapt and alter the espoused ethos and desire levels on the change ladder is what leads to the complex game playing that underpins many corporate failures. Consider the examples in Table 8.1 of common problems encountered in organizational change.

Table 8.1	D–E dissonance games		
	Customer focus	*Quality focus*	*People focus*
Ethos: espoused What people say is important and drives current behaviour	The customer is king	We strive for quality focus and have instigated a statistical process control programme	Our people are our greatest asset
Ethos: actual What is really important and drives current behaviour	Cost (which led to the use of automated customer response systems)	The organization is led by barons who protect their empire so will subvert figures	10% yearly growth on revenue and 4% cost reduction targets set by head office
Desire: primary What people say they want to do	We want to improve the customer response process	We are going to publish all quality results to customers	We want to create a more open environment by using a 360-degree leadership review
Desire: secondary What they really want to do	We want to reduce costs even more	We will hide bad figures and only present favourable outcomes	Local managers tightly manage the completion of leadership forms to ensure that positive messages are sent to head office

In each of the three examples indicated in Table 8.1 it is possible to see the conflict and tension that can exist. If the suggestion made by Leon Festinger is true, then the senior team will in some way or form need to modify either what they are saying and doing or what they are thinking.

Managing dissonance

This D–E dissonance will be experienced as an uncomfortable state in which people are motivated to reduce the discomfort. There are three strategies that can be used to manage the dissonance:

■ **Change beliefs:** If two beliefs are acting in opposition, we can simply change one to make it consistent with the other. Or we can change each idea in the direction of the other. Consider the MD who has instigated a new global strategy that is based upon the argument that it is right to move away from a niche product set and migrate to commodity level. The MD proclaims this strategy as the only one that will save the company from future incursion by cheap imports. So their espoused belief or ethos is that the market for niche products will be eroded and that the company can compete on a different low-cost base. However, after a few years this strategy does not seem to be working. So the MD realizes that the company needs to re-enter the niche market and withdraw from the commodity area. The problem is reconciling the dissonance between what they believed last year and the new desire without creating internal pain and public humiliation.

■ **Add beliefs:** If two opposing beliefs cause tension the dissonance can be reduced by adding one or more consonant cognitions. The non-smoker who has a cigarette can reduce his dissonance if he can believe that he only had the cigarette because he was with a group of people who could help with his career, so he wanted to fit in with them.

■ **Alter belief importance:** Since we all consciously and subconsciously weight our beliefs it may be advantageous to alter the importance of the various cognitions. The person who is in debt and needs to control costs might come to believe that the debt is trivial compared to the gain from purchasing something on sale. The importance of the positive belief (the one-day sale that helps save money) can be magnified and the importance of the opposing cognitions (in debt) can be minimized. When the new, altered importance weightings are placed against each other the idea of saving money acts as a higher priority than the need to save money. Thus the magnitude of dissonance will be decreased.

Consultant challenge

The need to challenge the client's willingness to focus on sustainable change has to start from the very outset of the change process. It is no good waiting until the change has been made to see if the client is serious; in the same way, the doctor who wishes to help someone with heart disease must challenge the patient's willingness to modify their life style before the treatment commences.

Hence the Continue stage actually starts in the Client stage of the Seven Cs process and is a part of the very first meeting. You must seek to probe and test the client's stated desire to make a change and form (sometimes quite quickly) an assessment of the seriousness of their intent to stick with the change. If you are unable or unwilling to make this kind of challenge then it might be possible to generate short-term revenue but at huge cost to your long term brand. If you deliver yet another change programme that the client will fail to maintain then your brand will suffer as people blame you for the failure of the change to last. You must be ready to test and measure the client against the four key levels on the change ladder and as shown in Table 8.2.

Table 8.2   **D–E dissonance test of client**

D–E levels	D–E dissonance test
Ethos: espoused What the client says is important and drives current behaviour	■ Budget plans and forecasts ■ Stated MD proclamations ■ Mission statement ■ Public debate ■ Values statements ■ Product and project plans
Ethos: actual What is really important and drives current behaviour	■ What do they do at present ■ Tangible evidence ■ How money is spent ■ How time is allocated ■ What they will fight for ■ What they say no to ■ How choices are ranked (In a preference test which options win?) ■ Private debate
Desire primary: What the client says they want to do	■ Vision proclamations ■ Strategy papers ■ Forecasts
Desire: secondary What they really want to do	■ Diary entries ■ Actual spend against projects ■ The doorman and PA test – what do they tell you? ■ Times they have tried and failed before ■ Willingness to stand on a soapbox in the office and shout out their dreams

However, let us not put all the blame and pressure on the client. In just the same way, the client must be prepared to challenge and confront the consultant on the consultant's desire and capability to deliver sustainable change. The consultant is being paid to deliver value through sustainable change and so should be able to demonstrate the competence and character to ensure that they are able to fulfil their part of the contract (*see* Table 8.3).

Table 8.3   **D–E dissonance test of consultant**

D–E levels	D–E dissonance tests
Ethos: espoused What the consultant says is important and drives current behaviour	▦ Company brochures ▦ Missions and purpose statement ▦ Opening pitch ▦ Focus on sustainable language
Ethos: actual What is really important and drives current behaviour	▦ What they do ▦ How they allocate their time with you ▦ How they allocate money and investment with you ▦ Willingness to reject the contract if the client is not serious ▦ Level of senior team involvement ▦ Level of support from back office ▦ Documentation standards ▦ Response time ▦ The questions they ask ▦ Previous case histories
Desire: primary What the consultant says they want to do	▦ Pitch presentation ▦ Formal submission ▦ Contract
Desire: secondary What they really want to do	▦ Prior contracts ▦ Type of language used ▦ Willingness to share risk ▦ Willingness to challenge in sensitive areas

Serious is as serious does. The dieting model is entirely appropriate in this context. The failure rate of diets is a huge testament to the difficulty associated with losing weight but also the inability (or unwillingness) of the diet industry to challenge people's intent before they embark on a weight-loss regime. The trouble is that after three or four failed diets people can become upset, dependent and almost resign themselves to never being able to manage their weight. This is no different to organizational change. Talk with any engineer, sales representative, clerical assistant or doorman: in most cases, they are fed up with the constant barrage of stories from the latest MD who promises that nirvana is just around the corner.

Of all the skills and traits that a consultant needs, the most important one is courage. It is having the guts and audacity to challenge whether if the client is serious about the change and will pursue it through to the logical conclusion, even if things get difficult. It is the constant failure to ensure sustainability that creates misery for the front-line worker, malaise in the ranks of middle management and what seems to be an increasingly suspect business model for the consultant.

Listen to the language

The extent to which change has been bedded can be determined by the shift in people's language. The quality consultant will hear a greater use of words like 'customer needs', 'cost of quality' or 'agreed standards'. The marketing strategist will hear words like 'customer segmentation', 'value chain' or 'brand development'. By changing the language, you will help ensure continuance of change. Although this is not guaranteed in all contexts, it does offer a good indication of the effectiveness of the transformation. Just listen to the way that children will adopt the language of their favourite cartoon character. The ability to mimic and copy the latest buzzword offers the child membership to a select band of friends and peers.

This power of language to influence how people behave should never be underestimated. We often think that language is simply a way of describing something to another person. However, communication is a magical process that takes the ideas and schematic models from one person's mind and recreates them in the mind of someone else. By the use of words, patterns, inflections and sounds an individual builds something new and original in someone else's mind. So as an idea is socialized through an organization, it is not the case that it is being passed from one person to another like a relay race. At each juncture, the idea is reborn and recreated in another person's mind. Each time this creation takes place, it will be subject to amplification, distortion and attenuation. Like the game of Chinese whispers, the language element of the socialization process can have a significant impact on the way in which knowledge is received and changed behaviours are eventually delivered.

The embodiment of new language into the culture of an organization is seen and heard in many different ways. The use of shared metaphors can help to explain a particular idea in terms of another experience. The metaphor is used in two ways: first as an implied analogy, where comparison is drawn between two similar things (for example Ford and General Motors); alternatively, it is in the nature of a figurative analogy that draws a comparison between two seemingly different things (for example musician and manager). You can often use metaphors when trying to explain a complex subject. The test of the metaphor's success is when you hear it being passed on to other people. Alternatively, jargon and catchphrases help to frame an idea in a set of words or context that help the recipient feel comfortable.

Finally, think about 'spin'. Spin is a process whereby you can take an idea and deliberately offer it in a positive or negative light. This is used sometimes by politicians as they try to angle a story so that it looks favourable to their party. It can also be used when people talk about the role they took in a transition programme – often escalating their importance when the change has been successful.

The ability to lock in change through the modification of a company's language base can offer immense value. By changing how people talk you are effectively modifying the corporate DNA. So by effecting a change in the client or consumer language, you can modify the organizational genes that describe how the business operates. As changes become embedded in language, so will the associated behavioural transformation. This changed behaviour becomes the norm and is accepted as part of how things are naturally managed. The net result is that continuance is locked in through the shared language and mental models, rather than having to rely on an overt control system that checks that people are changing their behaviour.

> **changing how people talk you are effectively modifying the corporate DNA**

Gravitational pull

To ensure the continuance of the change, it is important to focus on the intent driving the transition. For example, in writing this book there was a clear intent to produce something new and original about the field of consulting and change management. In theory, fulfilling the intent is quite easy – just sit down and write a chapter every month and out pops the finished book. However, nothing is quite so simple. Along the way different things occur that both slow the process down and cause energy to be diverted from writing the book. The children's homework, family problems, boredom and so on all conspire to drag the author away from the original plan.

In the same way, your client might have an overt goal to implement a new programme, but along the way things occur that cause a deviation. The greatest cause of intent corruption can be the organization itself. In many cases the weight of the structure and the bureaucracy built around a change process can take energy away from the transformation.

In the case of the sole trader everything that the individual does contributes to the declared goal to deliver a profitable return on the investment. Effective management of the customer interaction generally delivers this return. There is a straight line that connects the energy of the individual to the customer and the intent is clear and understood (*see* Figure 8.3). Once the business starts to grow, people will be recruited and the birth of a new organization takes place. However, at this point it is possible to see activities that are not directly related to the delivery of customer service. These will include the occasional meeting to discuss missing stock, forms to fill out to satisfy tax officials and agreeing who will provide cover when people are ill. The end result is that the intent is still in place, but the energy is slowly being drained away.

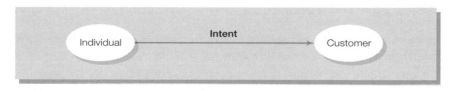

Figure 8.3   Connecting the individual to the customer

After a year or two, a full-blown organization is in place with over a hundred people and all the associated trappings that go with it. Now it is possible to see the effect of organizational gravity acting on the planned intent. The weight of the business systems makes it harder for the service to be delivered. The business has people whose sole responsibility is to deal with internal matters – half-day meetings on budget preparation, two-day workshops on setting the vision and resolving problems that the organization created for itself. It is at this stage that the weight created by organizational gravity can stop the change process from taking place.

Figure 8.4 shows how the energy is focused more upon the needs of the organization than those of the intended outcome. This is seen in many change programmes. Supporting bureaucracy often surrounds total quality and cumbersome systems are regularly built to achieve such standards as ISO 9000 registration.

You must ensure that the change intent is always at the forefront of people's minds. If someone wants to install a bureaucratic system then challenge the need for such systems. Every time that a participant is asked to fill in a form or report on progress to the board then this is energy being taken away from the desired goal. You must make sure the client and consumer are aware of the impact of such activities and how they can destabilize the change process.

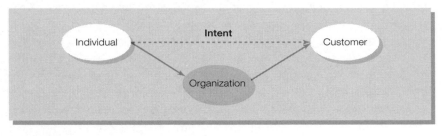

Figure 8.4   Gravitational pull

Knowledge transfer

As a consultant, you might have been employed because a company does not have the necessary skills or knowledge. Both you and the client have a responsibility to ensure that a learning transfer takes place during the change cycle so that the benefits of the contract are maximized. Your goal is to make sure that the essential elements of your competencies remain in the business. There are three types of knowledge that the client should seek to retain once you have left:

- **Tacit:** The skills and knowledge that are used naturally without any overt thought.
- **Explicit:** The codified skills and knowledge that you bring to the business.
- **Relational:** Wisdom that emerges as a result of the social interaction between the client, consultant, consumers and any other players in the engagement.

You must work with the client to understand what skills they want to retain and how best that transfer can be made during the engagement.

Tacit knowledge

Tacit knowledge is formed by the thoughts, feelings and intuition that go on in the background while people are performing a task. At an organizational level, it is characterized as routines, which are the rules, procedures, conventions, strategies and technologies that act as building blocks for an organization (Levitt and March, 1996). It might also be regarded as the beliefs, frameworks and general cultural artefacts that make up the softer elements of an organization.

Although the creation and exploitation of tacit knowledge is desirable from a commercial viewpoint, it does have a major drawback in that it is difficult to transfer within an organization. The reasons for this include a number of factors:

- **Context dependent:** For example, the musician who is only able to shine with a certain group of other musicians.

- **Difficult to articulate:** For example, the chef who is unable to describe what makes the difference between a good and a great meal.

- **Hard to facilitate collaboration:** Since tacit knowledge is often thought of in terms of personal metaphors and symbols, a metaphor shared between two people might have a totally different connotation to each.

- **Requires presence:** Although it is possible for a skilled pilot in a control tower to talk down a novice in a plane, it is very difficult. Some skills and knowledge are not readily transferred without immediate and close visual contact.

- **Emotional barriers:** Tacit knowledge has a deep personal meaning. If an expert is to share knowledge that they have spent years gathering, the recipient must be trusted not to abuse the learning.

- **Complexity:** Knowledge is not always readily identifiable in a distinct form. It is like a pot-pourri – a mix of different sets of knowledge, experiences and feelings.

Although these factors can make tacit knowledge difficult to transfer, it is the fountain of wisdom. A large element of knowledge innovation will originate from a tacit level and it grows in value as it is transferred from the tacit to explicit level and from person to person.

Explicit knowledge

Explicit knowledge is something that is easily talked about, codified and documented. It is a commodity that is readily shared with other people, stored, retrieved and embodied in tangible products, services or processes. Examples that display the attributes of explicit knowledge include training manuals, newspapers, equipment user guides and college lectures.

While explicit knowledge has the benefit of being readily communicated, stored and retrieved, the downside is that it is easily lost to competitors. It is transferred over the internet at the touch of a keystroke, overheard in a bar or simply deduced by analyzing a company's products. One common example of this can be seen in the automobile market: companies will regularly purchase their competitors' products, rip them apart and extract the embedded knowledge for their own products.

Relational knowledge

Knowledge is created or discovered when you interact with your client. There are times when something inexplicable happens between two people – an idea that would not have come to an individual. Every time you sit down to discuss options and ideas with a client, you have the chance to create new relational capital. It is the existence of this social asset that offers so much hidden value. All organizations have particular capabilities for creating a market advantage and this is often found in the space between the people. Your role is to grab the capital that exists in your relationship with your client and use it to fuel change.

> **monitor your relationship with the client and consumer and grasp knowledge opportunities wherever you can**

The relational discovery process can take place in two forms:

- **Tacit relational knowledge:** This exists where people that work together over a period of time will improve their working methods but may not recognize or discuss the improvement. Examples include musicians who play together for a long period or comedians who intuitively develop their appreciation of each other's style and preferred methods of working.

- **Relational knowledge:** This can exist at the explicit level. Examples include researchers writing a paper together or a project team in which people share ideas in building the project plans.

You need constantly to monitor your relationship with the client and consumer and grasp knowledge opportunities wherever you can. Perhaps you have a shared friend who might help develop a new operational procedure; or your shared interest in sailing can be used to develop a team-building event; or you both studied at the same college so can look at problems in a similar way. Whatever the capital asset, just ensure that you actively use it to aid the change.

Learning levels

All change interventions should be designed to help the client and consumers achieve a specific level of knowledge that will result in improved and sustainable personal or business performance. This residual knowledge is not some add-on that can be included as an afterthought in the tender document or initial proposal. It must be an integral part of the change intervention. Without such knowledge of how to self-maintain, then what chance is there for the client or consumer to develop and hold on to the change?. In the same way that schools, colleges and universities seek to measure the students' retained knowledge before allowing them to leave the programme, as consultants we should aim to develop processes that will help us to determine the level of retained knowledge before leaving the client.

There must be a clear line of sight, across three primary areas:

- **Knowledge level:** The learning that will take place during the engagement and the resulting knowledge.

- **Performance level:** What performance capability the new knowledge will deliver.

- **Business value:** The business value this will generate through enhanced performance.

At this stage, we are clearly delineating the knowledge gained in the engagement and trying to understand and ensure that value has been derived from the acquisition. If all change activities involve people in some way or form, then it might be acceptable to assume that as part of this change process the knowledge or capability of the individuals will be transformed. For the new computer system to work the users have to acquire a new set of cognitive capabilities; for the revised engineering guidelines to work the technician must learn a new set of processes; and for the new merger to be successful the manager must learn new capabilities.

The question is deciding the level of learning that is desired and what has been achieved once the change is complete. Have people just learnt enough to describe how to do something; can they translate the learning into action; or perhaps have they become experts as a consequence of going through the change process?

It is possible to create a hierarchy that shows the translation of knowledge into business performance (*see* Figure 8.5). At the lowest level of knowledge acquisition is someone who reads a book, visits a seminar or uses a website. They may have discovered some new knowledge and can describe this to others. The value is that they now have a language by which they can have productive conversations through the use of a shared language and mental map. At the next level is someone who can use their knowledge to apply or actively use their knowledge at an operational level. This step process continues up to the highest level where someone is seen as an authority or expert in the field. This incremental process can be seen in detail in Table 8.4.

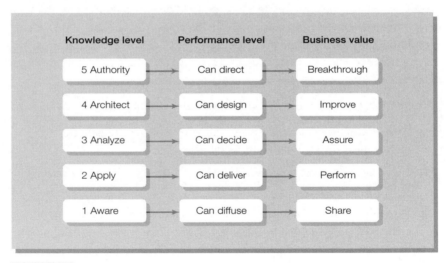

Knowledge level	Performance level	Business value
5 Authority	Can direct	Breakthrough
4 Architect	Can design	Improve
3 Analyze	Can decide	Assure
2 Apply	Can deliver	Perform
1 Aware	Can diffuse	Share

Figure 8.5   Learning levels

As you use the learning levels model you need to consider the following factors:

- **Transfer complete:** Has the necessary transfer of capability taken place to the agreed level on the learning levels framework? Do you need to ensure that you leave architects in place who can develop further support processes downstream, or is it sufficient just to leave analysts who can measure the continuance? If you have only moved the client to the apply level, what capability do they have to take themselves up to the high levels on the hierarchy, or will they need to purchase some of your time and capability at a later date?

■ **Who needs the knowledge:** Are you sure that the right people have been taken to the correct learning level? All too often consultant will leave the client group with key people at a higher level on the model but the senior team are left way down at the aware level. If the decision makers are at the lower level they might not engage emotionally with the change and so can fail to appreciate its importance in the next round of budget allocations.

■ **Internal transfer capability:** Does the client group also have the capability to take other people in the organization up the learning levels? No matter how many architects you leave in the business, at some point they will be promoted or will leave the company. Once they walk out then the expertise goes with them and the client group is

Table 8.4   **Learning levels**

Knowledge level	Performance level	Business value
At the end of the engagement I want someone who might be viewed as:	. . . and they are able to:	. . . that will create value by:
5 An authority	Judge other people's work from a position of authority and against accepted criteria	Setting new business performance standards against wider markets and business trends
4 An architect	Originate, integrate and combine ideas into a new product, plan or proposal	Improving business benchmarks and performance
3 Able to analyze	Compare, contrast and classify information in order to form a performance judgement	Ensuring and assuring that performance standards are being maintained
2 Able to apply	Use the knowledge to resolve operational problems	Delivering improved performance
1 Aware	Explain what they know and how it might be used.	Facilitating productive conversations within the company and with customers

left in a potentially non-sustainable position. The answer is to ensure that the client group has the capability to take its own members up the learning levels and so become self-sufficient.

■ **Future knowledge levels:** It is also important to help the client appreciate what learning level they are being left at but also what level they might need to achieve if they are to hold on to the gains and beat the competition. If the change was to install a new procurement system, the chances are that its leading-edge processes will soon be commonplace in the industry and within a few years it will be outdated. The client group will need to build on the retained expertise and understand where its learning level might need to be in a few years' time if it is to keep ahead of the pack.

Knowledge does not come for free. If I asked the local plumber to teach me how to repair my own leaky valves rather than paying him to come round, he would want to charge me for that knowledge. Consultancy is a business, not a charity: intellectual capital has value and it is the foolish consultant who does not understand the market value of their talent.

From the very outset of the engagement it is important to consider the issue of learning levels with the client – to help them understand where they want and need to be at the end of the engagement and consequently how much they will need to pay to gather such knowledge. For most consulting engagements there will be a step increase in the level of work required to get the client group up the five levels. It is relativity easy to get someone to the aware level and the apply level can be often managed with workshops, training courses and processes. But the moment the client want you to leave them with people at the analyze, architect or authority level, there will be a hefty price to pay. The benefit of the learning levels framework is that it offers a powerful way in which you can explain why the development of such capability will cost.

Table 8.5 gives an indication of the types of learning techniques that can be used at each level. Clearly, the level 1 options are commonly found in any organizational intervention and are used to underpin and drive most training processes around the world. But as we start to go up the levels, many of the techniques are more specialized in their context and content and will need the corresponding levels of sophisticated support. The other factor must be considered as you go higher up the levels is time. The lower levels tend to be heavily compressed, since time is money and the goal is to transfer the optimum level of knowledge in minimum time. But processes like mentoring, academic study and peer verification, are all very costly because of the time involved, and any drive to compress the time taken will reduce the quality.

Table 8.5 Learning techniques

Level	Learning processes
5 Authority	Mentoring
	Training and assessing others
	Authoring of critical papers
	Academic verification
	Peer verification
	National and international publication
	Citation from other authorities and authors
	Public scrutiny
4 Architect	Composition of original papers
	Academic study
	Research programmes
	Longitudinal studies
	Cross-boundary integration
	Cross-cultural experiences
	Peer presentations
3 Analyst	Expert assessment
	Case study development
	Site visits
	Peer validation processes
	Academic research
	Context-specific tests
	Benchmarking assignments
2 Application	Workshops
	Coaching
	Peer assessment
	Post-event web support
	Post-event peer workshops
	Applied accreditation
1 Awareness	Seminars or conferences
	E-learning
	Written material such as books or web

This is why it is so important that you have a discussion with the client about the level of learning that will be necessary and agree how much they are able and prepared to pay to attain such capability. The conundrum will be when the client wants sustainable change that is based on internal knowledge capability but is not willing or able to pay to raise people to the necessary learning level. Unfortunately there is no simple answer to this – it is either a case of helping the client to understand why they need to find the money or helping them to understand why it might be better to defer the change until they are really ready to make the necessary investment.

Sell the story

Building on the theoretical model offered in the previous section, you might need to undertake an analysis of the organization's practical capability to diffuse and sell the new ideas across the organization.

Ideally, you should map the transport mechanisms and consider how effectively they will expand and share knowledge. For example, consider the product team that has discovered a great new method for reducing quality costs on the production line. In an ideal world, this innovation would be rapidly transported across the business so that other teams can reap the benefits. Yet although organizations might suggest that their internal communication processes are open, speedy and flexible, they are often clogged up and slow. It is important to develop a clear picture of the channels as they are – not how the client or consumer thinks they are.

> **it is important to develop a clear picture of the channels as they are – not how the client or consumer thinks they are**

As you try to map how new ideas or knowledge will flow across a business after you have departed, it can help to consider the impact that the various channels will have on the diffusion process. The definition of a channel is any system, process or medium used to transport a piece of information from one part of the organization to another. It might be an internal newspaper, monthly team meeting, intranet system or grapevine. All will be tools to help continue the work undertaken by the consultant in the change project. The question you must ask is: What effect will the channel have on the knowledge as it is dispersed around the business? The following list takes the example of the introduction of a new quality programme and how the different channels will modify the knowledge flow:

■ **Amplify:** Knowledge channels rarely transmit information without changing its intensity. Often what is a relatively innocuous piece of information will be exploded beyond all expectation. The fact that the quality programme will include an audit process might well be interpreted by a militant staff association as a way in which senior managers will subject their members to oppressive supervision.

■ **Attenuate:** Conversely, some channels will take a relatively important piece of information and cause it to lose power and energy. Although the quality initiative might be commissioned as a way to respond to market pressures, this message might well be lost as the communication channels place greater emphasis on the practical aspects of the change programme. The commercial imperative that has driven the programme becomes overtaken by the project-management aspects, thus diminishing the power of the original message.

■ **Adapt:** Any newspaper or in-house journal will adapt and modify a story to fit the profile of the target audience. The engineering journal will offer details of the project in relation to the quality targets that have been set for the engineers. The marketing division will sell it on the basis of 'it is what our customers want'. Although this adaptive process is useful in diffusing the knowledge, you must be careful that the information does not become overly diluted or distorted.

■ **Accelerate:** Some processes will change the speed of diffusion of knowledge. If you are working in a more traditional organization, then diffusion will probably be through paper-based systems and the transmission time will be measured in terms of days rather than minutes. In an organization that has adopted IT within its core infrastructure, the diffusion of knowledge will be measured in minutes and hours. So whereas the time between a quality audit and the final programme assessment being presented would have been measured in weeks, with many new systems the board can monitor the result dynamically, mapping how different business units are faring in the quality assessment process.

■ **Abuse:** Many channels abuse the knowledge as it flows through. One prime example is seen with the political systems that fuel the grapevine. As people become aware of the impending quality system, so they will reinterpret the message to favour their position. The senior manager who is opposed to the rigour that the system will bring might choose to spread rumours about problems with it and in particular how it will drive up costs.

As these examples indicate, to make sure that the engagement continues after their departure, consultants must pay close attention to the channels within the business and attempt to map how they affect the change process. Wherever possible, your goal must be to understand how the change will be affected and to put in place compensating action to ensure the messages are not corrupted.

One tool that might help is the channel matrix (*see* Table 8.6), a simple process by which you can set out what core outcomes need to be maintained after you have closed the contract. With this, you can map the primary channels that will be used to share the knowledge. So for each cell on the matrix, you will attempt to indicate how the channel will deal with the change outcome, categorizing how it may modify the knowledge flow (amplify, alternate, adapt, accelerate, or abuse).

Table 8.6   **Channel matrix**

	Channel 1	*Channel 2*	*Channel 3*	*Channel 4*
Outcome 1				
Outcome 2				
Outcome 3				
Outcome 4				

For example, assume that outcome 1 is head office relocation, complete and delivered within the financial year. The consultant considers the various channels and maps the impact that three of them will have on the process as seen in Table 8.7. The conclusion might be that further work would have to be undertaken with the staff association. Unless it is convinced of the wisdom of the relocation, then problems might be stirred up that could affect the date of the final move.

The effective diffusion of ideas and knowledge will have a critical impact on their sustainability. Like the commuter running to catch a train, chasing through corridors that are clogged up with debris and people heightens the risk of missing the train. Your role is to ensure that the communication channels are free of such debris and that knowledge will flow through the organization and underpin and sustain the transformation.

Table 8.7	Channel matrix example

	Company newspaper	*Staff association*	*Project instructions*
Relocation delivered on time and to budget	**Amplify:** As with most good internal magazines, there will be a positive spin applied to the change, with all the up-side issues promoted	**Abuse:** This is only likely to happen where the staff association opposes the relocation project; in this case, it has significant power to distort the message	**Accelerate:** A good set of project instructions will help to speed up the rate of transmission; the use of e-mail, team meetings and project reviews can ensure that news is speedily transmitted around the team

Stage seven: Close

This is not the end. It is not even the beginning of the end;
but it is perhaps the end of the beginning.

Winston Churchill

The contract is over, it is time to say goodbye and move on. But like watching a good play or tasting a fine wine, it is that last memory that will remain and which may cloud the recollection of the total experience. This 'recency' factor means that the last items presented are more likely to be recalled than those that went earlier. Therefore it is important for you to manage the exit carefully and not just assume that it will be OK to ask for the money and leave.

Failure to stage-manage the closure process has led and will continue to lead to many disasters:

- Consultants were convinced that since the project action had been completed no formal review was necessary with the client. Although they were paid, no further contracts were offered because the client felt that the consultants had not been prepared to listen to the client's view of the outcomes.

- Although the board was happy with the new processes that consultants had helped to deliver, it was starting to question the real value of the change. It believed that it could have made the change itself and so saved substantial amounts of money. The problem was that the consultants focused on telling the board what had been delivered. If they had communicated how the company had changed as a result, the board might have understood that there were elements that it could not have delivered itself.

■ The consultants had finished a great piece of work and the client and consumer were happy and keen to build on the work. However, the consultants were relatively new to the consulting world and felt that they should not be trying to sell on the back of success. They believed that if the client wanted some further work this would indicated that as part of the relationship. The end result was that both parties spilt with an unspoken desire to work together again and hence there was a lost opportunity.

■ The consultants closed their project down and left to work on another project. But many parts of the client's organization had built a close working relationship with the consultants and tended to call on them for advice on many of the core issues within the project. Their departure meant that people felt slightly let down and were not keen to make use of their services again.

So, when closing an engagement, you must avoid the entirely natural urge to say goodbye with a cheery wave on the assumption that everything will be all right because the project outcomes have been achieved. There are many tangible and intangible issues that need to be addressed at this stage and you must work with the client to ensure that time is made available for the closure process.

Within this stage of the Seven Cs cycle, the following issues need to be considered:

■ **Look back and learn:** Encourage your client to consider what has been learned over and above the planned outcomes of the change.

■ **Look to let go:** The onus is on you to ensure that at the point of departure all unnecessary levels of dependence have gone from all sides of the relationship. The key question is can they fly solo?

■ **Look at the value:** It is important to understand how the outcomes from the change have tangibly delivered improvement to the operational or commercial viability of the organization.

■ **Look forward:** On the assumption that the consultancy assignment has been handled professionally and delivered the appropriate outcomes, then it may be appropriate to investigate what opportunities might exist for further work.

Look back and learn

The consultant is responsible for ensuring not just that the job is done, but also helping the client group understand how it was done, why it worked and how the client can repeat the same exercise by flying solo. A key component in the Close stage is the ability to learn and reflect on what actually happened rather than what people think happened in the project.

The after action review (AAR) is a powerful tool that can assist you with managing this process. It does this by eliciting feedback under a relatively controlled process. Typically, all the key participants who supported the engagement or operation will take time out to examine – in a non-incriminating manner and with the objective of organizational learning – how the project was managed. Their aim is to identify learning points and suggest ways that the next cycle can be improved.

The whole AAR process is designed to be simple so that it can be easily used in any sitatuion. It follows a set of five primary questions:

1 What did we expect to happen?
   - What was the objective of the piece of work?
   - Did we have a clear outcome?
   - Were the players involved clear about the change?
   - Were the measures communicated and understood?
   - What are the different perceptions from each member of the review?

2 What actually happened?
   - What was the outcome?
   - How do we know?
   - What does each person perceive to be the outcome and what are the perception gaps?
   - What explicit evidence do we have?
   - What anecdotal or intangible evidence do we have?

3 What worked and what did not work?
   - Was there any gap between what we expected to happen and what actually happened?
   - How would we rate the outcome against our expectations, the client's expectations and the consumer's expectations?
   - What helped the good to be good?
   - What caused the bad to be bad?
   - What helped the success or caused the failure?
   - What alternative courses of actions might have been more effective?

4 What have we learned?

5 What should we take forward to use next time?

The AAR creates a safe container, where people are able to express freely what they perceived to have happened without fear of recrimination. Although it would be foolish to think that this can always be guaranteed – because people are people – but the use of a formal agenda and structure with defined ground rules about behaviour and desired outcomes can go a long way towards facilitating an open learning process. The key factor is that is should always deal with the process and not the people. If the review begins to focus on 'who' rather than 'what' then it is heading down a spiral of recrimination and blame that will kill any chance for real tangible learning.

The primary benefits of any effective AAR will be that it:

■ creates a temporary pause where people can take a breath;

■ allows the client to test intended against actual outcomes;

■ allows for triangulation of data – pulling together different sources into a single document;

■ identifies what to keep, what to let go and what to amplify next time round;

■ links the three threads of operational, tactical and strategic change under a single review process;

■ captures and communicates learning based on fact rather than fantasy;

■ allows for immediate fixes rather than waiting for lessons to go round the bureaucratic structure;

■ signals a deep desire on the part of the change team to learn.

The US Army has been using this process as a way to manage learning after missions. The Army began the AAR process in the 1980s and has been refining it over the years. It was used first shortly after the Vietnam War in the Mojave Desert, where 8,000 US soldiers were conducting battle training, and it has been suggested that much of the US Army's success in the Gulf War came from its use (*Financial Executives International*, 2002). For many consultants the process of engaging a client group will be very similar to an army mission, so the AAR is a powerful tool that can help the consultant to take learning into new client engagements and help the client to bring learning back into the business for free.

Look to let go

All through the life of the change process, the drivers tend to be based around growing the relationship – improving the association so that the consultant develops a high degree of trust and responsiveness with the client. However, as this relationship grows, so the level of dependence grows between the various players. The problem is that at the end of the day both you and the client have to let go and break away from the relationship. The onus is on you to ensure that at the point of departure all unnecessary levels of dependence have gone from the relationship, because 'To have a situation where there is chronic dependence on consultants is an implicit admission of ineptitude in management' (O'Shea and Madigan, 1997).

> **you must be close enough to develop a trust-based association, but distant enough to allow independence and freedom**

At the start of the relationship you are often seen as 'the expert', someone who has all the right answers and will be able to solve the problems. While this can help to ensure that buy-in takes place, the danger is that a dependent relationship is formed – one in which the client is sometimes unwilling to let go of your perceived expertise. This can be seen in the patient who will only go to see one particular dentist or the preference that you might have for a particular car mechanic. However, a problem can arise when the dentist or mechanic decides to move. You are left high and dry, without anywhere to turn when the next problem surfaces. Thus there is a difficult balance in any client relationship. You must be close enough to develop a trust-based association, but distant enough to allow independence and freedom.

A common pattern in consulting projects is shown in Figure 9.1. The first stage is where you meet the client. There is still a freedom of choice about the relationship, like a couple out on a first date sizing each other up. Once there is an agreement that a relationship will be formed, you will typically have quite a high level of dependency on the client. You will need help to understand the working of the system (at the Clarify stage), access to the right people and confirmation that the initial work seems to be effective. However, once the process goes into the Create and Change stages, there is a shared dependency – both parties have invested time and reputation in the relationship and cannot afford to see it fail. Beyond this, in the Confirm and Continue stages, you are probably coasting and might well be starting to think about the next project. However, now the client has a strong depen-

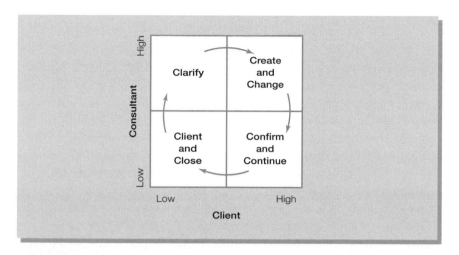

Figure 9.1   Dependency loop

dency on you to prove that the outcome is as agreed, since otherwise it
might reflect poorly on them. At the final Close stage, both you and the
client should be back at the start of the loop, able to reflect on the relationship in the cold light of day. It is from this rational position that any
decision is taken to pursue further options for working together.

Problems can arise where you try to close the relationship while the client
is still dependent on you. Change projects often fail because the consultant
has gone and the client and the consumer are left high and dry without the
real confidence or ability to run with the change. As a result, one of several
things can happen:

■ the client's organization reverts back to the state that existed before
  the change;

■ the client re-employs the consultant to return and fix some of the
  problems again;

■ the client turns against the consultant and employs a different firm to
  fix the problems.

Whichever option is followed, the end result is unsatisfactory and one that
you should avoid. Dependence is a positive state only when both parties are
aware of the condition. If one or both groups is unaware of the reliance,
then this can only lead to an unhealthy situation. Your goal is to develop a
relationship that is based upon a spirit of mutual interdependence.

Look at the value

The bottom line for any change must be to add value to the system being changed. This might be through modifications to people's behavioural routines, the implementation of a new information system, or the completion of a strategy to meet an international standard. If the core value cannot be extracted from the outcome then it becomes difficult for the management team to justify the time and expense of the change to the stakeholders of the business. In the closure stage, you must ensure that the added value is clearly understood by and communicated to the client and the end consumer. The notion of recency is paramount at this stage, because their lasting memory of you and the consulting engagement will be heavily influenced by the final messages and signals that you send out. Hence, you must ensure that the message of positive added value is included in all interactions with the client (Lascelles and Peacock, 1996). It is important that you present your role in developing this added value in as simple a form as possible. Developing grand outcome statements or strategic presentations is useful for those people who have been involved in the change, but will mean little to those in other parts of the organization. It is essential that you leave the client with a simple message that can be readily shared across the organization.

There are two aspects to the value management process:

- **Value management:** Identifying the area of the business value improvement that has been managed.
- **Value differentiation:** Counteracting the impact of value shift in the mind of the client and consumer.

Value management

Value management is about the ability to understand clearly and communicate where value is being created. Value in this sense is a tangible function – something from which the client will receive benefit, be it commercially, emotionally or physically. Nagle and Holden (1995) define it as the total savings or satisfaction that the customer receives from the product. Economists refer to this as the use value or utility gained from a product. In consulting terms, it might be defined as the benefit or gain that the client receives following the change engagement. Although your contract will clearly indicate the change that must be made to satisfy the commercial or social relationship, it might not include a specific focus on the value that will accrue on conclusion of the change.

Although there will be commercial consulting engagements that fall outside this definition, the vast majority of programmes will realize value from the change. As an example, typical consulting actions have been listed in Table 9.1. By allocating actions to simple headings it allows a consistent message to be communicated to the client and consumers. Although your engagement might be highly complicated and detailed, unless you are able to offer the end consumer (and other stakeholders) a clear and succinct reason for the change, then your action might fade into history along with all the other change programmes.

Table 9.1 Value-added categories

Added value	Consultant action
Increased revenue	■ Product enhancement
	■ Selling/marketing strategy
	■ Competitor response
	■ Business acquisition
Reduced costs	■ Buying policies
	■ Operating strategy
	■ Process simplification
	■ Use of materials
	■ Reduced overhead
	■ System integration
Effective people	■ Organizational effectiveness
	■ Work scheduling
	■ Headcount levels
	■ Pay rates
	■ Training and development
Effective assets	■ Use of fixed assets
	■ Gearing levels
	■ Stock levels
	■ Credit control
	■ Material management
	■ Interest levels

Value differentiation

In many cases, just offering the customer a review that sets out the value delivered is not sufficient. Consulting is a trade-based operation where the ability to sell products and services is a core competency. You must ensure that the closure process not only reinforces what you have delivered but shows how your services stand apart from what a competitor might have delivered. The art of the closure is in reinforcing the factors that differentiate your outcome from that of your competitors, as well as confirming what might be perceived as the commodity element of your proposition (*see* Figure 9.2). Value differentiation might be seen as the difference between the value of the work that you have undertaken and that which might be delivered by a comparable competitor.

> **" the art of the closure is in reinforcing the factors that differentiate your outcome from that of your competitors "**

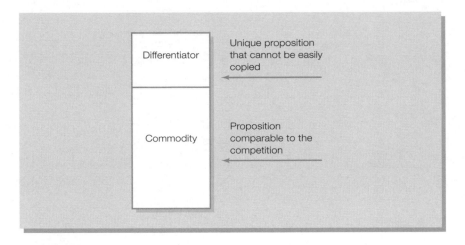

Figure 9.2   Differentiated delivery

Value, like beauty, is in the eye of the beholder and is not always an absolute element. Although value might be defined as the savings or satisfaction that the client and consumer receive from the engagement, there are many factors that drive this level of satisfaction. Consider the cost of a litre of petrol. This is a commodity that sells within a narrow price band, no matter where you might be. You might quite easily define the value of the product and equate it as being equal to the economic cost. Now switch to a different scenario: you have run out of petrol and the garage is a mile down the road.

How much would you be prepared to pay for the fuel now? The guess is that most people would be prepared to pay a price premium of 50 per cent to save the effort of walking down the road to get some more fuel. Now consider that you have run out of fuel on the way to an important client meeting. This meeting will be the final clincher in what has been a prolonged and difficult sales process and unless you are there to close the sale there is every chance that the client will switch to a competitor. What value does a litre of fuel now hold? In cold economic terms, it can equate to a percentage of the revenue that you will receive from the client contract, which in many cases might be the price of a new car.

Thus value must be measured from the perspective of the client and consumer, not from your perspective. Value is driven by the availability of comparable alternatives. So even if you have delivered exactly what has been specified in the contract, if the client feels that they could have achieved the result at lower cost via an alternative route, then your sense of value contribution will be minimized. In a simple world, this would not be a problem because the client's view of the perceived value would be constant over the course of the change. However, the reality is that over the life of any change project the client's perception of the value that you are adding could well change. By the end of the project they may be willing to pay the bill, but do so with a sense that true value has not been delivered.

Imagine you are walking down the high street and you see a shop that is selling your favourite brand of jeans at a third discount to the normal price. You decide to buy a pair and at the moment of decision you are convinced that this is a fair transaction and one where you will receive value from the purchase. However, as you walk out of the door, you notice that the shop on the other side of the street also has a sale but it is offering the same jeans for half price. Your sense that the jeans were a good purchase will be immediately reduced and in many ways you might blame the shop for ripping you off.

The same can happen in one of your consulting assignments. You begin the engagement on the clear understanding that you are responsible for re-engineering one of the company's core processes. All goes well, but at the end of the assignment the client starts to ask questions about the bad press that process re-engineering has received. They even start to question if the change was really necessary after all. Although they know in their head that you have delivered the agreed value, their heart tells them that something does not feel right and the only person they can blame is you. Here lies the quandary. From your perspective the appropriate and agreed value has been delivered, but from the client's perspective the value is suspect.

Clearly, you cannot prevent a change in the environment or how the client sees the world, but you can have an array of arguments that will help to ensure the client and consumer are made aware of the unique value that you have offered as part of the transformation. These arguments can be used to help the client to realign their understanding of value and in particular to see the value that your project has realized – even if there has been a significant change in the environment. Examples of the differentiated propositions might include:

- **Service performance guarantees:** If the client is not satisfied with the final outcome, any part of the delivery will be reworked free of charge.
- **Faster delivery:** Your ability to mobilize resources is such that any client demands are met without delay.
- **Licensed proposition:** You own the rights to the intellectual capital and no other provider is able to deliver the same product.
- **Trusted client relationship:** The closeness of the relationship means that no other supplier is able to get close to the client.

These differentiators are crucial because they offer options that the competition might not be able to replicate. Although they are not in themselves unique, any competitor wishing to replicate the proposition will have to mobilize the necessary resources – and this takes time.

So, when an engagement is being closed, it is important to ensure that the core added-value elements are communicated. But it is also important to ensure that the client understands how your particular differentiated proposition is embedded in your delivery. This reinforcement must be communicated on a logical and emotional level. The client must understand the cold logic of your differentiator, so that they are able to compare it with the competition. Second, they must feel how your service is different so that they can sell you and your ideas to others with a sense of passion. Finally, wherever possible, encourage the client to touch the difference. Wherever your solution has a tangible factor, ensure that the client touches, smells or feels how it is different from your competitors' offering. By ensuring that they understand the differentiated value there is a greater chance that the closure is successful and further repeat business can be won.

Look forward

No matter what the scenario, the best time to make a sale is the point when the customer voluntarily says how great the previous product or service has been. At this point they are happy, have found benefits with your offering and might already have made the decision to purchase again – so your sale process is simply a question of 'What they will buy?' rather than 'Will they buy?'. From a commercial perspective, when this happens the cost of sale is so low as to be negligible. Logically the point on the Seven Cs life cycle where this will happen is in the Close stage.

Although this may be the logical thing to do, now be honest and think about the following:

■ How many of the recent change programmes in your organization have been properly closed?

■ How hard is it to get a repeat sale if you don't know what the client thinks or feels about the current engagement?

■ How many of your recent engagements have you 'properly' closed down?

■ To what extent do you actively and consciously use the Close stage to trigger a repeat engagement?

There is plenty of evidence that both the client and consultant consistently underplay the Close stage. In many cases this because all the effort is placed on the early stages. We all aspire to meet our new client (for potential revenue), create a relationship, understand the problem and then help develop a sustainable solution. The trouble is that this is where it often stops: so many change programmes follow the pattern of Client, Clarify, Create, Change and runnnnnn ... (*see* Figure 9.3). There is often little measurement post-implementation, and neither the client nor the consultant rush to deal with the factors that help the change to be sustainable. There is certainly an almost complete absence of an effective Close stage.

As a consultant myself, I do feel bad making such audacious statements, suggesting that as an industry we are not professional and fail to take the engagement through to its logical and natural conclusion. But after running many events, seminars and client meetings where this issue is raised, I can count on one hand the number of clients who have said that I am wrong.

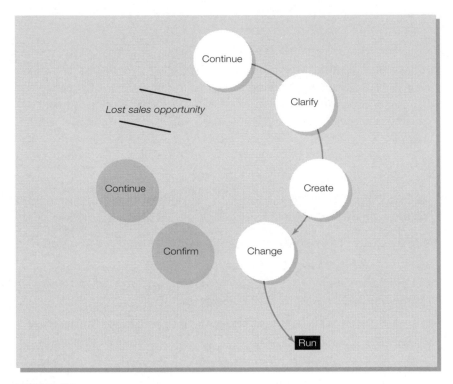

Lost sales opportunity

Continue

Clarify

Continue

Create

Confirm

Change

Run

Figure 9.3   Incomplete change programme

At one consultancy conference I heard a financial director of a large company say that over the course of a year not one consultancy engagement had delivered any of the anticipated benefits. And what is worse is that all the delegates (consultants) nodded their head and agreed that that happened all the time. The failure to close an engagement effectively is one of the primary reasons for the poor brand reputation of the change industry and will eventually lead to its destruction.

It is the courage to build on the current engagement that is key to any successful (and profitable) client partnership. Most consultants will allocate time to find new clients and work to promote a product or service, but this is costly and takes valuable time away from the real work. The effort needed to keep identifying new prospects can be quite draining, so the alternative approach is to focus on the development of high-value, long-term, profitable partnerships. A useful model is the Build framework, which defines the journey that an effective client–consultant partnership might follow. The framework is outlined below, together with advice on how to guide the client through the journey.

The build framework

The build process is built around the following three factors:

■ **Build dimensions:** The dimensions indicate how you help facilitate a desire on the part of the client to enter into a partnership relationship. Any relational process is built around three elements: the buying behaviour, an intellectual appreciation of the product and an emotional appreciation of the consultant or their product.

■ **Build steps:** These are the differing stages needed to progress the client from stranger to valued partner.

■ **Build drivers:** The drivers are the specific action you can take to manage each step change and so help people move along the partnership journey.

The build dimensions

There are three primary dimensions that underpin any commercial relationship:

■ **Cognitive or head:** What the client is thinking.

■ **Affective or heart:** What they are feeling.

■ **Behaviour or hand:** What they actually do.

A human being is a complex system involving an interaction between these three dimensions (*see* Figure 3.2). The effective consultant makes sure that they understand how all three interrelate and impact upon the nature of their commercial relationship with the client. By understanding the three dimensions it is possible to build a series of actions that will help manage the migration of a client from someone who has no interest in purchasing your services to a partner who passionately promotes you or your services in to their colleagues.

The build steps

The first time we meet a potential client it might be fair to assume that they have little desire to work with us; in many cases they might be anti the whole notion of using the services of an external agent. Certainly, the collective brand of the consultant it is often seen in very poor light. The jokes, bad press, corrupt working practices and other problems that seem to surface on a regular basis all come together to create a negative brand

> **❝ however, our goal must be to run an engagement that delivers value through sustainable change ❞**

image. However, our goal must be to run an engagement that delivers value through sustainable change and as a consequence move the client away from this perception and ideally help them to value our services. Over time and repeated engagements the hope is that the client will become even more enamoured with the value that we can provide, and eventually reach a point where the relationship might be viewed as a trusted partnership – similar to that you might have with a cherished doctor or financial adviser. Our goal might be to help the customer to progress effortlessly from a position where they might be fiercely opposed to the product or service, through to a position where they are a keen market advocate. So the journey might be one of a managed shift from 'anti' to 'educator' (*see* Figure 9.4).

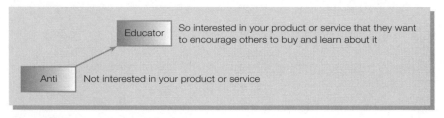

Figure 9.4   **Building the relationship**

However, the journey from anti to educator, albeit powerful, is rarely taken in a single step. To help the client make this shift they will often have to go through a number of steps:

- **Anti to ambivalent:** The client does not really have a strong belief either way.
- **Ambivalent to believer:** The client accepts the general need but not necessarily for the consultant's service.
- **Believer to buyer:** The client is prepared to make a single transaction purchase.
- **Buyer to customer:** An ongoing relationship has developed with the client.
- **Customer to champion:** The client will happily promote the consultant's proposition.
- **Champion to defender:** The client is such a strong advocate that they will counter any criticism against the product.

▨ **Defender to disciple:** The client's belief is such they want to learn more about the product.

▨ **Disciple to expert:** The new knowledge puts the client in a commanding position as an authority figure.

▨ **Expert to educator:** The client has the capability and desire to help others make a similar journey.

The build drivers

These build steps offer a powerful way to categorize the client's progression towards a partnership relationship. Although the steps do not provide a scientific or accurate portrayal of exactly what the client is thinking and feeling at any time, they offer a simple and symbolic analysis of the client and their relationship with you.

Once you understand the stages at which the client can be within the relationship, the next step might be to understand what you need to do to migrate them along the journey. How can you manage the relationship to help move to a partnership level (if that is what you want the relationship to look like)? We do this by understanding the drivers that impact upon the two dimensions of heart and head:

▨ What is it that we need to do to help improve how the client feels about us or our services?

▨ How can we help them to see the rationale for purchasing our services?

Each of the build steps is indicated below with the driver that might be used to help the client step to the next level. Each step is also categorized as a head or heart action.

▨ **Anti to ambivalent (head: offer evidence):**

As with a consumer who is opposed to any use of the product, the first logical step may be to offer logical evidence to demonstrate that no harm will come to the client from the association with the consultant. This is generic data and not necessarily data specific to the consultant's product or idea.

■ **Ambivalent to believer (heart: reason to believe):**

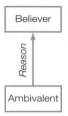

In the words of that great bard Rod Stewart, there must be 'a reason to believe'. The emotional shift from ambivalent to believer is indicative that the person believes in the need for the benefits associated with the service but has not yet bought into the need to make a purchase. The risk of getting the client to this stage is that once they believe in the need then a competitor may come along and steal them. This is why it is important not to lose sight of the next stage and ideally move the client to buyer as quickly as possible by offering firm evidence why the service offers the best value in the market.

■ **Believer to buyer (head: offer value):**

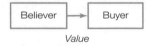

The shift from a position where someone believes in the need for a product and actually buying the service is driven by the logical appreciation that they will derive a benefit – that there might be a financial, emotional or rational payback resulting from the cost of sale. Interestingly, although it might be that the decision to buy is driven by an emotional pull, generally the customer will be able to rationalize the decision.

■ **Buyer to customer (heart: make it personal):**

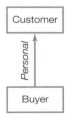

The buyer stage can be seen as a transactional position. This is where cost will take precedence over the nature of the relationship as a buying determinant. The shift to a customer level comes once the

relationship is personal. At this stage the buyer wants to come back
rather than purchasing from one of the competitors. Cost becomes less
of a logical decision criteria; instead the nature of the relationship
becomes more dominant. Research has revealed that up to 80 per cent
of repeat client purchases are driven by the nature of the relationship
rather than the quality of the previous project.

■ **Customer to champion (head: personal payback):**

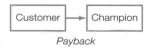

The logical shift from customer to champion is a subtle but important
one. It is the point where the client is prepared to tell others in their
organization about their experience and its value. This helps to
increase market penetration and starts to reduce the cost of sale. The
customer will often make this shift because they see some form of
personal payback from promoting the service. This might be in the
form of brand association or political power.

■ **Champion to defender (heart: stakeholder):**

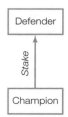

The emotional shift from champion to defender is indicated by the
willingness of the client to act as protector in cases where other
people criticize the proposition. The drive for this will often be
because they have a personal stake in the ideas associated with the
offering and view any attack as a personal criticism of their decision
to support the idea.

■ **Defender to disciple (head: lead though learning):**

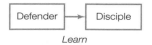

At this level the customer sees sense in learning more about the
proposition and so takes on a disciple or committed student role. Their
goal might be to acquire knowledge so they can deploy it for personal
or business gain.

- **Disciple to expert (heart: reframe):**

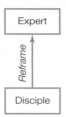

The step from disciple to expert is where the learner is able to take the ideas associated with the product and use it in a new way or direction. They do this by adding value through reframing the basic concept and presenting it to the market in a different form. At this stage they have internalized the learning and may start to present it using their own maps. This indicates immense buy-in – but the risk is when they get it wrong.

- **Expert to educator (head: recognition):**

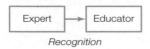

The final stage from expert to educator is where the client has acquired so much expertise that they are selling the proposition to their peers. At this level the cost of sale has been almost eliminated and the client is acting as a market advocate. There is often a need at this stage to shift the nature of the relationship from teacher or guide to that of a professional peer, where their value and expertise is openly acknowledged.

We can step back and see how the client will ideally progress up the build levels as shown in Figure 9.5.

Close by building

The build model is designed to help people make choices in how they develop a successful partnership and to understand how to progress people through the various levels on the build framework – possibly to take someone who is an anti all the way through to the educator level.

However, it is a rare occasion when a client can be taken through all levels of the framework in one engagement. The ultimate goal of the build framework is to ensure that when closing the current engagement, the client is helped to understand the value that has been delivered. By helping the client understand and appreciate the value at an emotional and cognitive level it becomes possible to step the client up a level on the build model. Thus if the client started the current engagement as a buyer, then aspire to get them on to the customer level; if they started the existing engagement at champion, use the project as an opportunity to migrate them to defender level. There is no optimum approach, the goal is simply to be aware of the current level, the level to which they should be migrated, and what action will help them make the shift.

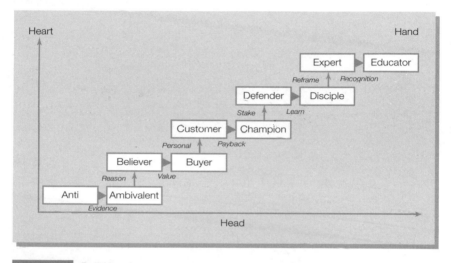

Figure 9.5   Build levels

The closure stage is not the point to say goodbye – it is the point to say hello. In saying hello it makes inherent sense for the client and the consultant to reflect upon their relationships and jointly decide if they want to move towards to a partnership: one that will create shared success for both parties (*see* Figure 9.6).

The danger at this stage is that you might decide to use the warmth of the closure as a chance to sell a new set of services to the client. Although this might be appropriate in a few cases, the broad principle must be that taking this action will sour the relationship. If you have not re-engaged the client by this stage, then it is better to walk out as a friend, and then re-enter the door at a later date with a new offering.

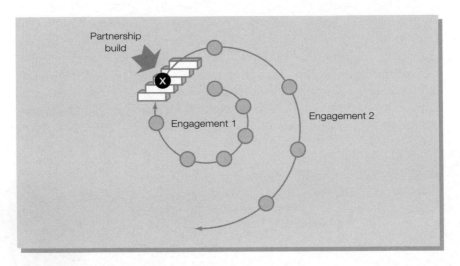

Figure 9.6   Partnership build

10

The consultant's capital

So just how do consultants create value? How do they pay the mortgage, feed the kids, buy the latest toys and pay for next year's holiday? Like all professionals, they go to market with their talent and tools.

All professionals will have their natural set of tools. These are the assets that you would expect to find being used by anyone, irrespective of the context or domain in which the work is undertaken. The doctor might have a stethoscope, the plummer a wrench, the carpenter a hammer, the architect a pencil or the musician an instrument. But what is the natural tool or asset that you might expect to find a consultant using? Although there might be domain-specific tools that are used operate in a particular context, there is no one natural tool or asset that all consultants will always have in their back pocket.

So what do consultants need to do? Often it is to simply to ask questions that follow the natural Seven Cs life cycle:

1 **Client:** Meet the customer, build a relationship and understand the initial position.

2 **Clarify:** Delve deeper to understand and map the real problem.

3 **Create:** Work with the client group to develop a sustainable solution.

4 **Change:** Help deploy the solution.

5 **Confirm:** Ensure that the solution does what it is supposed to do.

6 **Continue:** Work with people to ensure the change will last.

7 **Close:** Wave goodbye and say hello.

None of the seven stages has any great need for specific tools, instruments or assets. What each needs is the consultant's ability to build a trust-based relationship, diagnose the problem, and then be creative, challenging and brave. So whereas the plumbers, doctors and dentists may include some form of fixed asset base in their annual accounts, the consultant has little need to do this. The consultant's only real capital base is talent – and this is where the difficulty arises. The challenge is for the consultant to understand how to manage, measure and market this intangible capital base.

Unfortunately, this is where the dilemma often sits. Of all the different commercial factors that will drive a consultant's thoughts and feelings, time is the most critical. Whether you are an internal change agent, external consultant, personal coach or account director, time is generally the factor that is measured because that is what drives the billing or charge cycle. Time is the commodity that is measured most, but the paradox is that effective consultants do not sell time – they sell knowledge.

Knowledge as capital

Time management is a personal discipline that can be seen to blossom, even from school. As children we are forced to manage blocks of time at school; at college, one of the first guiding rules offered by the tutor is about the need to manage study time; and at work, some people now micro-manage themselves down to the minute. In this rush to manage time, where is the desire to manage knowledge? Generally, it is subordinate to time in terms of importance. However, the effective consultant can create a greater market value by selling one hour's worth of knowledge than they can one hour of their physical time.

> **smarter consultants help build smarter organizations**

In the same way that it has become accepted that people need to manage their time to become effective, so consultants must shift to a mental map where personal knowledge management is seen to be important. They must shift to a stage where personal knowledge management courses – programmes where they are taught how to map, measure, manage and market their personal capital – are viewed as crucial in their personal development plan.

The need for this shift has been re-emphasized by the recent suggestion of McKinsey & Co. that the most important corporate resource over the next 20 years will be talent. It's also the resource in shortest supply. Over the past decade, talent has become more important than capital, strategy or research and development. Think about the sources of competitive advantage that companies have. Capital is accessible today for good ideas and good projects. Strategies are transparent: even if you have got a smart strategy, others can simply copy it. And the half-life of technology is growing shorter all the time. For many companies, that means that people are the prime source of competitive advantage. Better consultants produce better results. Smarter consultants help build smarter organizations.

Hence, the capability to manage effectively personal capital at an individual level will provide a differentiator for the consultant and the client's company. In the same way that people now manage their time, we need to develop a business ethos where consultants actively create and manage their personal capital and use their talent to create value for themselves and their company (*see* Figure 10.1).

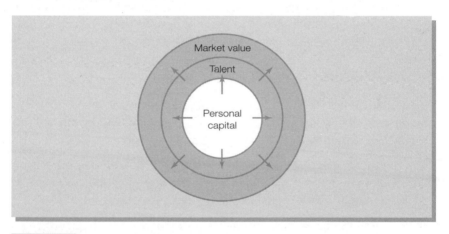

Figure 10.1   Personal capital into market value

Personal capital

Let us consider this idea of personal capital. Hidden behind the word 'personal' is the challenging idea that we are responsible for the choices we make. Your choice to work for a particular company, take a certain course, accept a certain wage are just that – your choice. In the same way that you make choices about the clothes you wear, the food you eat or the car you buy, you must now make choice about the way to manage your personal capital. These are the same decisions that any general manager makes in the day-to-day running of a business. Where should investment take place or where should investment be reduced?

The word 'capital' is not generally linked with the word 'personal'. Capital is normally something that companies need to fund investment or use to define their market value. However, as we shift to a world where the individual reigns supreme, so we must each control our personal capital in the same way that a financial director will jealously guard the financial assets of the business. Yet fewer than 1 per cent of the population, if asked, could say how they truly measure their capitalized value: how much it is worth and how they market it to the world. Instead, so many of us take the easy way out and let the company define our market value. When you do that the company will often not understand the value of your capital and so devalue your worth in the market.

Personal capital can be viewed in two primary dimensions:

■ **Knowledge stock:** We hold a stock of knowledge in either explicit or tacit form.

■ **Knowledge currency:** We acquire or sell our knowledge as a form of currency. This can be viewed in terms of how we think, behave or feel, or the cognitive, behavioural and affective elements.

Personal knowledge bandwidth

By synthesizing these two factors into a single framework, we can develop a pictorial or schematic representation of our knowledge bandwidth and how it might be deployed.

This idea of a personal bandwidth will help you take control of your knowledge. It offers a simple but powerful system to define your personal capital and build processes to enhance its value over time:

■ **Knowledge stock:** How knowledge is stored (*see also* Chapter 3):
  - **Explicit knowledge:** Can be expressed in words and numbers and can be easily communicated and shared in the form of hard data, scientific formulae, codified procedures or universal principles. This is the hard and tangible knowledge that can be codified, replicated and readily transferred across an organization.
  - **Tacit knowledge:** The informal, hard-to-pin down ability. It is a fingertips or muscle capability – where people can perform a task, but find it difficult to explain. It can be the knowledge that you do not recognize that you have, for example how to open a door may not seem like 'knowledge' until you meet somebody who has never seen a door.

■ **Knowledge currency:** How you present the knowledge to the market:
  - **Head:** Our cognitive ability, which is often viewed as our

intelligence or general mental ability. It refers to the capability of people to process information and to use such information to manage their behaviours.
- **Hand:** A generic term covering behaviours, physical activities, responses, reactions, movements, operations etc. It is any measurable response by an individual. This might be a sportsperson's ability to score goals or break records; a manager's ability to lead a team; or the way that a mechanic is able to repair the body work of a damaged car.
- **Heart:** Used to indicate the emotions that we use to manage ourselves and our relationship with others. This intrapersonal capability might be seen in the ability to manage personal motivation and inner leadership. It is the ability to resolve situations by dealing with others in an open and honest way, using the skills of trustworthiness, political astuteness, self-confidence and personal drive.

The combination of these elements can be viewed as the consultant's personal capital. This is the personal asset that we use to create value in the market.

Figure 10.2 illustrates this model. There are six levels, ranging from explicit head down to tacit heart:

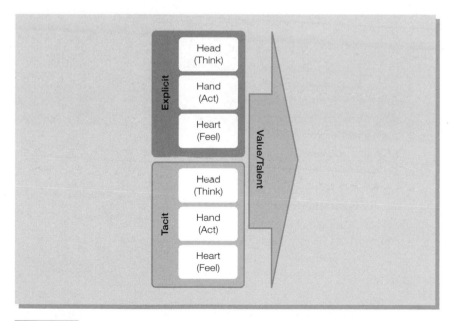

Figure 10.2   Knowledge bandwith

▦ **Explicit head:** What ideas and models are used to create value in the market? What future ideas are required by the market?

▦ **Explicit hand:** What are the behaviours that are of most value? What skills will be needed in your next job?

▦ **Explicit heart:** What techniques and actions do you use to manage relationships? How do you motivate yourself?

▦ **Tacit head:** What mental models drive how you operate? What are your personal assumptions and rules of thumb?

▦ **Tacit hand:** What intuitive behaviours help you to create value in the market? What attributes and capabilities do others admire in you?

▦ **Tacit heart:** How do you build long-term sustainable relationships? How do you maintain spirit and drive under pressure?

This knowledge bandwidth is taken to market in the form of our personal talent – and it is this that creates market value.

Consultant's bandwidth

Although there is no single or prescriptive model that describes the bandwidth to be developed by a consultant, the following list serves as a useful guideline:

▦ **Explicit head:**
- intervention/change frameworks
- business organization knowledge
- measurement techniques
- industry/sector knowledge
- diagnostic and clarification strategies
- negotiation strategies
- financial models
- influencing/political strategies
- decision-making tools
- modelling frameworks
- ethical criteria
- information technology
- case history/stories.

▦ **Explicit hand:**
- general consulting skills
- specific functional or technical skills

- ability to produce reports/presentations etc.
- listening strategies
- relational or rapport-building strategies.

■ **Explicit heart:**
- espoused or stated values
- customer relationship strategies
- sales techniques and strategies
- ability to map the emotional needs of the moment
- inner-security strategies – personal mantras.

■ **Tacit head:**
- knowing when not to intervene
- intuitive problem-solving approach
- knowing when not to give the answer
- giving a sense of assurances that have seen it before
- ability to make intuitive links and synthesize
- using the right language (social, political, organizational)
- rules of thumb associated with previous experiences
- knowing when to bluff and when to concede in negotiation
- financial prudence
- deep influencing patterns
- ability to identify intuitively the optimum choice
- knowing what pricing strategy to employ
- ethical choices and consequences.

■ **Tacit hand:**
- facilitation skills – putting people at ease
- open/closed body language as necessary
- doing the right thing at the right time
- intuitive bridge building
- kinaesthetic skills.

■ **Tacit heart:**
- charisma that gets you through closed doors
- self-confidence or inner-security
- knowing when someone is faking it or lying
- broad shoulders to take the flack meant for the client
- ability to empathize with the clients' and consumers' pain during the change
- independence
- values and integrity
- social responsibility and feeling for the right thing to do.

Conclusion

The age of the individual has arrived with a vengeance. This is because ultimately learning and knowledge will be discovered and delivered by individuals, not faceless corporate bodies. Hence, if individuals are not motivated to acquire or trade their personal capital, then little learning can or will take place at an organizational level.

Personal knowledge management is crucial because what worked yesterday may not work tomorrow. Companies that were manufacturing the best quality have become obsolete regardless of the efficiency of their processes – because their product definition did not keep up with the changing needs of the market. However, we must now move beyond the notion of knowledge management at a corporate level and take it down to the level of the individual.

> **knowledge management is crucial because what worked yesterday may not work tomorrow**

Unless you, too, take urgent steps to manage your knowledge, then you might be consigned to the sidelines while peers and junior colleagues achieve their goals and you can only look on with envy and regret.

The personal knowledge bandwidth framework will prevent you falling into this trap. It is a practical tool that will help you enhance your capability to learn, manage and market your personal capital. Part of this process includes asking yourself questions every day as you master your personal knowledge management processes. Questions such as:

- How do I create new knowledge?
- What investment strategies do I employ that ensure I acquire value-added knowledge?
- How effective is my memory as a storage system?
- How do I use systems to retain information?
- What impact do emotions have on my storage capability?
- How do I store knowledge in partnership with other people?
- Have I developed my capability to unlearn?
- How do I manage the pain that goes with letting go?
- What strategies do I have to ensure that I can modify knowledge on my terms rather than being forced by someone else?
- What explicit and intuitive processes do I use to share and transfer knowledge with colleagues?

- To what extent do competitive forces impact on my ability or desire to share knowledge?
- To what extent do I buy and sell knowledge?
- How do I use communities of interest to amplify and enhance my personal capital?
- Can I place a market value on my personal capital?
- How do I balance the relationships with my employer and the market?
- Where do I position my personal capital in the market?

As a consultant your value comes from what you think, feel and do and is not dependent on the use of assets of blueprints. Therefore the onus is on you to ensure that you map, manage and market your personal capital effectively. If you don't, then who else will? If you don't know your value, then who does?

Bibliography

Argyris, C. (1992) *On Organizational Learning*. Oxford: Blackwell Business.

Battram, A. (1999) http://world.std.com/vlo/96.09/0589.html, 10 December.

Birch, P. and Clegg, B. (1996) *Imagination Engineering*. London: Pitman Publishing.

Buchanan, D. and Body, D. (1992) *The Expertise of the Change Agent*. London: Prentice Hall.

Capra, F. (1997) *The Web of Life*. New York: HarperCollins.

Carter, S. (1999) *Renaissance Management*. London: Kogan Page.

Choo, Chun Wei (1998) *The Knowing Organisation*. New York: Oxford University Press.

Cooper, K. and Sawaf, A. (1997) *Executive EQ*. USA: Orion Business Books.

Cope, M. (1998) *Leading the Organisation to Learn*. London: FT Prentice Hall.

Cracknell, D. (1999) *Sunday Business*, 7 February, 1.

Czerniawska, F. (1999) *Management Consultancy in the Twenty-First Century*. London: Macmillan Business.

De Bono, E. (1992) *Serious Creativity*. London: HarperCollins Business.

The Economist (1984) 'Mad dogs and expatriates', 3 March, 67.

Egan, G. (1994) *Working the Shadow Side*. San Francisco: Jossey-Bass.

Financial Executives International (2002) http://www.fei.org/magazine/Exclusives/AAR_7_01.cfm, October.

Goldstein, J. (1994) *The Unshackled Organization*. Portland, Oregon: Productivity Press.

Gordon, J. E. (1978) *Structures or Why Things Don't Fall Down*. Harmondsworth: Penguin.

Hersey, P. and Blanchard, K. (1972) *Management of Organizational Behaviour*. Englewood Cliffs: Prentice Hall.

Juster, N. (1971) *The Phantom Tollbooth*. New York: Random House.

Kauffman, S. (1995) *Order for Free*. Harmondsworth: Penguin.

Kotter, J. (1999) in Senge, P., Kleiner, A., Roberts, C., Roth, G. and Ross, R. *The Dance of Change*. London: Nicholas Brealey Publishing.

Kubr, M. (1976) *Management Consulting*. Geneva: International Labour Office.

Lascelles, D. and Peacock, R. (1996) *Self Assessment for Business Excellence*, London: McGraw-Hill.

Levitt, B. and March, G. (1996) 'Organizational learning' in Cohen, M. and Sproull, L. (eds) *Organizational Learning*. London: Sage.

Lissack, M. and Roos, J. (1999) *The Next Common Sense*, London: Nicholas Brealey Publishing.

Meznar, N. (1995) 'The social construction of organisational learning: conceptual and practical issues in the field', *Human Relations*, 48(7).

Michalko, M. (1998) *Cracking Creativity*. Berkeley, California: Ten Speed Press.

Michalko, M. (1991) *Thinkertoys*. Berkeley, California: Ten Speed Press.

Nagle, T. and Holden, R. (1995) *The Strategy and Tactics of Pricing*. New Jersey: Prentice Hall.

The New York Times (1996) obituary of Arthur Rudolph, 3 January.

Nonaka, I. and Takeuchi, T. (1995) *The Knowledge Creating Company*. Oxford: Oxford University Press.

O'Shea, A. and Madigan, C. (1997) *Dangerous Company*, London: Nicholas Brealey Publishing.

Randall, J. (1999) 'Survival can be a loss', *Sunday Business*, 31 January.

Sanchez, R. (1997) *Strategic Learning and Knowledge Management*. New York: John Wiley & Sons.

Schein, E. (1993) 'How can organizations learn faster? The challenge of entering the green room', *Sloan Management Review*, Winter.

Schein, E. (1994) 'Organizational and managerial culture as a facilitator or inhibitor of organizational learning', MIT internet paper' http://learning.mit.edu/res/wp/10004.html

Senge, P., Kleiner, A., Roberts, C., Roth, G. and Ross, R. (1999) *The Dance of Change*. London: Nicholas Brealey Publishing.

Senge, P. (1990) *The Fifth Discipline*. London: Century Business.

Smith, G. (2000) *Knowledge Management*, 3(5), February.

Stessin, L. (1979) 'Culture shock and the American businessman overseas', in Smith, E. and Luce, L. (eds) *Towards Internationalism: Readings in Cross Cultural Communication*, Rowely, Massachusetts: Newbury House.

Wheatley, M. (1994) *Leadership and the New Science*. San Francisco: Berrett-Koehler Publishers Inc.

Wolfe, T. (1987) *The Bonfire of the Vanities*. London: Picador.

Wren, D. and Greenwood, R. (1998) *Management Innovators*. New York: Oxford University Press.

Index

clients 18–84
change ladder 20, 47–77
compound contracting 20, 77–84
head-heart negotiation 19, 23–7
MPH client mapping 20, 35–44
OUTCOME testing 20, 44–7
push-pull relationships 19, 31–4
rapid mapping 11
seriousness test 41–4
spiral building 14–15
trust index 19, 27–31
understanding clients/problems 18–20,
39, 40–1
close 260–80
after action reviews (AAR) 262–3
building on the relationship 271–80
dependency loop 264–5
rapid mapping 12
spiral building 16–17
value differentiation 268–70
value management 266–7
cockpit confirmation 208, 215–20
cocktail capabilities 55, 60–2
cognitive behaviour 23
cognitive dissonance 239
command change process 186, 187–8
competing preferences 24
competitive advantage 139
complementary resources 165
compound contracting 20, 77–84
confirm 207–33
change ladder 208, 210–15
cockpit confirmation 208, 215–20
cost confirmation 208, 230–3
measurement process 208, 226–30
quantitative-qualitative mix 208, 220–6
rapid mapping 12
responsibilities 208–10
spiral building 16
conflict 24
consequences and choices 157–9
consistency 28, 30
consultant misalignment 21
consumer misalignment 21
consumer segmentation 168, 190–2
contingency responses to risk 137
continue 234–59
desire-ethos (D-E) dissonance 234,
238–45
gravitational pull 235, 246–8
knowledge transfer 235, 248–51
learning levels 235, 251–6
listening 235, 245–6
rapid mapping 12
selling the story 235, 256–9
spiral building 16
sticky steps 234, 235–8
contracts 20, 77–84
and measurement 207
negotiating 80
and shared success 80–3
control 115, 152–3
controlled change model 196
convergent choice 138, 151–62

consequences and choices 157–9
control over outcomes 152–3
end game fit 159–60
hungry for success 153–4
internalization of responsibility 156–7
options for action 154–6
solution test 160–2
conversation 33
Cooper, K. 150
Cope, M. 173
cost confirmation 208, 230–3
create 138–66
convergent choice 138, 151–62
divergent scanning 138, 148–51
managed creativity 138, 139–48
rapid mapping 12
resource management 138, 164–6
solution storyboard 138, 161–4
spiral building 15
CREATE model 139–48
cults 70–1
cultural attributes 115–16
cultural diversity 118–20
culture 86, 114–20, 227
audits 114–17
merging 197
culture blindness 116
culture paradox 116
customer databases 97
customer facing groups 203
Czerniawska, F. 234

D-spot 183–4
data
analysis 98–100, 222–6
gathering 89, 93, 95–8, 222
qualitative 221, 223
quantitative 221–2, 223
requirements 90–4
richness 93–4
source checks 101
validity 97–8
databases 97
De Bono, E. 147
dead choices 154–5
debate change model 197–8
decision makers 86, 120–2
decision rules 155
decision-making 19–20, 141–2
deflection 112
delays 113
delivery costs 231
demarcating resources 165
dependency loop 264–5
deployment costs 231, 232
descriptive statistics 97
design costs 231, 232
desire for change 54, 73, 74, 76
double desire 55, 63–5
measurement 212
desire-ethos (D-E) dissonance 234, 238–45
development costs 232
diagnosis 86–101
data analysis 98–100, 222–6